Hot Jobs

College & Career Press
Chicago, Illinois

Editorial Staff

Andrew Morkes, Publisher/Managing Editor
Amy McKenna, Publisher/Editor
Felicitas Cortez, Writer/Editor
Nora Walsh, Writer/Editor
Jon Bieniek, Proofreader
Kevin Meyers Design, Cover Design

Library of Congress Cataloging-in-Publication Data
Morkes, Andrew.
  Hot jobs : more than 25 careers with the highest pay, fastest growth, and most
new positions / by Andrew Morkes and Amy McKenna.
      p. cm.
  Includes bibliographical references and index.
  Summary: "Provides an overview of more than 25 careers that have been identified by the U.S. Department of Labor as offering the highest pay, fastest
employment growth, and most new jobs through 2018. Each article provides an
overview of job duties, educational requirements, interviews with workers in the
field and more"--Provided by publisher.
  ISBN 978-0-9745251-6-7
  1.   Vocational guidance--United States. 2.   Occupations--United States.   I.
McKenna, Amy, 1969- II. Title.

  HF5382.5.U5M665 2011
  331.7020973--dc22

                                        2010032794

Published and distributed by
College & Career Press, LLC
PO Box 300484
Chicago, IL 60630
773/282-4671 (phone/fax)
amorkes@chicagopa.com
www.collegeandcareerpress.com

Printed in the United States of America

11-10

TABLE OF CONTENTS

Introduction v
Accountants and Auditors 1
Advanced Practice Nurses 10
Carpenters 18
Civil Engineers 26
College Professors 35
Computer Network, Systems, and Database Administrators 41
Computer Support Specialists 47
Computer Systems Analysts 53
Construction Managers 60
Cost Estimators 69
Counselors 75
Dental Hygienists 86
Financial Planners 92
Management Analysts 100
Marketing Research Analysts 110
Medical Scientists 117
Paralegals 124
Pharmacists 133
Physical Therapists 144
Physicians 153
Public Relations Specialists 162
Registered Nurses 171
Renewable Energy and Green Industry Workers 180
Software Engineers 192
Special Education Teachers 201
Teachers—Kindergarten, Elementary, and Middle School 208
Index 215

Other Products From College & Career Press:
College Exploration on the Internet, 2nd Edition
They Teach That in College!?, 2nd Edition
They Teach That in Community College!?
They Teach That in College!?—Midwest Edition
Nontraditional Careers for Women
College Spotlight newsletter
CAM Report career newsletter

INTRODUCTION

Competition for jobs is increasingly strong, and it is important to know which careers offer the best employment opportunities. The editors of *Hot Jobs* have chosen 26 careers that will grow most quickly [with employment growth of at least 13 percent (carpenters) and as high as 53 percent (network systems and data communication analysts and network architects and engineers), employ the largest number of people, and offer higher-than-average median salaries (the average salary for all workers in May 2009 was $43,460).

Twenty-seven percent of the careers listed in *Hot Jobs* are found in the health care industry, 15 percent in the computer and information technology industry, and 12 percent in educational services. These industries are some of the strongest in the United States and offer a wealth of career options. In addition to these fields, hot jobs are found in the business, construction, financial planning, marketing, law, public relations, and renewable-energy industries. Opportunities are available for people from all educational backgrounds—from apprenticeship training to a medical degree.

The following paragraphs provide more information on the sections in each career article and other features in the book.

The **Fast Facts** sidebar appears at the beginning of each article. It provides a summary of recommended high school classes and personal skills; the minimum educational requirements to enter the field; the typical salary range; employment outlook; and acronyms and identification numbers for the following government classification indexes: the Occupational Information Network (O*NET)-Standard Occupational Classification System (SOC) index; the Guide for Occupational Exploration (GOE); the Dictionary of Occupational Titles (DOT); and the National Occupational Classification (NOC) Index. The O*NET-SOC, GOE, and DOT indexes have been created by the U.S. government; the NOC index is Canada's career classification system. Readers can use the identification numbers listed in this section to obtain further information about a career. Print editions of the GOE (*Guide for Occupational Exploration.* Indianapolis, Ind.: JIST Works, 2001) and DOT (*Dictionary of Occupational Titles.* Indianapolis, Ind.: JIST Works, 1991) are available at libraries. Electronic versions of the DOT (www.oalj.dol.gov/libdot.htm), NOC (www5.hrsdc.gc.ca/NOC), and O*NET-SOC (http://online.onetcenter.org) are available on the Internet. When no O*NET-SOC, GOE, DOT, or NOC numbers are listed, this means that the U.S. Department of Labor or Human Resources and Skills Development Canada have not created a numerical designation for this career. In this instance, you will see the acronym "N/A," or not available.

The **Overview** section provides a capsule summary of work duties, educational requirements, the number of people employed in the field, and employment outlook. **The Job** provides a detailed overview of primary and secondary job duties and typical work settings. The **Requirements** section features four subsections: **High School** (which lists recommended high school classes), **Postsecondary Training** (which lists required post-high school training requirements to prepare for the field), **Certification and Licensing** (which details voluntary certification and mandatory licensing requirements, when applicable), and **Other Requirements** (which lists key personal and professional skills for success in the field). **Exploring** provides suggestions to young people about how they can explore the field while in school. Examples include books and magazines, websites, information interviews, membership in clubs and other organizations, hands-on activities, competitions, and summer and after-school programs. **Employers** lists the number of people employed in the occupation in the United States and details typical work settings. **Getting a Job** provides advice on how to land a job through employment and association websites, career service offices, networking, career fairs, and other methods. The **Advancement** section provides an overview of typical ways to move up at one's employer or via other means (such as opening a consulting firm or entering academia). **Earnings** provides information on starting, median, and top salaries for workers. Information on salaries in particular industries is also provided for many careers. The **Employment Outlook** section provides an overview of the outlook for the career through 2018. It lists the factors that are causing employment to grow and details career areas in which there will be especially strong growth. Outlook information is obtained from the U.S. Department of Labor and is augmented by information gathered from professional trade associations. Job growth terms follow those used in the *Occupational Outlook Handbook* (http://stats.bls.gov/search/ooh.htm). Growth described as "much faster than the average" means that employment will increase by 20 percent or more from 2008 to 2018. Growth described as "faster than the average" means an increase of 14 to 19 percent. Growth described as "about as fast as the average" means an increase of 7 to 13 percent. Each article ends with **For More Information.** This section provides contact information for professional associations that provide details on educational programs, career paths, scholarships, publications, youth programs, and other resources.

Additionally, most articles in *Hot Jobs* features one or more interviews with professionals and educators in that particular field, who provide useful advice on what it takes to land a job and be successful in the field. Other features include informative sidebars, photographs, and a career title and association index.

We hope that *Hot Jobs* provides you with some great ideas for possible career paths. But this book is just the beginning. Contact the professional associations listed at the end of each article to obtain more information; perhaps they can even help arrange an information interview with a worker in a field that interests you. Follow the suggestions in the Exploring section of each article to get hands-on experience. That way, you will be able to try out each field before making the big decision of choosing a career. Learning about careers can be fun, and we hope this book is useful to you as you begin your search. All the best to you during your career exploration!

ACCOUNTANTS AND AUDITORS

OVERVIEW

Accountants and auditors maintain financial records and monitor transactions for individuals and government, nonprofit, or corporate clients. Some examine the tax implications of financial transactions. A minimum of a bachelor's degree is required to enter the field. Approximately 1.3 million accountants are employed in the United States. Employment opportunities for accountants and auditors will be favorable through 2018.

THE JOB

Accountants and auditors analyze financial statements to see whether an organization is running efficiently and utilizing its financial resources effectively. They also serve as watchdogs to ensure that no illegal or fraudulent activities are taking place in an organization or government agency. Their job duties depend largely on which area of accounting or auditing they are employed.

All auditors and accountants must be comfortable working with numbers, but they must also be good communicators. They spend a good amount of time traveling from one client to the next or in meetings or on the phone with their clients discussing their clients' financial statements. The remainder of their time is spent completing paperwork, writing reports, reviewing documents, and making mathematical calculations.

The major fields of accounting and auditing include *public accounting, government accounting, corporate accounting,* and *internal auditing.*

The career of *public accountant* includes a broad category of professionals who work for corporations, government agencies, nonprofit organizations, and individual clients. They provide a wide range of accounting, auditing, tax review, and other financial consulting services. *Tax consultants* advise businesses on how to reduce their taxes and help companies file their tax returns. Other accountants are hired on a contract basis as *financial consul-*

FAST FACTS

High School Subjects
Business
Economics
Mathematics

Personal Skills
Communication
Critical thinking
Time management

Minimum Education Level
Bachelor's degree

Salary Range
$37,000 to $60,000 to $104,000+

Employment Outlook
Much faster than the average

O*NET-SOC
13-2011.00, 13-2011.01, 13-2011.02

GOE
13.02.03

DOT
160

NOC
1111

tants, advising on employee payroll and benefit issues as well as other topics. *External auditors* review corporate filings and other financial records and then make written or verbal statements to investors or state and federal government authorities on whether the organization's financial records are sound and accurately reported. Auditing work is becoming increasingly computerized, and auditors increasingly rely on sophisticated random-sampling methods for efficiency and accurate reporting. *Forensic accountants* are hired by government agencies and independent investigators to help law enforcement identify criminal activity, such as money laundering, tax fraud, or embezzlement. They also consult with lawyers regarding bankruptcies and contract disputes.

Government accountants and *auditors* are employed by federal, state, and local agencies. They may work as *general accountants,* reviewing a government agency's financial statements, analyzing budgets, and making financial recommendations. Many others are employed by the Internal Revenue Service to review corporate and individual tax returns.

Corporate accountants, also referred to as *cost, industrial, private,* or *managerial accountants,* are on staff at corporations to focus on their financial information. They may consult with the executive team on budgeting, cost analysis, employee payroll and performance review, mergers and acquisitions, and asset management. They focus on making long-term financial projections to help their employers make wise business decisions.

Internal auditors are employed by businesses as internal watchdogs to ensure against fraud or financial mismanagement. After reviewing financial records, management procedures and processes, and internal controls, they produce reports for executives that detail the financial condition of the business. They also ensure that corporate policies and government regulations are being followed. Internal auditors may also have special titles such as *compliance auditor, information technology auditor,* and *environmental auditor.*

In addition to these four major groupings, there are also opportunities with nonprofit and educational institutions. Accountants may work as *college or university professors,* teaching accounting, auditing, corporate ethics, taxation law, business, and other related topics. Accountants and auditors are also employed by nonprofit organizations in the same fashion as corporations. Nonprofit organizations seek their advice on making sound financial decisions to make their dollars go further and make the greatest impact.

There are also opportunities for auditors and accountants in environmental areas. Corporations now have new rules and regulations in regard to environmental issues, such as taxes on air pollution. *Environmental accountants* are hired to help ensure that companies comply with these new state and federal taxes. They also consult with executives on how making "green" choices can help a company save money.

Accountants and auditors work in offices, but they may travel often to meet with clients. Many have the traditional 40-hour workweek, but those focusing on taxation issues are busy during traditional tax filing time (April 15th) as well as during quarterly deadlines. The number of hours accounting professionals work depends largely on the type and volume of clients.

REQUIREMENTS

HIGH SCHOOL

In high school, take as many business, accounting, and mathematics courses as possible. Since you will use spreadsheets, databases, and other computer programs frequently in your work, take computer science courses. Finally, accountants and auditors need excellent communication skills. Take as many English and speech classes as possible to hone these skills. Other recommended classes include economics, history, and government.

POSTSECONDARY TRAINING

A bachelor's degree in accounting is required by all states before applicants can take the licensing examination. Top employers may require a master's degree in accounting or a master's degree in business administration with a concentration in accounting. Some colleges offer specialized degrees, concentrations, or minors in specialty areas such as internal auditing. AACSB International—Association to Advance Collegiate Schools of Business offers a list of accredited accounting programs at its website, www.aacsb.edu/accreditation/AccreditedMembers.asp.

CERTIFICATION AND LICENSING

A large percentage of accounting professionals are certified. Certified public accountants (CPAs) must pass an examination and receive licensure from their state board of accountancy. All states use the four-part Uniform CPA Examination prepared by the American Institute of Certified Public Accountants (AICPA). Most states require CPA candidates to have a college degree, but some allow the substitution of a number of years of public accounting experience in lieu of a college degree. In addition, the U.S. Department of Labor reports that "46 states and the District of Columbia require CPA candidates to complete 150 semester hours of college coursework—an additional 30 hours beyond the usual four-year bachelor's degree. California, Colorado, New Hampshire, and Vermont are the only states that do not require 150 semester hours for certification."

In addition to certification, members of the AICPA with valid CPA certificates can earn specialty credentials such as accredited in business valuation, certified information technology professional, and personal financial specialist.

There are many accounting specialties, and some accountants and auditors pursue specialized credentials to demonstrate their knowledge to prospective employers. The following associations also offer certification programs to accountants and auditors: the Institute of Management Accountants; the Accreditation Council for Accountancy and Taxation; the Institute of Internal Auditors; the ISACA; and the Association of Certified Fraud Examiners.

OTHER REQUIREMENTS

The American Institute of Certified Public Accountants says that most successful accountants and auditors have a combination of strong leadership skills, business savvy, technical know-how, and communication skills.

Other important traits include mathematical acumen, honesty, patience, organizational skills, the ability to solve problems, and a willingness to work long hours under deadline pressure.

Books to Read

Alba, Jason. *Vault Career Guide to Accounting.* 3rd ed. New York: Vault Inc., 2008.

Gaylord, Gloria, and Glenda Ried. *Careers in Accounting.* 4th ed. New York: McGraw-Hill, 2006.

Goldberg, Jan. *Great Jobs for Accounting Majors.* 2nd ed. New York: McGraw-Hill, 2005.

Gulko, Candace S. *Field Guides to Finding a New Career: Accounting, Business, and Finance.* New York: Ferguson Publishing Company, 2010.

EXPLORING

There are many ways to learn more about accounting and auditing. You can read books and magazines (such as *Forbes, Fortune,* and *Bloomberg Businessweek)* about accounting and business, participate in information interviews with accounting professionals, join your high school's business club, or even ask your business teacher to arrange a tour of an accounting firm. You can also visit association websites, which provide information on education and careers. One recommendation is Start Here, Go Places (www.startheregoplaces.com), which is sponsored by the American Institute of Certified Public Accountants. At the site, you will learn more about accounting specialties, recommended educational paths, and why accounting is such an exciting career; and you can read interviews with certified public accountants and look up accounting-related terms in a glossary. You can also read copies of the *Going Places* e-zine and *Start Here* magazine. Finally, the American Institute of Certified Public Accountants offers a membership option for high school students.

EMPLOYERS

Approximately 1.3 million accountants are employed in the United States. Accountants and auditors work at public accounting firms, government agencies, nonprofit organizations, auditing and bookkeeping firms, and any other organization that requires accounting and auditing services. Twenty-four percent work for accounting, tax preparation, bookkeeping, and payroll services firms. Eight percent of accountants and auditors are self-employed.

GETTING A JOB

Many accounting professionals obtain their first jobs as a result of contacts made through college internships, career fairs, and networking events. Others seek assistance in obtaining job leads from college career services offices, newspaper want ads, and employment websites. Additionally, the

Career Planning & Development section of the AICPA website www.aicpa.org/YoungCPANetwork/Planning_Developing.htm) provides information on accounting careers, job search strategies, cover letters and résumés, and job interviews, as well as job listings and a section where you can post your résumé. Those interested in positions with the federal government should visit www.usajobs.opm.gov.

ADVANCEMENT

Within a year or two of being hired, skilled public accountants can advance to positions that involve more responsibility. The next step would be to advance to a senior-level accounting position, then to a position as a supervisor, manager, or partner. Some accounting professionals start their own accounting firms. Others become corporation executives or teach accounting at colleges and universities.

EARNINGS

Salaries for accountants and auditors vary by type of employer, geographic region, and the worker's experience level and skills. Accounting graduates with a bachelor's degree in accounting received average starting salary offers of $48,993 a year in July 2009, according to the National Association of Colleges and Employers. Those with master's degrees were offered $49,786.

Median annual salaries for accountants and auditors were $60,340 in 2009, according to the U.S. Department of Labor (USDL). Salaries ranged from less than $37,690 to $104,450 or more. The USDL reports the following mean annual earnings for accountants and auditors by specialty: federal government, $88,190; securities and commodity contracts intermediation and brokerage, $80,780; postal service, $79,600; accounting, tax preparation, bookkeeping, and payroll services, $73,920; management of companies and enterprises, $66,330; insurance carriers, $66,520; local government, $57,490; and state government, $54,040.

Employers offer a variety of benefits, including the following: medical, dental, and life insurance; paid holidays, vacation, and sick and personal days; 401(k) plans; profit-sharing plans; retirement and pension plans; and educational assistance programs. Self-employed workers must provide their own benefits.

EMPLOYMENT OUTLOOK

Employment for accounting professionals is expected to grow much faster than the average for all careers through 2018, according to the U.S. Department of Labor. High-profile corporate accounting scandals and government legislation to better regulate the accounting industry have created strong demand for accountants and auditors. Forensic accountants and auditors will be in especially strong demand. Other hot industries for accountants include health care, hospitality, and financial services.

According to Robert Half International, the world's largest specialized financial recruitment service, there is strong demand for professionals "who can help manage costs and enhance profitability," as well as those who "possess deep technical expertise, are excellent communicators, and collaborate effectively with colleagues across multiple departments." It reports that tax accountants, compliance directors, credit managers/supervisors, and senior financial analysts will have the best job prospects in coming years.

Opportunities will be best for those who are certified (especially as certified public accountants), have a master's degree in accounting or a master's degree in business administration with a concentration in accounting, experience with computerized accounting and auditing software and information systems, and specialized expertise—such as knowledge of international financial reporting standards or international business.

FOR MORE INFORMATION

For certification information, contact
Accreditation Council for
Accountancy and Taxation
1010 North Fairfax Street
Alexandria, VA 22314-1574
888-289-7763
www.acatcredentials.org

For information on scholarships for high school and college students, membership for high school students, careers, and certification, contact
American Institute of
Certified Public Accountants
1211 Avenue of the Americas
New York, NY 10036-8775
212-596-6200
www.aicpa.org

For information on accredited programs, contact
Association to Advance
Collegiate Schools of Business
777 South Harbour Island Boulevard,
Suite 750
Tampa, FL 33602-5730
813-769-6500
www.aacsb.edu

For certification information, contact
BAI
115 South LaSalle Street, Suite 3300
Chicago, IL 60603-3801
info@bai.org
www.bai.org

For information on careers for women in accounting, contact
The Educational Foundation
for Women in Accounting
136 South Keowee Street
Dayton, OH 45402-2241
937-424-3391
info@efwa.org
www.efwa.org

For information on certification, contact the following organizations
Institute of Internal Auditors
247 Maitland Avenue
Altamonte Springs, FL 32701-4201
407-937-1100
iia@theiia.org
www.theiia.org

Institute of Management Accountants
10 Paragon Drive
Montvale, NJ 07645-1718
800-638-4427
ima@imanet.org
www.imanet.org

ISACA
3701 Algonquin Road, Suite 1010
Rolling Meadows, IL 60008-3124
847-253-1545
www.isaca.org

For a wealth of educational and career information, visit
Start Here, Go Places
www.startheregoplaces.com

Interview: Maya Chahine Khan

Maya Chahine Khan is a certified public accountant. She discussed her career with the editors of *Hot Jobs*.

Q. Where do you work? How long have you worked in the field?

A. I work at a mid-size (approximately 300 employees) accounting firm in New York City. I've worked at this firm for about 4.5 years.

Q. What made you want to enter this career?

A. I went to college and graduated with a bachelor of science in business management. After graduation, I had no idea what type of career I wanted. I obtained a job as an accounts payable clerk at a lumber company on Long Island. I worked for a year before realizing that I would be very bored working in accounts payable for the rest of my life. After discussing several options with friends and family, I decided to try accounting. I found a job at a small accounting firm and gave it a shot. After several months, I knew this was the field for me. I enjoyed the work, working with clients and being constantly challenged. After several months of working, I went back to school, part-time, so I could qualify to sit for the CPA exam.

Q. What is one thing that teens may not know about a career in accounting?

A. A lot of people think that accountants are "good in math." That is not true. Accounting is simple mathematics, not solving complex math problems. Accountants don't solve math problems, but rather analyze the numbers. For example, a tax accountant will prepare a projection of an individual's income for a specific year. From that projection, the accountant will advise the client about different options in minimizing his or her tax. Also, accountants do not sit at a desk all day, every day. We often visit clients and do work at their offices. Accounting is not a "desk job."

Q. What are your typical and secondary job duties?

A. I am a real estate accountant. My clients own real estate in the New York area. The great thing about my position is that I get to do a little of everything, from auditing and preparing financial statements to tax returns. A typical job duty is preparing work papers and financial statements or tax returns. A secondary job duty is researching tax statutes or auditing standards.

Q. What are the most important qualities for accountants?

A. As a personal quality, it's important to be a people person. When it comes to dealing with clients' money, clients have to feel comfortable with you. Clients want accountants who can answer their questions and listen to their specific situation. As for a professional quality, it is extremely important to be and remain 'professional.' Since clients trust their accountant with important information, the accountant must act with professionalism in any situation.

Q. What are some of the pros and cons of your job?

A. Pros: working with clients, interacting with various people in the field, dealing with various business problems and analyzing them. Cons: The hours! During tax season, we work about 60 hours a week from January to April 15th.

Q. What advice would you give to young people who are interested in the field?

A. Accounting is a great career—from the job duties to the salaries. A person can live a financially stable life as an accountant. My advice is to intern during your college or high school years. It's important to find out if you personally like the career. If you don't, then no matter what, you will hate your job. During your internship, ask a lot of questions, talk to all staff about their career and job duties. It is wise to take advantage of the opportunities you may have as a young person.

Interview: Luke Sniewski

Luke Sniewski is a certified public accountant (CPA) as well as a personal trainer. He discussed his careers with the editors of *Hot Jobs*.

Q. Where do you work? How long have you worked in the field?

A. I am a self-employed CPA. I acquire, maintain, and grow with my 100 or so clients. I have been an accountant for four years and a CPA for two years.

Q. What made you want to enter this career?

A. I entered this field for a multitude of reasons. My older brother was an influence for sure. But the most significant reason why I entered accounting was its applicability to any avenue of business. The accounting degree may be the most versatile degree available to a business major. It reveals so many aspects of business practices, that most accountants can literally do anything for a business. And when it comes to teaching personal financial responsibility, nothing beats an accounting degree.

Q. What is one thing that young people may not know about a career in accounting?

A. The running joke is that a social accountant is one that stares at your feet, rather than his own. Though funny, this stereotype of accountants being locked in a small room behind a desk is very far from true. The often ignored soft skills separate the successful accountants from the ones who may have lost their jobs during the recession. The ability to communicate cannot be overstated. As accountants, we must communicate complex accounting scenarios to clients who want simple explanations. This requires clear and concise communications, whether it is written or verbal.

Q. What are your typical and secondary job duties?

A. As with most professions, the typical secondary duties involve a combination of continued education and networking. As the old adage goes: Your education begins after you graduate. After an accountant leaves the sanctuary of his or her classroom, the true tests begin. Networking events and continued education courses will become second nature to successful accountants. This is actually a fantastic opportunity for accountants to separate themselves from competition. They are constantly provided with opportunities to improve their soft skills and build upon their foundation of knowledge.

Q. What are the most important qualities for people in your career?

A. If an accountant really wants to climb the ladder to becoming a partner, there are certain intangibles that must be present. The obvious quality is to be a knowledgeable resource to clients and fellow peers. This, however, is not an intangible quality and is earned after years of focus, determination, and continual education. The ironic thing is that the eventual knowledge base is actually the direct result of the personal and professional qualities instilled in successful accountants. This includes timeliness, drive, and organization. All three of these qualities are the catalysts that ensure the accountant learns, grows, and avoids the common burnout so often seen in a profession dominated by strict deadlines.

Q. What are some of the pros and cons of your job?

A. The most obvious con of being an accountant is the inevitability of clients determining the timing of workload and job completion. Even though accountants would love to finish the majority of their workload well before tax deadlines, this is often not the case. Clients seem to procrastinate much more than they need to—which places additional pressures on accountants to finish the work. This problem is significantly amplified when multiple clients decide April 14th is an appropriate time to get you their documents.

Q. What advice would you give to young people who are interested in the field?

A. Young people should forget about all the stereotypes that have haunted the accounting industry for decades past. The path to being a partner used to be paved by 14-hour days, unhealthy lifestyles, and a complete disregard for anything that is closely considered a quality life. Times have changed, and so has the accounting industry. Drastic focus has been placed on work/life balance, a step that makes accounting one of the most forward-thinking industries in America. With health care costs being the highest in the world, the accounting industry has taken steps to keep its kind healthy by recognizing that personal time may be the most important variable in keeping employee turnover down and productivity up.

Q. Can you tell us a little about your other career as a personal trainer?

A. I was a professional football player prior to becoming a trainer. After I witnessed more injuries behind a desk of a cubicle than on a football field, I decided I wanted to figure why a computer desk could be such an anti-productive environment and lead to so many work-related injuries. What I found astounded me and motivated me to teach CPAs everywhere about the completely real dangers of working in front of a computer for hours on end. That is when I created my company, LEAF (www.leaflifestyle.com), which educates CPAs on the importance of their proactive lifestyles and their link to improved productivity. As a trainer who focuses on business professionals, which essentially includes everyone that sits for a living, I focus on fixing underlying postural issues, improving inconsistent energy levels, and ensuring that proper nutritional plans are in place for not only a successful work life, but also an improved personal life. This is truly the epitome of the work/life balance.

ADVANCED PRACTICE NURSES

OVERVIEW

Advanced practice nurses (APNs) are registered nurses who provide specialized health care, promote health, prevent and treat disease and injuries, and help patients cope with illness. APNs have earned master's degrees and certifications to become either a *certified nurse-midwife,* a *clinical nurse specialist,* a *certified registered nurse anesthetist,* or a *nurse practitioner.* There are more than 259,500 advanced practice nurses employed in the United States. Employment for APNs is expected to be excellent through 2018.

THE JOB

What makes nurses unique from other health care professionals? Many agree it is the job of the nurse to treat the individual—not just the presenting health problem. In addition, nurses are often tasked with caring not only for the patient, but for his or her loved ones and family, keeping them comfortable and "in the know" about a health crisis of a loved one. Finally, nurses are stewards in their community, keeping the public informed on ways to get and stay healthy. Advanced practice nursing is an umbrella term given to registered nurses who have completed a master's degree and passed additional clinical practice requirements specific to their chosen career path. Advanced practice nursing specialties are detailed in the following paragraphs:

Certified nurse-midwives (CNMs) provide gynecological wellness checks and consultations on conception and pregnancy, and they assist in childbirth. Approximately 7.4 percent of U.S. births are attended by certified nurse-midwives. CNMs work in hospitals and birthing centers, and they conduct home visits for women who want to deliver their babies at home. The common misconception is that all these professionals do is deliver babies. In fact, they spend only about 10 percent of their workday assisting in childbirth. The majority of their work involves providing routine annual exams and giving primary, preventive care to women of all ages.

FAST FACTS

High School Subjects
Biology
Chemistry
Mathematics

Personal Skills
Active listening
Communication
Critical thinking
Judgment and decision making

Minimum Education Level
Master's degree

Salary Range
$71,000 to $100,000 to $174,000+

Employment Outlook
Much faster than the average

O*NET-SOC
29-1111.00

GOE
14.02.01

DOT
075

NOC
3152, 3232

Clinical nurse specialists (CNSs) specialize in a wide range of physical and mental health areas. Their area of clinical expertise may be in a setting such as emergency room nursing, a type of health problem such as stress or wounds, a population such as pediatrics or the elderly, or a type of care such as rehabilitation. In addition to direct care, they may serve as consultants, researchers, educators, and medical administrators. CNSs work in clinics, offices, community centers, hospitals, and other medical facilities.

Nurse anesthesia is the oldest advanced nursing specialty. *Certified registered nurse anesthetists (CRNAs)* administer anesthesia to patients undergoing surgery or other medical treatments. They also provide pain management and emergency services. CRNAs administer approximately 30 million anesthetics to patients annually in the United States. Men make up 44 percent of nurse anesthetists, according to the American Association of Nurse Anesthetists. Fewer than 10 percent of workers in all nursing fields are men. CRNAs work alongside surgeons, anesthesiologists, dentists, podiatrists, and other health care professionals in hospitals, in medical offices, and in other settings.

Nurse practitioners (NPs) are qualified to provide some of the direct health care services that are generally performed by physicians. They treat illnesses ranging from the common cold to diabetes. NPs have a variety of duties, including diagnosing and treating minor illnesses or injuries and prescribing medication. They also conduct physical examinations; provide immunizations; help patients manage high blood pressure, diabetes, depression, and other chronic health problems; prescribe medications; perform certain medical procedures; order and interpret lab results, x-rays, and EKGs; and educate and counsel patients and their families. Nurse practitioners can write prescriptions in all 50 states and practice independently from physicians in nearly 20 states. While many NPs focus on primary care, others—with additional training—become *pediatric, gerontological, oncology, neonatal, acute care, school, occupational health, psychiatric,* and *women's health care nurse practitioners.* NPs work in hospitals, offices of physicians, clinics, nursing homes, pharmacies with health clinics, and other medical facilities.

Work settings for advanced practice nurses vary based on their specialty, but they generally work in medical offices or hospitals. Since there is a 24-hour demand for health care, some of these professionals work nights, weekends, and holidays. Regardless of the shift, APNs find their work rewarding. They enjoy caring for patients and their families and promoting wellness education in the field and in the community.

REQUIREMENTS

HIGH SCHOOL

Take health, mathematics, biology, chemistry, physics, English, speech, business, and sociology classes in high school to prepare for a career in advanced practice nursing.

POSTSECONDARY TRAINING

The first step to become an APN is to complete training to become a registered nurse. Prospective RNs have the option of pursuing one of three training paths:

Calling Dr. Nurse!

The nursing field is adding yet another specialty—doctor of nursing practice, or DrNP. DrNPs are graduates of a two-year doctoral program (that includes a one-year residency), which advocates believe allows them to enter the medical field with the training, skill, and medical experience of a primary care physician. There are currently 1,874 students enrolled in DrNP programs throughout the country—more than double the number enrolled in 2006, according to the American Association of Colleges of Nursing.

associate's degree, diploma, and bachelor's degree. Associate's degree programs in nursing last two years and are offered by community colleges. Diploma programs in nursing typically last three years and are offered by hospitals and independent schools. Bachelor of science in nursing programs are offered by colleges and universities. They typically take four—and sometimes five—years to complete. Graduates of all three paths are known as graduate nurses and must take a licensing exam in their state to obtain the RN designation. Visit Discover Nursing (www.discovernursing.com), for a database of nursing programs.

Graduates of midwifery education programs must have a master's degree in order to be able to take the national certifying exam, which is offered by the American Midwifery Certification Board (www.amcbmidwife.org). The Accreditation Commission for Midwifery Education has accredited nearly 40 nurse-midwifery education programs in the United States. Visit www.midwife.org/map.cfm for a list of programs.

Clinical nurse specialists need at least a master's degree to work in the field. The National Association of Clinical Nurse Specialists offers a list of educational programs at its website, www.nacns.org.

Nurse anesthetists must have at least a master's degrees to practice. The Council of Accreditation of Nurse Anesthesia Educational Programs has accredited more than 100 programs. Visit the American Association of Nurse Anesthetists' website, www.aana.com, for a list of programs.

You will need a master's degree to work as a nurse practitioner. Visit the website (www.aanp.org) of the American Academy of Nurse Practitioners for a searchable database of education programs.

Doctorate degrees (such as a Doctor of Nursing Practice) are typically required for those who want to work in top levels of administration, in research, or in education. These degrees normally take four to five years to complete.

CERTIFICATION AND LICENSING

Voluntary certification is available for all four advanced practice nursing specialties. The American Midwifery Certification Board offers certification to midwives. Clinical nurse specialists can become certified by the American Nurses Credentialing Center (ANCC), the American Association of Critical Care Nurses Certification Corporation, the Oncology Nursing Certification Corporation, and the Orthopaedic Nurses Certification Board. Nurse anesthetists can become certified by the Council on Certification of Nurse Anesthetists and the American Society of PeriAnesthesia Nurses. Nurse practitioners can obtain certification from such organizations as the American Academy of Nurse Practitioners, the ANCC, the American Nurses Association, the Oncology Nursing Certification Corporation, and the Pediatric Nursing Certification Board. Contact these organizations for more information.

Nurses must be licensed to practice nursing in all states and the District of Columbia. Licensure requirements vary by state, but they typically include graduating from an approved nursing school and passing a national examination. Visit the National Council of State Boards of Nursing's website, www.ncsbn.org, for details on licensing requirements by state.

OTHER REQUIREMENTS

Successful APNs are detail oriented, caring, sympathetic, responsible, and emotionally stable. They need excellent communication skills in order to interact well with patients and coworkers. They have good judgment, are able to remain calm and decisive under pressure, have good leadership abilities, and are willing to continue to learn and upgrade their skills throughout their careers.

EXPLORING

Read books about nursing, talk with your counselor or teacher about setting up a presentation by a nurse, take a tour of a hospital or other health care setting, or volunteer at one of these facilities. Nursing-related websites, including those of professional associations, can also be a good source of information. Here are a few suggestions: Cybernurse.com (www.cybernurse.com), Discover Nursing (www.discovernursing.com), and Nurse.com (www.nurse.com).

EMPLOYERS

There are more than 259,500 advanced practice nurses employed in the United States. Fifty-two percent of this total work as nurse practitioners, 27 percent as clinical nurse specialists, 17 percent as nurse anesthetists, and 4 percent as certified nurse-midwives. The following paragraphs provide information on work settings for the four advanced practice nursing specialties.

Certified nurse-midwives work in hospitals and birthing centers, and they conduct home visits for women who want to deliver their babies at home.

Clinical nurse specialists are employed in clinics, offices, community centers, hospitals, and other medical facilities.

Certified registered nurse anesthetists work in hospitals; outpatient surgery centers; and offices of dentists, ophthalmologists, plastic surgeons, podiatrists, and pain management specialists.

Nurse practitioners are employed in hospitals, clinics, nursing homes, mental health centers, colleges and universities, student health centers, home health agencies, hospices, offices of physicians, community health centers, rural health clinics, prisons, and industrial organizations.

Advanced practice nurses also work for government agencies, including the U.S. Department of Veterans Affairs, U.S. Public Health Services, and the U.S. military. They also teach at colleges and universities.

GETTING A JOB

Many APNs obtain their first jobs as a result of contacts made through college internships or networking events. Others seek assistance in obtaining job leads from college career services offices, nursing registries, nurse employment agencies, state employment offices, newspaper want ads, and employment websites. Additionally, professional nursing associations (such as the National Association of Clinical Nurse Specialists and the American Academy of Nurse Practitioners) provide job listings at their websites. See For More Information for a list of organizations. Those interested in positions with the federal government should visit the U.S. Office of Personnel Management's website, www.usajobs.opm.gov.

ADVANCEMENT

The position of advanced practice nurse is not an entry-level career. Most APNs enter the field after working as registered nurses and obtaining several years of experience and advanced education and certification. APNs can eventually advance to managerial or senior-level administrative roles. These positions often require APNs to earn a doctorate degree in nursing or management. The U.S. Department of Labor reports that some APNs are hired by hospitals, pharmaceutical manufacturers, insurance companies, and managed care organizations to provide health planning and development, policy development, marketing, consulting, and quality assurance consulting. Other APNs work as teachers at colleges, universities, and teaching hospitals.

EARNINGS

Median annual salaries for registered nurses were $63,750 in 2009, according to the U.S. Department of Labor. Salaries ranged from less than $43,970 to $93,700 or more. Salaries for APNs are typically higher. Salary.com reports the following salary ranges for APNs by specialty in October 2010: certified nurse-midwives, $76,650 to $105,604; clinical nurse specialists, $71,536 to $100,417; nurse anesthetists, $135,421 to $174,889; and nurse practitioners, $74,793 to $101,029. APNs usually receive benefits such as health and life insurance, vacation days, sick leave, and a savings and pension plan. Self-employed workers must provide their own benefits.

EMPLOYMENT OUTLOOK

Employment for registered nurses is expected to be excellent through 2018, according to the U.S. Department of Labor (USDL). The USDL reports that these professionals "will be in high demand, particularly in medically underserved areas such as inner cities and rural areas. Relative to physicians, these RNs increasingly serve as lower-cost primary care providers." APNs with doctoral degrees and certification will have the best employment prospects.

FOR MORE INFORMATION

For information on opportunities for men in nursing, contact
**American Assembly
for Men in Nursing**
PO Box 130220
Birmingham, AL 35213-0220
www.aamn.org

For information on accredited nursing programs, contact
**American Association
of Colleges of Nursing**
One Dupont Circle, NW, Suite 530
Washington, DC 20036-1135
www.aacn.nche.edu

For more on certification, contact
**American Nurses
Credentialing Center**
c/o American Nurses Association
8515 Georgia Avenue, Suite 400
Silver Spring, MD 20910-3492
www.nursecredentialing.org

For information on gerontological advanced practice nursing, contact
**Gerontological Advanced
Practice Nurses Association**
East Holly Avenue, Box 56
Pitman, NJ 08071-1735
www.gapna.org

For general information about nursing, contact
National League for Nursing
61 Broadway, 33rd Floor
New York, NY 10006-2701
www.nln.org

For information on membership, contact
**National Student
Nurses' Association**
45 Main Street, Suite 606
Brooklyn, NY 11201-1099
nsna@nsna.org
www.nsna.org

For resources for aspiring and current nurses with disabilities, visit
ExceptionalNurse.com
www.exceptionalnurse.com

NURSE-MIDWIVES
For information on education, careers, and certification for certified nurse-midwives, contact the following organizations
**American College
of Nurse-Midwives**
8403 Colesville Road, Suite 1550
Silver Spring, MD 20910-6374
www.acnm.org

**American Midwifery
Certification Board**
849 International Drive, Suite 205
Linthicum, MD 21090-2228
www.accmidwife.org

**Midwives Alliance
of North America**
611 Pennsylvania Avenue, SE, #1700
Washington, DC 20003-4303
www.mana.org

CLINICAL NURSE SPECIALISTS
For information on education and careers, contact
**National Association
of Clinical Nurse Specialists**
100 North 20th Street, 4th Floor
Philadelphia, PA 19103-1462
www.nacns.org

NURSE ANESTHETISTS
For information on education, careers, and certification, contact the following organizations
**American Association
of Nurse Anesthetists**
222 South Prospect Avenue
Park Ridge, IL 60068-4037
info@aana.com
www.aana.com

**American Society of
PeriAnesthesia Nurses**
90 Frontage Road
Cherry Hill, NJ 08034-1424
www.aspan.org

NURSE PRACTITIONERS
For information on education,
careers, and certification for nurse
practitioners, contact the following
organizations
**American Academy
of Nurse Practitioners**
PO Box 12846
Austin, TX 78711-2846
512-442-4262
admin@aanp.org
www.aanp.org

**American College
of Nurse Practitioners**
1501 Wilson Boulevard, Suite 509
Arlington, VA 22209-2403
www.acnpweb.org

**National Association of Nurse
Practitioners in Women's Health**
505 C Street, NE
Washington, DC 20002-5809
www.npwh.org

**National Association
of Pediatric Nurse Practitioners**
20 Brace Road, Suite 200
Cherry Hill, NJ 08034-2634
856-857-9700
www.napnap.org

Interview: Nina Ortegon

Nina Ortegon is a nurse practitioner in the Pediatric Intensive Care
Unit at Advocate Hope Children's Hospital in Oak Lawn, Illinois. She
discussed her career with the editors of *Hot Jobs*.

Q. What made you want to enter this career?

A. I always wanted to be a nurse and after becoming a nurse, I wanted to
advance in the profession and obtain my nurse practitioner (NP) certification. I wanted the opportunity to help people in the time of need and
make an impact on their lives.

Q. What are the most important qualities for nurse practitioners?

A. An NP has to have a strong nursing foundation. It is important to develop your basic nursing skills before moving on to an NP program. An NP
also has to be independent and confident enough to care for patients on
their own. It is also important for the NP to know when to ask for help.
The NP can't be afraid to collaborate with his or her supervising doctor.
The NP also has to be compassionate and have the desire to make a difference in his or her patients' lives.

   My motto is to treat every patient like I would like my family treated.
I also believe it is important to take my time when interacting with my
patients. I want to provide the bedside manner that makes my patients
know that I am there to listen and address their needs.

Q. What do you like most and least about your job?

A. I love having the opportunity to care for people in their time of need. I
enjoy saving people's lives and making them feel better. I like the challenge in figuring out what is wrong with patients. At times you feel like a
detective. I also enjoy treating patients' illnesses.

I dislike the fact that many hospitals are overcrowded and busy, which makes it difficult to provide the quality care that you would like to provide with every patient. You can't always spend the extra five to 10 minutes explaining something to the patient or family because you have many other patients that need to be seen. It is also hard to see people in pain or dealing with death.

Q. **What advice would you give to young people?**

A. Take science classes, and continue to work on your people skills. It is also helpful to learn a foreign language, since many of the patient populations don't speak English. After you enter college, I would recommend getting your undergraduate nursing degree. I would work as an RN for several years before starting any graduate classes. You need to find the area of nursing that you enjoy before starting with your advanced nursing education.

Q. **What is the employment outlook for nurse practitioners?**

A. There are many jobs available as an NP. You have the opportunity to work in various settings, as well. As a NP, you always have the option to work as a RN as a backup plan. Being a NP opens so many more doors for your career as a nurse.

Interview: Tara Seider

Tara Seider is a pediatric nurse at Children's Memorial Hospital in Chicago. She is currently studying to become a pediatric nurse practitioner. She discussed her career and her educational journey with the editors of *Hot Jobs*.

Q. **What made you want to become a nurse? Can you tell us what prompted you to decide to transition from work as an RN to an advanced practice nurse (APN)?**

A. I have always loved the idea of helping others. Nursing seemed to be a natural fit for me.

I decided to advance my nursing career because I realized I had more to give. Being a staff/bedside nurse is wonderful and an honor, but I know with an advanced degree I can use the knowledge that I obtain to better serve my patients. I am also excited at the prospects of more responsibility and autonomy that the APN role will provide.

Q. **Can you tell us a little about your training to become an APN?**

A. I am just starting! I have three classes completed and a whole lot left. I will be taking theory classes, as well as science courses. I will also work alongside a current APN and learn hands on.

Q. **What are the most important qualities for nurses?**

A. Personal: One must have compassion, honesty, and a good sense of humor! A good nurse should be flexible and be able to relate to all types of people.

Professional: One should have integrity, good judgment, excellent communication skills, and patience.

Q. **What advice would you give to young people?**

A. Enjoy it! Be honest to your patients, be good to yourself, and take care of you. Study and ask many questions.

CARPENTERS

OVERVIEW

Carpenters are skilled tradesworkers who cut, form, fit, install, and repair items typically made from wood, but also made of metal, glass, tile, or other materials. They work in the manufacturing and construction industries. About a third of carpenters are self-employed and work as subcontractors employed by home or business owners or construction managers. Carpenters train for the field by attending vocational schools or technical colleges or formal apprenticeship programs, which often last three to four years. Others learn the trade through on-the-job training. Approximately 1.3 million carpenters work in the United States. Employment opportunities for carpenters should be good through 2018.

FAST FACTS

High School Subjects
Mathematics
Technical/shop

Personal Skills
Communication
Critical thinking
Technical

Work Environment
Indoors and outdoors
Primarily multiple locations

Minimum Education Level
Apprenticeship

Salary Range
$24,000 to $45,000 to $70,000+

Employment Outlook
About as fast as the average

O*NET-SOC
47-2031.00

GOE
06.02.02

DOT
860

NOC
7271

THE JOB

The majority of carpenters work in construction. Their duties vary based on the project and where they are employed. They may help construct buildings, roads, bridges, docks, industrial plants, boats, and many other structures. In general, their job consists of cutting, sizing, and constructing wood or other building materials. A growing number of building managers are hiring carpenters who specialize in building structures such as scaffolds, constructing and installing staircases, building with concrete, installing wood trim, fitting windows, and making and installing custom cabinetry, among other skills. Some carpenters are multiskilled, which makes them very marketable.

Carpenters have to be familiar with building regulations because they often determine the materials that are used in construction. Although every job carpenters perform is different, most jobs have the same basic steps. The initial steps are typically handled in a workshop or manufacturing room offsite. First, carpenters review blueprints and measure, mark, and organize materials. Next, they size, form, and cut the items, whether made of wood, fiberglass, drywall, or another building material. To accomplish this, they use a variety of hand tools, such as chisels, saws, and hammers, as well as power tools such as drills, sanders, and electric saws. Once they build the items, they travel to the job site to fit and install the materials. They use adhesives or nails, depending on the material, to fit pieces together. Some jobs do not require pieces to be made but simply require installation. Staircases and cabinets are often premade and can be installed more quickly onsite than custom jobs. The last step in every carpentry project is reviewing the work. Carpenters make sure everything is straight and smooth using levelers, sanders, and rulers.

Some carpenters remain workshop-based and are responsible solely for manufacturing items such as furniture or wooden molds for pouring concrete. Some make doors, staircases, or scaffolds. Other carpenters travel to job sites and fit and install such items or do finishing jobs such as laying hardwood floors or installing wood trim.

Some carpenters specialize in remodeling jobs rather than new construction. These workers may need to work around occupants and owners of the house or commercial building, so they must be careful, clean, and conscientious in their work.

Not all carpenters work in construction. Some repair materials such as glass, furniture, or hardwood floors. Others install locks, doors, or windows. Manufacturing firms hire carpenters to install or move machinery or structures.

The work of carpenter is physically demanding and the risk of injury in this career is fairly high. Inhalation of wood or fiberglass dust is a side effect of working in enclosed spaces with machinery, so carpenters typically wear face masks to protect themselves. They also wear protective gear such as hard hats, goggles, work gloves, and steel-toed boots to avoid injury. The work is strenuous, and carpenters spend a lot of time standing, kneeling, bending, and crouching.

At construction sites, the number of daylight hours affects the length of the working day (if the project is outside). As a result, early starts are common for carpenters. Some carpenters that specialize in manufacturing remain in their workshops, but most carpenters perform their work onsite, so travel is a must. Most carpenters work a standard 40-hour week; however, some work additional hours depending on their workload and deadlines.

REQUIREMENTS

HIGH SCHOOL

In high school, take classes in algebra, geometry, physics, English, mechanical drawing, blueprint reading, and general shop.

POSTSECONDARY TRAINING

Carpenters train for the field by attending vocational schools or technical colleges or formal apprenticeship programs, which often last three to four years. The United Brotherhood of Carpenters and Joiners of America offers a searchable database of training programs at its website, www.carpenters.org. Information on training can also be obtained from the Home Builders Institute (www.hbi.org).

CERTIFICATION AND LICENSING

The United Brotherhood of Carpenters and Joiners of America offers voluntary certification to carpenters in several specialty areas, including scaffold building, high-torque bolting, or pump work. Contact the union for more information.

OTHER REQUIREMENTS

Successful carpenters have good eye-hand coordination, manual dexterity, and a good sense of balance. They are physically fit and have good endurance. Other important traits include mathematical acumen, problem-solving skills, the ability to follow instructions, strong communication skills, and the ability to work as a member of a team, but also independently, as needed. Carpenters who wish to become foremen or construction managers should be proficient in Spanish, since many construction workers today speak Spanish as a first language.

EXPLORING

One of the best ways to learn more about a career as a carpenter is to actually do carpentry work. Ask your shop teacher or parents to provide some age-appropriate activities that will help you hone your carpentry skills. You can also read books and magazines about carpentry, visit carpentry-related websites, and talk to a carpenter about his or her career. Finally, consider volunteering with Habitat for Humanity. This nonprofit organization offers volunteer opportunities for young people between the ages of five and 25. Visit www.habitat.org/youthprograms for more information.

EMPLOYERS

Approximately 1.3 million carpenters are employed in the United States. Thirty-two percent work in the construction industry, and another 22 percent are employed by specialty trade contractors. Others are employed by government agencies, manufacturing firms (such as shipbuilding or aircraft production), retail establishments, theater organizations, movie and television production companies (as set builders), convention halls, and a variety of other industries. Approximately 32 percent of all carpenters are self-employed—a percentage that is much higher than the average for all occupations.

GETTING A JOB

Contact the local office of your state's employment service to learn more about available apprenticeships. Job leads can also be obtained from contractors, newspaper classified ads, and the local offices of the United Brotherhood of Carpenters, and by contacting potential employers directly. Those interested in positions with the federal government should visit the U.S. Office of Personnel Management's website, www.usajobs.opm.gov.

ADVANCEMENT

With experience, carpenters can advance to the position of carpentry supervisor or general construction supervisor. Others work as independent con-

Did You Know?

Women make up about 51 percent of the U.S. population, but only 10 percent of workers in the construction industry. Although this number is growing, women in construction still face many challenges (such as unequal pay and sexual harassment on the job). The following organizations provide support to women in the construction industry: National Association of Women in Construction (www.nawic.org); Nontraditional Employment for Women (www.new-nyc.org); Tradeswomen, Inc. (http://tradeswomen.org); Tradeswomen Now and Tomorrow (www.tradeswomennow.org); Women Construction Owners and Executives, USA (www.wcoeusa.org); Hard Hatted Women (www.hardhattedwomen.org), and Women Contractors Association (www.womencontractors.org).

tractors or teach at high schools or in apprenticeship programs. Carpenters who can speak Spanish, are able to estimate the cost and duration of a job, and have excellent communication skills will have the best chances of obtaining managerial positions or opening their own business.

EARNINGS

Salaries for carpenters vary by type of employer, geographic region, and the worker's experience level and skills. Earnings for carpenters ranged from less than $24,600 to $70,750 or more in 2009, according to the U.S. Department of Labor (USDL). The USDL reports the following mean annual earnings for carpenters by industry: electric power generation, transmission and distribution, $64,770; motion picture and video industries, $58,170; nonresidential building construction, $48,500; building finishing contractors, $45,870; foundation, structure, and building exterior contractors, $41,180; and residential building construction, $40,950.

Apprentices earn starting salaries that are about 50 percent of a journeyman carpenter's earnings. This wage increases gradually as the apprentice gains experience. By the fourth year of work, apprentices earn 90 to 95 percent of the journeyman carpenter's salary.

Employers offer a variety of benefits, including the following: medical, dental, and life insurance; paid holidays, vacations, and sick days; personal days; 401(k) plans; profit-sharing plans; and pension plans. Fringe benefits are typically guaranteed by union contracts. Approximately 19 percent of all carpenters are members of unions. Non-union workers typically receive fewer or no benefits. Additionally, self-employed workers must provide their own benefits.

EMPLOYMENT OUTLOOK

Employment for carpenters is expected to increase about as fast as the average for all occupations through 2018, according to the U.S. Department of Labor. Population growth, an increasing emphasis on energy conservation

FOR MORE INFORMATION

For information on accredited educational programs, contact
**American Council
for Construction Education**
1717 North Loop 1604 E, Suite 320
San Antonio, TX 78232-1570
acce@acce-hq.org
www.acce-hq.org

For information on K-12 programs, contact
**Associated General
Contractors of America**
2300 Wilson Boulevard, Suite 400
Arlington, VA 22201-5426
info@agc.org
www.agc.org

For information on state apprenticeship programs, visit
**Employment &
Training Administration**
U.S. Department of Labor
www.doleta.gov

For information on apprenticeships and training programs, contact
Home Builders Institute
1201 15th Street, NW, Sixth Floor
Washington, DC 20005-2842
postmaster@hbi.org
www.hbi.org

For information about careers in the construction trades, contact
**National Association
of Home Builders**
1201 15th Street, NW
Washington, DC 20005-2842
www.nahb.com

For information on apprenticeships and union membership, contact
**United Brotherhood of
Carpenters and Joiners of America**
Carpenters Training Fund
6801 Placid Street
Las Vegas, NV 89119-4205
www.carpenters.org

Contact the following organizations for information on youth training programs in the construction trades
Job Corps
U.S. Department of Labor
200 Constitution Avenue, NW,
Suite N4463
Washington, DC 20210-0001
national_office@jobcorps.gov
www.jobcorps.gov

Project CRAFT
Home Builders Institute
http://hbi.org/page.cfm?pageID=129

Youthbuild
Home Builders Institute
http://hbi.org/page.cfm?pageID=176

(especially in the industrial sector), and an increase in projects that improve our nation's infrastructure (bridges, highways, and public buildings) will increase demand for carpenters. Opportunities will also emerge as a result of turnover in this large career field—which is the second-largest building trades occupation—as workers retire or leave the field for other reasons.

Employment for carpenters—especially those who work in the construction industry—is tied to the health of the U.S. economy. When the economy is strong, more funding for construction projects is available, and opportunities are good. When the economy is poor, fewer jobs are available as the private and public sectors reduce funding.

Interview: Rocky Hwasta

Rocky Hwasta is a union carpenter (Local #212) in Cleveland, Ohio. She discussed her career with the editors of *Hot Jobs*.

Q. Why did you decide to enter this career?

A. In 1985 I was at a point in my life where I was working in a low-paying job with no benefits. I wanted to make a career change to a job that gave me more personal satisfaction, a higher wage, and benefits. Also, I believed I had a responsibility to provide my children with a better life.

I always enjoyed working with my hands and was always a sort of "tomboy," climbing trees, not afraid to get dirty, enjoying camping and the outdoors. As a carpenter I "made and built things" with my own hands; these accomplishments gave me a great sense of pride in my job. I gained skills that I continually improved and that no one can ever take away from me.

Q. Where do you work?

A. Presently, I am a foreman for a contractor at the new University Hospitals Cancer Hospital near Case Western Reserve University in Cleveland. I assign tasks daily to my crew and follow up on supervision. I read a blueprint for dimensions to transcribe to a layout for installation of various items. Daily, I assess material needs, produce a daily progress report, and project the number of carpenters needed for job completion. I have to think "on my feet" to solve problems that arise and cooperate with other trades on the job.

Q. How did you train for this career? What was your educational path?

A. To enter the carpentry apprenticeship, I had to make a commitment to the union-funded and -operated program. The apprenticeship is a four-year program where you learn and you earn. An apprentice attends the training center for classroom and hands-on skills building four weeks a year. The rest of the time is spent on a construction project, employed by a contractor, where an apprentice is paired with a journeyman who teaches him or her the trade.

Q. How do you enter an apprenticeship?

A. There are different ways in different parts of the country, but in this area one must contact the union hall or training center for a list of contractors. Then he or she has to get hired by one of these contractors. The contractor signs an "Intent to Hire" letter. The person must work for this employer for 90 days before he or she is indentured (accepted) into the apprenticeship program. Back when I got in, I took a written test and was placed in a five-week pre-apprenticeship (40 hours/week) with classroom and shop training with about 20 guys. I placed first in my class and was sent to a bridge job. The rest is "her"story!

Q. What are the most important qualities for carpenters?

A. Math and reading comprehension, plus any type of drafting or shop classes, are helpful for a firm foundation to the apprenticeship. At the training center an apprentice follows a structured program of classes, including knowledge of hand and power tools, roof framing, interior systems (building walls, hanging drywall, installing ceilings and doors), blueprint reading, stair building, and many others.

Carpenters should be able to motivate themselves, work well by themselves and with others in a crew, and work with pride. They should learn as many carpentry skills as they can and be proficient in blueprint reading and basic math calculations. All construction workers need common sense to perform their work productively and safely. A good attitude and attendance are important aspects of a high-quality work ethic and are noticed by an employer.

Q.   What are some of the pros and cons of work in this field?

A.   Over the course of my 25+ years of carpentry, I have performed a variety of tasks and worked on many different types of job sites: schools, shopping malls, hospitals, bridges, colleges, sports arenas, and office buildings. I have set wooden forms for concrete; built walls, roofs, and stairs; hung drywall; installed doors with their hardware; and installed cabinets, countertops, and fine trim and woodwork, such as crown mold, chair rail, and casing around windows and doors. I have had the opportunity to work as a *residential carpenter* (one who builds houses) and as a *commercial carpenter* (one who builds infrastructure and multipurpose structures, like office buildings, schools, and shopping centers).

This type of work keeps you fit and strong. There are all sizes of carpenters, and you can only do what your body allows you. As a woman, I try to do my best without injuring myself. That is all that can be expected of anyone on the job, so men who are stronger than me do not intimidate me. They come in all shapes and sizes, too.

Carpenters take pride in completing a job. They can identify buildings and projects on which they have worked. There is a great pride in possessing the skills of a carpenter. Once learned and acquired, you have them for life. I also enjoy teaching others my skills and "tricks of the trade."

The cons of the job are working in the heat and blistering sun in the summer or the cold, frigid air of the winter, or the muddy, rainy weather of the spring. Working indoors doesn't always solve that problem if the building isn't to the point of being heated or air-conditioned. I have worked in pleasant conditions, too, like in the outdoors on a fall day, or indoors with air-conditioning.

At some sites the use of portable bathrooms is the only option, and they can be disgusting. Some sites have separate facilities for men and women. That is an ideal situation, but not always the case.

Carpentry work is always physical and sometimes difficult. For instance, on some jobs a carpenter may work on a scaffold all day, climbing up and down a ladder for access. Bridgework puts a carpenter far off the ground with the use of safety harnesses that are sometimes uncomfortable and restricting, but necessary in case of an accidental fall. Some jobs require greater risks than others. Working on a ladder or in a hole provides bigger risks than working on the ground or standing on a floor.

Carpentry is sometimes seasonal where layoffs are common. All construction workers work themselves out of a job as a project is completed. A contractor has the option of sending its workers to another project or laying them off. Saving your money when you are working, and not living paycheck to paycheck, are important to being financially successful.

Construction work is not for everyone; weighing the pros and cons are important to job satisfaction. Also, remember that all carpenters do not perform all tasks. Some are highly skilled in some areas and perform only those parts of the job. For instance, some carpenters work only with finished wood products and cabinets, either preparing and building them or installing them, while still others work only on bridges, assembling "forms" for concrete pours. However, it is always most beneficial to steady and full employment to be as skilled as possible in all carpentry tasks.

Q.   Have you faced any challenges as a woman working in a male-dominated field?

A.   As a woman, I had to learn to work with mostly men. Sometimes I would be the only woman on a job of more than 100 construction workers. I learned to focus on my work and not the derogatory comments of some of the men. As I built my skills, my personal confidence increased. I developed a "thick skin" against the mean remarks and learned all I could, often taking on personal projects in my home and volunteer projects to practice my skills. I learned what I could from the carpenters who were willing to teach and steered clear of those who didn't want me there. My independent spirit and positive outlook guided me to continue and not be intimidated. That paid off in a decision I do not regret, as I cherish my career, am now well-respected, have multiple skills, and look forward to a financially secure retirement.

Q.   What advice would you give to high school students—especially young women—who are interested in this career?

A.   Women who are interested in pursuing a career in carpentry need to be determined and focused. The work is hard, but rewarding. Research the training, job tasks, and financial rewards/benefits that are offered by a career in carpentry to help make a decision. More women are entering the field, so a network of mentors and support systems now exists to help them be successful. My suggestion is to find a mentor. Young women today are more Internet savvy; there are tradeswomen organizations across the country that offer emotional, and sometimes financial, support to female apprentices. (For instance, I am board president of Allied Cleveland Tradeswomen (www.actw.org); we offer scholarships to female apprentices and mentor support to all tradeswomen. I also serve on the board of Hard Hatted Women (www.hardhattedwomen.org); this organization offers multiple tools for entry and success in building trades careers.)

The carpenters' union is designed to train its members, help them find work, and offer a network of support. Attending meetings and staying current with your dues are your responsibility as a conscientious member. I have found my union to be more supportive of women over the years because I became active in advocating for us: tradeswomen specifically and union carpenters in general. Our local and regional training centers now both have a mentor committee for all apprentices.

Q.   What is the future employment outlook for carpenters?

A.   The future employment outlook for carpenters is very good, as many are retiring with a secure pension at an early age. I will be eligible for full retirement benefits at the age of 57. The requirements for retirement vary regionally. In most cases, membership in the union allows for higher wages and more benefits than a non-union carpenter. A highly skilled, motivated carpenter will always be in demand. There are also numerous career paths a carpenter may take: foreman, superintendent, instructor, apprentice coordinator, union official, estimator, project manager, safety enforcement official, or self-employed contractor, to name a few.

CIVIL ENGINEERS

OVERVIEW

Civil engineers design and supervise the construction of a variety of structures, including buildings, bridges, dams, canals, tunnels, roads and highways. They improve people's quality of life and ease of transportation. Civil engineers work on large government projects such as a new highway extension, or on smaller private projects such as a single-family home. Major subspecialties in the field include *environmental, geotechnical, structural, water resources,* and *transportation engineering.* Civil engineers typically have at least a bachelor's degree in civil engineering or a related field. Approximately 278,400 civil engineers are employed in the United States. Employment in the field is expected to grow much faster than the average for all careers through 2018.

FAST FACTS

High School Subjects
Mathematics
Physics

Personal Skills
Complex problem solving
Judgment and decision making
Technical
Time management

Minimum Education Level
Bachelor's degree

Salary Range
$49,000 to $85,000 to $120,000+

Employment Outlook
Much faster than the average

O*NET-SOC
17-2051.00

GOE
02.07.04

DOT
055

NOC
2131

THE JOB

How do people living in Marin Country cross the bay into downtown San Francisco? How do people bypass rush-hour traffic and still travel from Detroit into Windsor, Canada? How do Arizona, Nevada, and many of their neighboring states get hydroelectric power, irrigation flow, and protection from floods? How do commuters from outlying suburbs get to their downtown Chicago offices? The answers: the Golden Gate Bridge, the Detroit-Windsor Tunnel, the Hoover Dam, and the many Chicago expressways. All these structures, while different in size, scope, and purpose, share one thing in common. They were all created in part by civil engineers. Civil engineers design and supervise the construction of structures to optimize the quality of life for people—whether to provide them with easy navigational means of transportation, a safe place to live and work, or an alternative energy source.

When beginning a project, civil engineers meet with a team of builders, architects, engineers, and members of the community to discuss the purpose of the project. For example, they may meet with government officials or community leaders to address the need for a bridge to connect surrounding towns located across a body of water. Civil engineers then visit the proposed site to study the area that is involved and determine if the project is achievable. They take into account the topography of the area, including the type of soil and rock found there and the depth of the water, before designing construction plans. Using mathematical and scientific principles, and with the help of computer-aided design programs, civil engineers make a preliminary drawing of the structure, taking into consideration the type of bridge that is being constructed and the construction materials that will be used. Many times, civil engineers build miniature models to prove their design will withstand meteorological and geological stresses and everyday wear and tear while staying within the proposed budget. Their analysis is tested, reviewed, and revised before construction plans are finalized.

Major subspecialties in the field include environmental, geotechnical, structural, transportation, and water resources engineering. They are detailed in the following paragraphs.

Environmental engineers are concerned with improving the environment, including providing access to clean water, controlling pollution, developing recycling programs, and creating waste disposal and management systems. They conduct tests to gauge the levels of hazardous waste at a chemical processing plant and suggest designs to better contain or avoid dangerous situations. For example, engineers may design a filter bed used to treat and convert wastewater into clean and safe drinking water.

Geotechnical engineers study the types of soil and rock that are present at a proposed building site. For example, in the planning stages of a harbor-front building, geotechnical engineers are consulted to conduct a soil mechanics analysis. They test the condition or any variables of the soil or bedrock found in the area and suggest the types of materials that should be used in the building's foundation. Their work is important in identifying the proper combination of steel and concrete needed to ensure a strong and reliable foundation; they may suggest the use of other stress-resistant materials or designs to withstand volume change, or to reduce problems caused by erosion or weather. They also take into account any existing variables such as possible landslides, sinkholes, or earthquakes.

Structural engineers design and supervise the construction of buildings, bridges, tunnels, as well as offshore structures such as oil and gas fields. When working on a new project, structural engineers first assess the structure and identify the type of load the structure must carry, as well as the stress and forces (weather, temperature, or potential stress from other natural phenomena such as hurricanes and earthquakes). Structural engineers closely study the type and magnitude of load, meaning the structure's material weight and the weight it must hold, including motor vehicles and their passengers and cargo. Live loads include moving weight and dynamic loads from wind or changes in temperature. Structural engineers create construction plans to make sure structures are functional, yet safe, considering factors such as a structure's overall construction costs, its aesthetics, and durability. Specializations in this field include *wind engineering* and *earthquake engineering*.

Construction engineers are involved in many different building projects, from multistory dwellings to a suspension bridge to a waterway. They conduct experiments and studies, interpret data, and make predictions on whether an apartment's design, for example, is strong enough to withstand environmental stresses, or whether the design of a suspension bridge is strong enough to handle the weight of its load. They draft and evaluate building contracts and estimate the cost of building supplies and equipment. Construction engineers may also interpret area zoning laws and other legal processes.

Transportation engineers design and supervise the construction of streets, roads, highways, airports, transportation systems, and ports and harbors. When designing a traffic management plan, for example, they conduct research to identify the needs of the community, then gather data on past accidents, the volume of traffic flow in the area, and any other relevant information. With this information, they work with a team of engineers to target certain intersections or certain areas, to time traffic signals or railway crossing signals, and to upgrade or widen lanes on frequently used roadways. They may also seek to improve pedestrian-heavy areas by introducing walking paths or extra pedestrian crossing signals or pavement markings.

Monuments of the Millennium

The American Society of Civil Engineers surveyed its members to determine the "10 civil engineering achievements that had the greatest positive impact on life in the 20th century." Here are the results (in alphabetical order): California State Water Project; Chicago Wastewater System; Empire State Building; Eurotunnel (between France and Great Britain); Golden Gate Bridge; Hoover Dam; Kansai International Airport (Japan); Panama Canal; sanitary waste disposal advances overall; and the U.S. Interstate Highway System.

Hydraulic engineers design and oversee the construction of any structure that deals with the flow and transportation of water, including dams, pipelines, bridges, levees, and canals. They use their knowledge of geology, hydrology, conservation science, resource management, meteorology, and the environment to predict the type and quantity of water in lakes, rivers, streams, and underground sources. They are concerned with the pressure and ease of water flow from these sources. After Hurricane Katrina struck the Gulf Coast, for example, hydraulic engineers in New Orleans were instrumental in overseeing the design and construction of a new levee system and floodwalls. This new system was designed to better withstand the high-power storm surges and the possible erosion of soil. Many hydraulic engineers are employed by the U.S. Army Corps of Engineers.

Full-time engineers work 40 hours a week, though oftentimes they clock in closer to 50 or even 60 hours a week. This is especially true when working to meet an important deadline or if complications arise on a project. Civil engineers work in clean, well-lit, and comfortable offices. Much of their work is done on computers, whether writing proposals, conducting research, or using the latest design program. However, engineers spend time in the field, as well. For example, a transportation engineer may visit extremely busy roads to identify the reasons for congestion and traffic. An engineer specializing in water and sewage may visit existing water treatment plants or water reclamation centers. A structural engineer may travel to potential sites to identify the best location for a new bridge or tunnel. If a project is located in another state, or perhaps even another country, civil engineers may have to temporarily relocate there until the project is well underway.

Civil engineers work with a variety of professionals including architects, designers, construction managers, engineering technicians, and other engineers. They may also be responsible for making presentations to business executives or government officials in order to win a bid or to receive funding for a project. Civil engineers often meet with private citizens, especially if the structure in question is close to a residential area, or if the structure will be used by the public.

REQUIREMENTS

HIGH SCHOOL

In high school, take the following classes: physics, algebra, geometry, trigonometry, calculus, computer science, foreign language (especially if you want to work abroad), and science (chemistry, biology, physics, earth science), as well as classes such as English and speech that will help you develop your communication skills.

POSTSECONDARY TRAINING

Most people enter the field by earning a bachelor of science in civil engineering and taking and passing the Fundamentals of Engineering examination and obtaining professional licensing. Most employers require an advanced degree for top positions. The Accreditation Board for Engineering and Technology (ABET) accredits civil engineering programs. Visit its Web site, www.abet.org, to access a searchable database of accredited programs in the United States and other countries. Students who plan to pursue study in environmental engineering can learn more about the field and access a list of accredited environmental engineering programs by reading the *Environmental Engineering Selection & Career Guide* (www.aaee.net/Website/SelectionGuide.htm), which is offered by the American Academy of Environmental Engineers.

CERTIFICATION AND LICENSING

The American Society of Civil Engineers (ASCE) offers voluntary certification via its sister organization, Civil Engineering Certification. This organization has partnered with the Environmental & Water Resources Institute, the Geo-Institute, and the Coastal Ocean Ports & Rivers Institute to create specialized certification programs. Visit the ASCE website for more information. Voluntary certification for environmental engineers is offered by the American Academy of Environmental Engineers, the Institute of Professional Environmental

Practice (www.ipep.org), and the Academy of Board Certified Environmental Professionals (www.abcep.org). Voluntary certification for transportation engineers is offered by the Institute of Transportation Engineers.

Civil engineers whose work affects property, health, or life must be licensed as professional engineers. According to the U.S. Department of Labor, "this licensure generally requires a degree from an ABET-accredited engineering program, four years of relevant work experience, and completion of a state examination. Recent graduates can start the licensing process by taking the examination in two stages. The initial Fundamentals of Engineering examination can be taken upon graduation. Engineers who pass this examination commonly are called engineers in training (EITs) or engineer interns. After acquiring suitable work experience, EITs can take the second examination, called the Principles and Practice of Engineering exam." Visit the National Council of Examiners for Engineering and Surveying website, www.ncees.org, for more information on licensure.

OTHER REQUIREMENTS

To be a successful civil engineer, you should be good at solving problems, have excellent communication skills, excel at mathematics, be able to work well with others, and have an inquisitive personality.

EXPLORING

There are many ways to learn more about a career in civil engineering. You can read books and magazines about civil engineering, talk to an engineer about his or her career, attend an after-school or summer engineering program (see www.careercornerstone.org/pcsumcamps.htm for more information), and join the Junior Engineering Technical Society and participate in its competitions and other programs. Additionally, the ASCE has created a website to educate people about the rewards of a career in civil engineering. It can be accessed by visiting ASCEville.org.

EMPLOYERS

Approximately 278,400 civil engineers are employed in the United States. According to the American Society of Civil Engineers, there are five main employment areas for civil engineers: government, education, consulting, industry, and construction. Civil engineers work for large international engineering companies, government agencies, and small regional construction companies. Others are employed as teachers at colleges and universities.

GETTING A JOB

Many civil engineers obtain their first jobs as a result of contacts made through college internships or networking events. Others seek assistance in obtaining job leads from college career services offices, newspaper want ads, and employment websites. Additionally, professional engineering associations—such as the American Society of Civil Engineers and the Institute of Transportation Engineers—provide job listings at their websites. See For More Information for a list of organizations. Those interested in working for

FOR MORE INFORMATION

For information on careers, certification, and the *Environmental Engineering Selection & Career Guide,* contact
American Academy of Environmental Engineers
130 Holiday Court, Suite 100
Annapolis, MD 21401-7003
info@aaee.net
www.aaee.net

For information about careers in engineering, contact
American Society for Engineering Education
1818 N Street, NW, Suite 600
Washington, DC 20036-2479
202-331-3500
www.asee.org

For information on education and careers, contact
American Society of Civil Engineers
1801 Alexander Bell Drive
Reston, VA 20191-5467
www.asce.org

For information on highway engineering, contact
American Society of Highway Engineers
65 Beacon Hill
Henderson, NC 27537-9448
www.highwayengineers.org

For information on water resources engineering, contact the following organizations
American Water Resources Association
PO Box 1626
Middleburg, VA 20118-1626
www.awra.org

American Water Works Association
6666 West Quincy Avenue
Denver, CO 80235-3098
www.awwa.org

For industry information, contact
Institute of Transportation Engineers
1627 Eye Street, NW, Suite 600
Washington, DC 20006-4087
www.ite.org

For information about civil engineering and student competitions and membership, contact
Junior Engineering Technical Society
1420 King Street, Suite 405
Alexandria, VA 22314-2750
www.jets.org

For information on structural engineering, visit
Structural Engineers Association-International
www.seaint.org

the federal government should visit the U.S. Office of Personnel Management's website, www.usajobs.opm.gov.

ADVANCEMENT

Civil engineers with considerable experience and certification can open up their own consulting firms. Others advance by receiving pay raises, by taking on managerial duties, or by pursuing job opportunities at more prestigious firms. Some civil engineers teach at the high school and college levels.

EARNINGS

Salaries for civil engineers vary by type of employer, geographic region, and the worker's experience level and skills. The median income for civil engineers was $85,000 in 2009, according to *The Engineering Income & Salary Survey,* ASCE/ASME. The median income for civil engineers with less than one year of experience was $55,160, while those more than 25 years of experience earned $120,050. Earnings also varied by educational attainment. Civil engineers with a bachelor's degree had median annual earnings of $85,000, while those with a doctoral degree in engineering earned $110,700.

Median annual salaries for civil engineers were $76,590 in 2009, according to the U.S. Department of Labor. Salaries ranged from less than $49,620 to $96,800 or more.

Civil engineers usually receive benefits such as health and life insurance, vacation days, sick leave, and a savings and pension plan. Self-employed workers must provide their own benefits.

EMPLOYMENT OUTLOOK

Our nation's infrastructure (bridges, roads, buildings, airports, tunnels, dams, harbors, and water supply and sewage systems) is deteriorating, but the population is increasing (which will require the construction of even more infrastructure). This is good news for civil engineers. Opportunities will be best for those with advanced education and certifications. Employment for civil engineers is expected to grow much faster than the average for all careers through 2018, according to the U.S. Department of Labor.

Interview: Fraser Howe

Fraser Howe, PE is a senior associate at T.Y. Lin International. He has worked in the field for 36 years. Fraser discussed his career with the editors of *Hot Jobs.*

Q. What made you want to enter this career?

A. I started taking drafting classes in high school (pencil & paper) and became interested in engineering. Initially I wanted to be an automotive designer but became more interested in the environment. At Michigan State University (MSU) I took several courses in water and waste water treatment and accepted an offer from a firm that designed industrial wastewater treatment systems. Basically, I became a civil engineer so I could help make the world a better place to live in.

Q. What is one thing that young people may not know about a career in civil engineering?

A. Civil engineers make the built environment. If you want to change the world, become a civil engineer! Once you have that powerful motivation, you will want to gain the skills needed to do it, i.e. the math and science education to learn the design principles.

Q. How did you train for this career? Did you participate in any internships?

A. After graduating from high school I was accepted at Tri-State College, now Trine University, in Angola, Indiana. I attended classes for a B.S. in civil engineering until I transferred to MSU in the spring of my sophomore year. That May I married my wife, a registered nurse. I did not do any internships, although now I recommend them to engineering students in their junior and senior years. During the summer after my junior year I worked full-time for a materials testing firm. I had just taken my geotech and concrete design courses so it was great to go into the field and use that knowledge.

Q. **What are the most important qualities for civil engineers?**

A. While most think of engineering as a technical profession a good engineer is a people-person. It takes a language skill to translate often complex technical issues into terms that a non-engineer can understand. I try not say that we must "educate" them because most intelligent people can understand the issues if we can put them into terms they can visualize or relate to their daily lives.

Q. **What advice would you give to young people who are interested in becoming civil engineers?**

A. Go for it! Seriously, they should try to meet practicing engineers or engineering students. This could be a local group of engineers from the American Society of Civil Engineers, the National Society of Professional Engineers, or a local engineering school that has an outreach program to high school or middle school students. Joining this will give them the opportunity to participate in programs like the West Point Bridge Design Contest (http://bridgecontest.usma.edu), MathCounts (http://mathcounts.org), Future City Competition (www.futurecity.org), or National Engineers Week (http://eweek.org) activities.

Interview: Maria Lehman

Maria Lehman, PE, F.ASCE is a civil engineer at Bergmann Associates. She has worked in the field for more than 29 years. Maria discussed her career with the editors of *Hot Jobs*.

Q. **What made you want to enter this career?**

A. I entered engineering because of a math teacher I had who happened to be the department chair, Mr. Thomas LaPenna. I believe he made us learn calculus through osmosis. The entire class grasped it and did well, and it didn't seem to be as hard as everyone thought it would be. His class motto was, "Cogitation and Tenacity." He told us if we lived up to the motto he would even forgive us for forgetting calculus. I still live by that motto. I went to a blue-collar neighborhood high school, John F. Kennedy High School in Cheektowaga, New York. Only 10 percent of my graduating class went on to college, and most of us went on to engineering due to Mr. LaPenna's influence.

Q. **What is one thing that young people may not know about a career in civil engineering?**

A. Civil engineering is really about helping people through a better built environment. Much of what we do is always there working to make people's lives better every day. I often challenge middle-school students to bring something up that they think is not tied to engineering and I tell them how it is. I have not yet been stumped. It's about the lights, radio, TV, and computer you turn on; it's about the house you live in; the school you learn in; the building you work in; it's about the transportation you take to where you are going; it's about the water you drink and the contaminated water you flush away; it's about energy generation and distribution; and it's about environmental clean-up and habitat restoration. Engineering is all around you, each and every day, and it is necessary for a safe, healthy, and prosperous today and tomorrow.

It is incredibly satisfying to see your ideas show up in a design and then be constructed. And many years later to hear from people who have been impacted by something you did a long time ago.

Q. How did you train for this career?

A. In high school, I took five years of math—algebra, geometry, trigonometry, coordinate geometry and probability (both 1/2 year courses), and calculus. I also took four years of science—biology, chemistry, physics, and advanced biology. In college I took the required curriculum, but also took business classes to understand that side of what I am doing today.

Q. Did you participate in any internships?

A. I did not participate in any internships in college, and felt woefully inadequate when I started my first job. So I committed to working with the School of Engineering at the University of New York at Buffalo (my alma mater) to make sure that students were linked to employers through our professional organization, the American Society of Civil Engineers (ASCE). As a young board member of ASCE, I worked as student liaison to get placements. And 15 years later when the school took internship to the next level, with a summer Engineering Career Institute, I worked with the school as a guest lecturer and helped with placements. I have been involved ever since graduation. I believe it is that important.

Q. What are the most important qualities for civil engineers?

A. Professional qualities that are important are technical expertise and integrity. The first few years out of school, engineers should try to get as much varied experience as possible, not only to have a better chance at passing their Professional Engineering exam to become a PE, but also to get a better feeling for where they'd like to be professional in five, 10, 20 years. After becoming an "engineering shortstop." Then you need to focus on a couple of core competencies and build your résumé. Throughout your career you need to network, to know your peers and bounce ideas off of them. Diversity always helps synthesize a better solution. And integrity is the most important core principle. Engineers by their cannons of ethics are to hold public health and safety paramount. Without that you have nothing.

Personal qualities are more dependent on the individual. I have always been what I call a "professional cliff diver." I try new things, take on new challenges, and volunteer for the assignments that no one else wants to take on. Sometimes it works out better than others, but you always learn in the process. As a whole, the personalities that migrate toward engineering tend to be risk adverse; we really need to step out of that comfort zone, as that is where you find true innovation and your career soars.

Q. What advice would you give to aspiring civil engineers?

A. Go for it, it's a great career that will always be in need.

COLLEGE PROFESSORS

OVERVIEW

College professors teach and advise students at the undergraduate and graduate levels, serve on department and university committees, conduct research in their concentration, write articles for scholarly journals and other publications, and promote higher education. Their job is as varied as the subjects they teach and the institutions for which they work. A minimum of a master's degree is required to work as a college professor; top colleges and universities typically require a doctorate. Approximately 1.7 million college professors are employed in the United States. They work for community colleges, vocational colleges, and four-year colleges and universities. Employment for college professors is expected to grow faster than the average for all careers through 2018.

THE JOB

College professors have a variety of duties, from instructing large undergraduate lectures, to hosting small seminar classes, to running laboratory experiments and supervising computer labs, to writing textbooks. Though the first thing that may come to mind when thinking of a college professor might be teaching, the average professor spends only a small amount of time each week in the classroom—from three hours a week for graduate-level professors to 12-16 hours a week for those teaching at the undergraduate level. College professors spend the rest of their time conducting research, preparing lesson plans, grading assignments, advising students, giving presentations, serving on department or university committees, and writing for publication.

FAST FACTS

High School Subjects
English
Speech

Personal Skills
Communication
Critical thinking
Leadership
Time management

Minimum Education Level
Master's degree

Salary Range
$52,000 to $79,000 to $108,000+

Employment Outlook
Faster than the average

O*NET-SOC
25-1011.00, 25-1021.00, 25-1022.00, 25.1031.00, 25-1032.00, 25-1041.00, 25-1042.00, 25-1043.00, 25-1051.00, 25-1052.00, 25-1053.00, 25-1054.00, 25-1061.00, 25-1062.00, 25-1063.00, 25-1064.00, 25-1065.00, 25-1066.00, 25-1067.00, 25-1071.00, 25-1072.00, 25-1081.00, 25-1082.00, 25-1111.00, 25-1112.00, 25-1113.00, 25-1121.00, 25-1122.00, 25-1123.00, 25-1124.00, 25-1125.00, 25-1126.00, 25-1191.00, 25-1192.00, 25-1193.00, 25-1194.00

GOE
12.03.02

DOT
090

NOC
4121

A professor advises students who are working on a group project. Nearly 257,000 new jobs are expected to be available for college professors by 2018, according to the U.S. Department of Labor. (Creatas Images/Thinkstock)

College professors typically focus on a particular subject, such as English, history, psychology, or mathematics, to name a few. The classes they teach can be general, such as Composition 101, or specific, such as British Survey: 1650-1700 or The Novels of Toni Morrison. This variety and uniqueness in subject matter afforded to college professors makes the job interesting and unique.

It can be challenging for professors just entering the field. Depending on their employer, there can be great pressure to get published in scholarly publications. Doing so creates credibility for the professor and brings esteem to the college or university for which he or she teaches. Getting published also helps to ensure a tenure-track position.

What is all the buzz about tenure? It is very difficult for a tenured professor to be fired without cause. However, tenure no longer means complete immunity; post-tenure review is now required at most universities. Tenured professors are granted a sort of academic freedom to teach what they want and how they want, without much regulation by administrators. They can largely set their own responsibilities and decide to a large extent how to divide time between teaching, writing, research, and administration.

Because of their flexible schedules and long spans of time off, many college professors have second jobs. For example, an English professor might write articles that appear in newspapers or scholarly publications. An economics professor might sit on the board of a corporation or work for a government agency. An archaeology professor might conduct fieldwork during winter or summer break in Peru, Iraq, China, or other foreign countries.

Online education has become a popular option in recent years for students. The cost savings are twofold. Student sometimes save money in tuition costs by enrolling in classes online, and colleges and universities save money in infrastructure costs, since they do not need to physically provide a classroom for the course. Today's college professors must be willing and able to convert any of their lessons to an online format if requested and answer emails as they would converse with students in class and after hours. Knowledge of technology, including that which is used to teach students in brick-and-mortar settings, is key to success for college professors.

While college professors' schedules are flexible, their hours can be long. Since much of their time is spent planning lessons, teaching, grading, and advising students, many professors conduct research and write on their own time, in the evenings and on weekends. The job can also be stressful, particularly for those striving for a tenure-track position. Between working toward that goal and submitting countless articles for publication, most of which will be rejected, the job is not for the thin-skinned.

However, ask any professor, and most will tell you it is rewarding to teach a subject they have expertise in, conduct research on new and existing topics within their discipline, help students make important educational and life choices, interact with colleagues in a highly intellectual work setting, and write for publication about topics that they enjoy. Another plus is the flexibility of their schedules. Yes, professors work hard, but they also have a fair amount of freedom in terms of when they work. Finally, let us not forget summer break and other long vacations! Not many other careers offer that many blocks of scheduled time off throughout the year.

REQUIREMENTS

HIGH SCHOOL

In high school, you should pursue a general college preparatory curriculum that includes courses in science, history, mathematics, foreign language, computer science, social studies, and government. Take English and speech classes to hone your communication skills.

POSTSECONDARY TRAINING

You will need at least one advanced degree in your specialty to work as a college professor. Having a master's degree will qualify you for some positions—especially at community colleges—but most colleges and universities require their teachers to have a doctorate.

The Council of Graduate Schools has prepared a useful publication, *Graduate School and You,* which provides information on choosing a graduate school, paying for school, and other topics. It is available for a small charge. Visit www.cgsnet.org for more information.

CERTIFICATION AND LICENSING

There is no certification or licensing available for college professors.

OTHER REQUIREMENTS

To be a successful college professor, you should have excellent communication skills and enjoy working with students. You should have an analytical mind, be self-motivated, enjoy conducting research, be comfortable in a position of authority, and have self-confidence.

EXPLORING

One excellent way to learn more about a career in education is to observe your high school teachers as they do their work. Try to arrange an information interview with your favorite teacher to learn more about teaching. You can also visit the websites of colleges and universities to read the biographies of teachers in your area of interest. You might even contact them via email to see if they are interested in talking with you about your career plans or set up an in-person appointment during your campus visits in your junior and senior years. You can also read books about teachers and visit education association websites. Try to gain some hands-on experience working as a teacher at a summer camp, in a community center, in a day camp, or with a religious organization. Finally, consider joining or starting a chapter of the Future Educators Association at your school (visit www.futureeducators.org for more information).

EMPLOYERS

Approximately 1.7 million college professors are employed in the United States. They work for community colleges, vocational colleges, and four-year colleges and universities.

GETTING A JOB

Many aspiring college professors obtain experience by working as graduate teaching assistants while still in school. They teach classes and perform other teaching-related duties, such as grading papers, preparing class presentations, and conducting laboratory sessions. As a graduate student, you should prepare for the hiring process by developing a curriculum vitae (an academic résumé), seeking recommendations from professors, and attending educational conferences, where students often meet with prospective employers for interviews. The Council of Graduate Schools and the Association of American Colleges and Universities have created a teacher-preparation program called Preparing Future Faculty (PFF). According to its website, "the program is a national movement to transform the way aspiring faculty members are prepared for their careers. PFF programs provide doctoral students, as well as some master's and postdoctoral students, with opportunities to observe and experience faculty responsibilities at a variety of academic institutions with varying missions, diverse student bodies, and different expectations for faculty." Visit www.preparing-faculty.org for more information.

You can also learn about job openings from professional education associations, such as the College and University Professional Association for Human Resources (www.cupahr.org), and by reading industry publications such as *The Chronicle of Higher Education* (www.chronicle.com).

ADVANCEMENT

The typical advancement path for a college teacher is from instructor, to assistant professor, to associate professor, and finally to professor—with an overall goal of attaining tenure. According to the U.S. Department of Labor, "tenured professors cannot be fired without just cause and due process." The tenure track is a difficult path. Because of stiff competition, most tenured professors at four-year colleges have a doctoral degree. This typically takes four to seven years to complete since it encompasses student teaching, writing, and defending a dissertation. At the end of this time period, a teacher's academic record, research and writing accomplishments, and overall contribution to the school is reviewed. If the review is positive, teachers are usually granted tenure. Teachers who do not receive tenure typically must leave the academic institution. While approximately 80 percent of college professors work for a four-year institution, about one-third are employed part-time or are in non-tenure-track positions. Once a professor is tenured, he or she might advance by serving as department head or becoming a dean or even college president.

EARNINGS

Salaries for college professors vary by geographic region, type of school (private, public, women's only, for example), and the teacher's experience level, position, skills, and professional achievements. The average yearly income for all full-time faculty was $79,439 in 2008-09, according to the American Association of University Professors, which also reports that professors earned the following average salaries by rank: lecturers, $52,436; instructors, $45,977; assistant professors, $63,827; associate professors, $76,147; and full professors, $108,749. Salaries for full-time faculty averaged $79,439. Full-time faculty at private independent institutions earned average salaries of $92,257; in public institutions, $77,009; and in religiously affiliated private colleges and universities, $71,857.

According to the College and University Professional Association for Human Resources, professors in the following disciplines received the highest average salaries in 2009-10: legal professions and studies, $102,101; business, management, marketing, and related support services, $91,886; and engineering, $90,208. The lowest salaries were found in the following fields: English language and literature/letters, $60,850; parks, recreation, leisure, and fitness studies, $61,709; and visual and performing arts, $61,898.

Colleges and universities offer a variety of benefits, including the following: medical, dental, and life insurance; paid holidays, vacations, and sick days; personal days; 401(k) plans; profit-sharing plans; retirement and pension plans; and educational assistance programs. Part-time teachers must provide their own benefits.

EMPLOYMENT OUTLOOK

Employment for college professors is expected to grow faster than the average for all careers through 2018, according to the U.S. Department of Labor. The increasing number of college students and an expected wave of retirements will create approximately 256,900 new jobs through 2018. There will also be a growing number of jobs available at community colleges and for-profit institutions because working adults are returning to school as a result of the recession and more young people are pursuing careers that require less than a four-year education. Some of the best opportunities for college professors will be in occupational fields that are experiencing strong growth, including computer science, business, nursing and other health specialties, and the biological sciences. Despite this prediction, competition for tenure-track positions will be strong. There will be more opportunities for those seeking non-tenure-track positions and part-time jobs. Professors who have Ph.D.'s will have the best job prospects.

FOR MORE INFORMATION

For information on careers and union membership, contact the following organizations

**American Association
of University Professors**
1133 Nineteenth Street, NW, Suite 200
Washington, DC 20036-3655
202-737-5900
aaup@aaup.org
www.aaup.org

American Federation of Teachers
555 New Jersey Avenue, NW
Washington, DC 20001-2029
202-879-4400
online@aft.org
www.aft.org

The following association represents the professional interests of female professors

**American Association
of University Women**
1111 Sixteenth Street, NW
Washington, DC 20036-4809
800-326-AAUW
connect@aauw.org
www.aauw.org

The following organizations are just a small sampling of educational associations that represent the interests of professors in a variety of academic disciplines. Visit their websites for more information.

**American Association
for Agricultural Education**
http://aaaeonline.org

**Association for Library and
Information Science Education**
www.alise.org

**Association of Environmental
Engineering and Science Professors**
www.aeesp.org

**Association of
Professors of Dermatology**
www.dermatologyprofessors.org

**Association of University
Professors of Neurology**
www.aupn.org

**Association of University
Professors of Ophthalmology**
www.aupo.org

**Computer Science
Teachers Association**
http://csta.acm.org

Journalism Education Association
www.jea.org

**National Association
of Geoscience Teachers**
www.nagt.org

**National Earth Science
Teachers Association**
www.nestanet.org

**National Marine
Educators Association**
www.marine-ed.org

**National Science
Teachers Association**
www.nsta.org

COMPUTER NETWORK, SYSTEMS, AND DATABASE ADMINISTRATORS

OVERVIEW

Computer network administrators, systems administrators, and database administrators design, install, manage, and provide support for computer systems at businesses, government agencies, schools, and other organizations. Depending on their specialty, these administrators manage databases; set up area networks, the Internet/intranet, and other data communication systems; and oversee network security. Educational requirements vary by specialty. Approximately 961,200 computer network, systems, and database administrators are employed in the United States. Excellent employment prospects are expected through 2018.

THE JOB

Many businesses, organizations, and individuals rely on the efficient and timely transmission, as well as the storage and safety of, electronic information. These duties are carried out by a variety of specialized computer administrators (detailed in the paragraphs below). Computer administrators play a key role in helping businesses and individuals share and store this important information.

Computer network and *systems administrators* design, install, and provide support for computer networks used by businesses and other organizations. They also establish local area and wide area networks and Internet/Intranet systems. Administrators identify what is expected of the system and network, and coordinate the acquisition and setup of all necessary components—both hardware and software—to meet these expectations. They monitor the performance of the network and make adjustments, installing updates and patches, and revising configurations as needed. Network and

FAST FACTS

High School Subjects
Computer science
Mathematics

Personal Skills
Communication
Complex problem solving
Technical

Minimum Education Level
Bachelor's degree

Salary Range
$40,000 to $75,000 to $116,000+

Employment Outlook
Much faster than the average

O*NET-SOC
15-1061.00, 15-1071.00,
15-1081.00, 15-1099.00

GOE
02.06.01

DOT
039

NOC
2172

Computerworld's Best Companies to Work For in Information Technology, 2009

1) General Mills, Inc. (www.generalmills.com)

2) Genentech, Inc. (www.gene.com)

3) San Diego Gas & Electric Company (www.sdge.com)

4) University of Pennsylvania (www.upenn.edu)

5) Monsanto Co. (www.monsanto.com)

6) Securian Financial Group, Inc. (www.securian.com)

7) Verizon Wireless (www.verizonwireless.com)

8) JM Family Enterprises, Inc. (www.jmfamily.com)

9) USAA (www.usaa.com)

10) University of Miami (www.miami.edu)

11) American Fidelity Assurance Co. (www.afadvantage.com)

12) Marriott International, Inc. (www.marriott.com)

13) Sun Microsystems, Inc. (www.sun.com)

14) Quicken Loans, Inc. (www.quickenloans.com)

15) Raytheon Company (www.raytheon.com)

systems administrators also perform periodic maintenance such as routine network startup and shutdown procedures, scheduled backups, and maintenance of control records. They respond quickly to problems reported by users and by automated network monitoring systems.

A database is a collection of electronic files holding information that is important to a company or organization, such as health care records, sales figures, or even police criminal records. *Database administrators* manage the storage and organization of this information. They use data management software to ensure secure storage of the data, and to allow users to quickly and easily retrieve information. The quick-responding database, such as one that retrieves files in real time, can be an important factor in the success of a company. Database administrators test modifications to the new system and troubleshoot for any potential problems. They also add new users to a system and ensure that the database is secure and protected from hackers or other unauthorized use. Those who specialize in computer and information security are known as *computer security specialists*.

Network systems and data communication analysts plan, design, build, maintain, and test networks and data communication systems of companies and organizations. They are often referred to as *network architects* or *network engineers*. Without them, it would be virtually impossible to easily share electronic information among departments or from satellite offices. They use special software to model and test upgraded or new networks or make needed changes to existing networks. Network systems and data communication analysts set up local area networks and wide area networks as well as interoffice email systems. They are also on call to help prevent viral threats to the system or other technological emergencies.

Administrators work in clean, comfortable offices or computer laboratories. Depending on their employer, some administrators are able to telecommute from home, or access their clients via remote technology. Much of their day is spent working on computers, either keyboarding programs or troubleshooting for glitches. However, there are many times administrators may need to get on the floor in order to maneuver around the main computer server or to set up pieces of hardware.

Most administrators work full time—about 40 hours a week. However, administrators are often on call, and they may be expected to work overtime and on weekends. It is not uncommon to log 50 or more hours a week, especially when facing a tough deadline, an unexpected system failure, or a crashed server.

REQUIREMENTS

HIGH SCHOOL

It should go without saying that you should take as many computer science classes as possible in high school. Courses that help you develop your problem-solving and critical-thinking skills will be most useful. Other important classes include mathematics, English, and speech.

POSTSECONDARY TRAINING

Network and systems administrators typically need a bachelor's degree in computer science, information science, or management information systems. Other companies may require applicants to only have an associate's degree, or extensive computer industry experience and professional certification.

Network architects and database administrators must have a bachelor's degree in a computer-related field, although some companies require workers to have a master's degree in business administration with a concentration in information systems.

Computer administrators continue to learn throughout their careers by taking seminars, classes, and other educational offerings from employers, colleges and universities, industry associations, hardware and software vendors, and private training institutions.

CERTIFICATION AND LICENSING

Certification, while voluntary, is highly recommended. It is an excellent way to stand out from other job applicants and demonstrate your abilities to prospective employers. Certification is offered by HDI (www.thinkhdi.com), the Institute for Certification of Computing Professionals (www.iccp.org), CompTIA (www.comptia.org), DAMA International, the IEEE Computer Society, other computer associations, product vendors, and training institutions.

OTHER REQUIREMENTS

Computer administrators are excellent problem solvers who are able to work well under pressure or when a computer crisis threatens productivity and deadlines. They have analytical personalities and are very attentive to detail. Other important traits include excellent communication and organizational skills and the ability to work both independently and as a member of a team.

EXPLORING

Read books and magazines (such as *Computerworld*) to learn more about the computer industry. Visit the websites of college computer science departments to learn about typical classes and possible career paths. Ask your teacher or school counselor to arrange an information interview with a computer administrator.

To help young people explore opportunities in computer science, the Association for Computing Machinery and other organizations have created a useful website, Computing Degrees and Careers (http://computing careers.acm.org), that provides a wealth of information about important skills, educational requirements, and career paths; interviews with computer science students and recent graduates; and answers to frequently asked questions about the field, such as Didn't the opportunities in the field disappear when the dot-com bubble collapsed in 2000? and Aren't computing jobs solitary and boring? Here are two other useful sites for those interested in learning more about computer careers: Why Choose Computer Science & Engineering? (www.cs.washington.edu/WhyCSE) and Sloan Career Cornerstone Center (http://careercornerstone.org). Finally, The Computing Technology Industry Association has created the CompTIA TechCareer Compass, which helps aspiring computer professionals assess their skills and interests, learn about certification, and plan for their careers. It can be accessed at http://tcc.comptia.org.

EMPLOYERS

Approximately 961,200 computer network, systems, and database administrators are employed in the United States. Computer administrators work for a variety of industries, including computer systems design and related services companies, financial firms, insurance companies, schools, government agencies, and telecommunications companies.

GETTING A JOB

Many computer administrators obtain their first jobs as a result of contacts made through college internships, career fairs, and networking events. Others seek assistance in obtaining job leads from college career services offices and newspaper want ads. Additionally, professional associations, such as the IEEE Computer Society, provide job listings at their websites. See For More Information for a list of organizations. Many computer professionals also seek out job opportunities at job-search websites such as Dice (www.dice.com), Crunchboard (www.crunchboard.com), Robert Half Technology (www.roberthalftechnology.com), and ComputerJobs.com (www.computerjobs.com). Those interested in positions with the federal government should visit the U.S. Office of Personnel Management's website, www.usajobs.opm.gov.

ADVANCEMENT

Computer administrators advance by receiving pay raises, taking on managerial duties, or promotion to positions such as chief technology officer. They also may open their own consulting firms and offer their services on a contract basis.

EARNINGS

Salaries for computer administrators vary by type of employer, geographic region, and the worker's education, experience, and skill level. The U.S. Department of Labor reports the following salary ranges for computer administrators by specialty in 2009: database administrators, $40,780 to $114,200; network and computer systems administrators, $41,940 to $105,970; and network systems and data communication analysts, $42,880 to $116,120.

According to *Computerworld*'s 2010 Salary Survey, network administrators earned an average base salary of $60,835 and an additional $2,192 in bonuses. Systems administrators averaged $69,029, with a bonus of $2,458. Network architects earned an average salary of $94,491, with an additional $4,351 in bonuses.

Computer administrators usually receive benefits such as health and life insurance, vacation days, sick leave, and a savings and pension plan. Self-employed workers must provide their own benefits.

EMPLOYMENT OUTLOOK

The employment of computer network, systems, and database administrators is expected to grow much faster than the average for all careers through 2018, according to the U.S. Department of Labor. Approximately 286,600 new jobs will be added from 2008 to 2018. The following paragraphs provide information on employment outlooks through 2018 for each specialty.

Job opportunities for computer network and systems administrators are expected to increase by 23 percent as a result of companies investing in new technologies and the use of mobile technologies that allow workers to use the Internet to conduct business.

Employment for database administrators is expected to grow by 20 percent. As advances in technology allow businesses to store, study, and manipulate more data, database administrators will be needed to help manage databases.

Employment of network systems and data communication analysts and network architects and engineers is projected to increase by 53 percent. The incorporation and upgrading of technology into business operations, and an increasing reliance on wireless networks, is fueling growth in these careers.

An increasing emphasis on computer security is also fueling growth for workers in all specialties. Large amounts of data—much of it industry-sensitive or the private information of customers (Social Security numbers, private medical information, etc.)—is being stored, analyzed, and transmitted over wireless and physical networks, and skilled computer administrators will be needed to safeguard this data.

Growth may be slowed by the outsourcing of positions to countries that pay workers lower salaries than those paid to U.S.-based workers, as well as by the consolidation of information technology services, which may reduce the number of workers needed in the field.

FOR MORE INFORMATION

For information on education and careers, visit the association's websites.
Association for
Computing Machinery
2 Penn Plaza, Suite 701
New York, NY 10121-0701
800-342-6626
http://computingcareers.acm.org
www.acm.org

For membership information, contact
Association for
Women in Computing
41 Sutter Street, Suite 1006
San Francisco, CA 94104-4905
info@awc-hq.org
www.awc-hq.org

For industry news, contact
Association of Information
Technology Professionals
401 North Michigan Avenue, Suite 2400
Chicago, IL 60611-4267
www.aitp.org

For certification information, contact
DAMA International
19239 North Dale Mabry Highway, #132
Lutz, FL 33548-5067
813-778-5495
info@dama.org
www.dama.org

For information about careers and scholarships, contact
IEEE Computer Society
2001 L Street, NW, Suite 700
Washington, DC 20036-4910
202-371-0101
www.computer.org

The LOPSA is a nonprofit organization committed to providing education and networking opportunities to further the advancement of professionals working in the field. Visit its website for more information.
League of Professional System
Administrators (LOPSA)
PO Box 5161
Trenton, NJ 08638-0161
202-567-7201
www.lopsa.org

For information on high school competitions and women in the computer industry, contact
National Center for Women
and Information Technology
University of Colorado
Campus Box 322 UCB
Boulder, CO 80309-0322
www.ncwit.org

COMPUTER SUPPORT SPECIALISTS

OVERVIEW

Computer support specialists help people use software or hardware. Many support specialists answer questions over the phone, via email, or through live help sessions when an individual visits a particular website. Others travel on-site to help an individual in person. Educational requirements for computer support specialists vary by employer. Approximately 565,700 support specialists work in the United States. Employment is expected to grow faster than the average for all careers through 2018.

THE JOB

Computer support specialists help people solve computer problems. They are typically divided into two groups: *help desk technicians* and *technical support specialists*.

Help desk technicians work on a help desk answering phone calls

or emails from end users with computer questions. They may also participate in live chats with users who are visiting a company's website. In this situation, the help desk technician and customer communicate through a text messaging program that pops up on the customer's computer.

Help desk technicians need to have some technical background but also must be good listeners and problem-solvers. They must be able to reduce technical information to simple language. Often a user calling with a problem has no computer background, and the problem might simply be tied to user error. To determine this, the support specialist listens to the user describe the problem as well as the exact steps that were taken to trigger the error. The support specialist often will log in remotely to the user's computer and try to repeat the exact steps described to try to duplicate the problem. If the problem is tied to user error, the specialist walks the user through the correct way to handle the issue and may direct the user to computer manuals for future reference. If it is determined that there is a legitimate bug or issue with the software or hardware, the specialist tries to isolate the issue. If the specialist cannot solve the problem, he or she may take the issue to a supervisor for assistance. Any technical issues with the programming code of the software will need to be brought to the attention of a software developer.

The Best Providers of Computer Support

The Association of Support Professionals creates an annual list of the best websites for online computer support. Here are the top sites for 2009 (in alphabetical order) in its Open Division: EMC Corp (www.emc.com); Hewlett Packard (consumer, www.hp.com/#Support); Juniper Networks (www.juniper.net/customers/support); Mentor Graphics (http://supportnet.mentor.com); Novell (www.novell.com/services); and Verizon (www.verizon.com).

At this point, most support specialists will take the contact information of their client and create a support ticket that is referred to by their supervisor. That way once the issue is addressed, the support specialist will know who he or she needs to inform of the fix.

Help desk specialists should have excellent communication skills and problem-solving abilities. Programmers and infrastructure engineers use reports written up by these support specialists to modify existing products or to help prevent similar problems when designing new products.

Not all support specialists troubleshoot problems. Technical support specialists install hardware such as servers, printers, scanners, and software. They may instruct users how to use the tools after installation. They may refer to manuals and other instruction documentation that they have created or a publication that came from the vendor.

Technical support specialists may be employed by companies to oversee the day-to-day operations of their computer systems. These specialists may check programs and hardware to make sure they are installed properly and are compatible with existing infrastructure or systems. They may check to see if upgrades are needed or if anything outdated needs to be replaced. For new projects, they may be asked to ensure that hardware and software are installed correctly and meet the company's needs and expectations. Finally, technical support specialists with programming skills might work with off-the-shelf software and modify it to fit the needs of a company.

Employers place a high value on the work of support specialists—who are the public face of a company. If a customer is unhappy with a product, the prompt assistance of a support specialist will encourage the customer to remain loyal to the company and not take his or her business to another company. Since they work with products daily, computer support specialists are great resources for information and feedback from customers on what they like or dislike about a product's design.

Most computer support specialists work in offices or computer labs. With the advent of remote desktop applications, as long as the specialist has an Internet connection, he or she is able to log onto a customer or coworker's computer or server from virtually anywhere. This reduces or eliminates travel to the customer's workplace and may allow some support specialists to work from home.

Like other IT jobs, support specialists spend much of their time in front of a computer, which can cause eyestrain or carpal tunnel syndrome in the wrists from too much typing.

Though most computer support specialists work a standard 40-hour workweek, some work second or third shifts. Help desks are sometimes staffed 24 hours a day, so specialists have to be available during evenings and weekends to take questions from end users after traditional work hours.

REQUIREMENTS

HIGH SCHOOL

Take as many computer science courses as possible in high school. Other useful classes include mathematics, psychology, English, and speech.

POSTSECONDARY TRAINING

Educational requirements for computer support specialists vary by employer. Some employers require a bachelor's degree in computer engineering, computer science, or information systems. At other employers, an associate's degree in a computer-related field and certification are sufficient credentials. Some people are hired with just strong technical skills and a degree in any field. Some companies hire workers with considerable computer experience and certification.

Once hired, support specialists usually participate in on-the-job training that lasts anywhere from one week to one year, but the typical length of training is three months. Support specialists continue to learn throughout their careers by taking seminars, classes, and other educational offerings from employers, colleges and universities, industry associations, hardware and software vendors, and private training institutions.

CERTIFICATION AND LICENSING

Certification, while voluntary, is highly recommended. It is an excellent way to stand out from other job applicants and demonstrate your abilities to prospective employers. Certification is offered by HDI, the Institute for Certification of Computing Professionals, CompTIA (www.comptia.org), and other computer associations.

OTHER REQUIREMENTS

To be a successful computer support specialist, you should be a good problem solver and have excellent analytical skills. You should be able to think quickly on your feet in order to provide solutions in a time-effective manner. Communication skills are also extremely important, since you will be constantly interacting with customers, colleagues, and managers via email and telephone, in person, and in live online chats. Good listening skills are key because you will need to analyze every bit of information provided to you to help troubleshoot a computer problem. You will need to be a good writer in order to effectively communicate via email and prepare user manuals and reports for customers.

EXPLORING

Read books and magazines (such as *Computerworld*) to learn more about the computer industry. Visit the websites of college computer science departments to learn about typical classes and possible career paths. Ask your teacher or school counselor to arrange an information interview with a computer support specialist. If you have the opportunity to interact with a support specialist due to a hardware or software issue on your computer, do so. Pay close attention to the questions they ask, but remember that they are doing their jobs and will not have time to answer questions about their work while on duty.

To help young people explore opportunities in computer science, the Association for Computing Machinery and other organizations have created a useful website, Computing Degrees and Careers (http://computing careers.acm.org), that provides a wealth of information about important skills, educational requirements, and career paths; interviews with computer science students and recent graduates; and answers to frequently asked questions about the field, such as Didn't the opportunities in the field disappear when the dot-com bubble collapsed in 2000? and Aren't computing jobs solitary and boring? Here are two other useful sites for those interested in learning more about computer careers: Why Choose Computer Science & Engineering? (www.cs.washington.edu/WhyCSE) and Sloan Career Cornerstone Center (http://careercornerstone.org). Finally, The Computing Technology Industry Association has created the CompTIA TechCareer Compass (http://tcc.comptia.org), which helps aspiring computer professionals assess their skills and interests, learn about certification, and plan for their careers.

EMPLOYERS

Approximately 565,700 computer support specialists are employed in the United States. They work for software and hardware companies, businesses that rely on computer systems, or for third-party consulting companies that run a help desk or hire out technology professionals on a contract basis. Approximately 18 percent of support specialists are employed in the computer systems design and related services industry. Other major employers include administrative and support services companies, financial institutions, health care organizations, insurance companies, government agencies, schools, software publishers, and telecommunications companies.

GETTING A JOB

Many computer support specialists obtain their first jobs as a result of contacts made through college internships or networking events. Others seek assistance in obtaining job leads from college career services offices and newspaper want ads. Additionally, professional associations, such as the Association of Support Professionals and HDI, provide job listings at their websites. See For More Information for a list of organizations. Many computer professionals also seek out job opportunities at job-search websites such as ComputerJobs.com (www. computerjobs.com), Robert Half Technology (www.roberthalftechnology.com), Dice (www.dice.com), and Crunchboard (www.crunchboard.com). Those interested in positions with the federal government should visit the U.S. Office of Personnel Management's website, www.usajobs.opm.gov.

ADVANCEMENT

Computer support specialists advance by earning higher salaries, by being asked to provide support for products that are more technically complex, or by taking on managerial duties. Others pursue additional education and certifications to become software or hardware engineers, computer programmers, or network and systems administrators.

EARNINGS

Salaries for computer support specialists vary by type of employer, geographic region, and the worker's experience, education, and skill level. Median annual salaries for computer support specialists were $44,300 in 2009, according to the U.S. Department of Labor (USDL). Salaries ranged from less than $27,200 to $72,690 or more. The USDL reports the following mean annual earnings for computer support specialists by industry: computer and peripheral equipment manufacturing, $61,780; professional and commercial equipment and supplies merchant wholesalers, $52,470; computer systems design and related services, $47,850; colleges, universities, and professional schools, $45,370; and elementary and secondary schools, $43,310.

According to *Computerworld*'s 2010 Salary Survey, help desk/technical support specialists earned an average base salary of $49,376 and an additional $988 in bonuses.

Computer support specialists usually receive benefits such as health and life insurance, vacation days, sick leave, and a savings and pension plan. Self-employed workers must provide their own benefits.

EMPLOYMENT OUTLOOK

Employment for computer support specialists is expected to grow faster than the average for all careers through 2018, according to the U.S. Department of Labor (USDL). More businesses and other organizations are introducing technology to help them save time and money, and support specialists will be needed to troubleshoot software and hardware that is installed incorrectly or that does not perform to expectations. Industries that rely heavily on technology will offer the best job prospects. These include the computer systems design and related services industry; the data processing, hosting, and related services industry; the software publishing industry; and the management, scientific, and technical consulting industry. Opportunities should also be good in the health care industry.

Growth may be slowed by the outsourcing of positions to countries that pay workers lower salaries than those paid to U.S.-based workers.

The USDL reports that "those who possess a bachelor's degree, relevant technical and communication skills, and previous work experience should have even better opportunities than applicants with an associate degree or professional certification."

FOR MORE INFORMATION

For information on education and careers, visit the association's websites.
Association for
Computing Machinery
2 Penn Plaza, Suite 701
New York, NY 10121-0701
800-342-6626
http://computingcareers.acm.org
www.acm.org

For information on earnings and companies that provide excellent computer support, visit the association's website.
Association of
Support Professionals
122 Barnard Avenue
Watertown, MA 02472-3414
617-924-3944
http://asponline.com

For information on training and certification, contact
HDI
102 South Tejon, Suite 1200
Colorado Springs, CO 80903
800-248-5667
support@thinkhdi.com
www.thinkhdi.com

For information about certification, contact
Institute for Certification
of Computing Professionals
2400 East Devon Avenue, Suite 281
Des Plaines, IL 60018-4629
800-843-8227
office2@iccp.org
www.iccp.org

For information on high school competitions and women in the computer industry, contact
National Center for Women
and Information Technology
University of Colorado
Campus Box 322 UCB
Boulder, CO 80309-0322
www.ncwit.org

For industry information, contact
Technology Services
Industry Association
17065 Camino San Bernardo, Suite 200
San Diego, CA 92127-5737
858-674-5491
info@thesspa.com
www.tsia.com

COMPUTER SYSTEMS ANALYSTS

OVERVIEW

Computer systems analyst is a broad term for the information technology professionals who assist organizations in improving their existing computer systems or plan and develop new solutions. They are essentially technology problem solvers. Most companies require computer systems analysts to have at least a bachelor's degree and relevant work experience. Approximately 532,200 computer systems analysts work in the United States. Employment opportunities for computer systems analysts should be excellent through 2018.

THE JOB

In the same way that organizations vary differently in what types of business they conduct, the computer systems that help organizations get their business done vary widely. It is the job of the computer systems analyst to help organizations find or create information technology (IT) solutions to maximize efficiency and profit.

For example, the editors of an online publication may need a system that can load text, photos, and videos quickly and track the number of online readers to their site. A retail company that sells clothing through the Internet needs a system that displays products and processes orders securely and quickly. A school district may need a system that stores student information securely and conveys grade and attendance data to parents. In sum, there is no one-size-fits-all software package for businesses and organizations. Analysts help custom-fit systems to the specific needs of their client.

Computer systems analysts must be excellent listeners in order to do their job right. In order to design or adjust a software solution to fit the needs of a business, they must do what is called requirements gathering—listening to the goals and needs of corporate executives, mid-level managers, and end users. Analysts organize these requirements into programmable features within an IT system. They have to consider workflows as the data is entered

FAST FACTS

High School Subjects
Computer science
Mathematics

Personal Skills
Communication
Complex problem solving
Technical

Minimum Education Level
Bachelor's degree

Salary Range
$47,000 to $77,000 to $119,000+

Employment Outlook
Much faster than the average

O*NET-SOC
15-1051.00

GOE
02.06.01

DOT
033

NOC
2162

Books to Read

Eberts, Marjorie. *Careers for Computer Buffs & Other Technological Types.* 3rd ed. New York: McGraw-Hill, 2006.

Kraynak, Joe. *The Complete Idiot's Guide to Computer Basics.* 5th ed. New York: Alpha, 2009.

Miller, Michael. *Absolute Beginner's Guide to Computer Basics.* 5th ed. Indianapolis, Ind.: Que Publishing, 2009.

into a system and also keep in mind any business reporting needs. Data fields that are important to a business must be captured within the system in some way. Computer systems analysts may work with *graphic designers* to design and implement screens and views for data input and collaborate with *software report writers* to design the data reports that come out of the system.

For those analysts working to improve existing IT solutions, time is spent checking whether there is an issue or "bug" in the system that needs to be resolved or check if users are actually using the system correctly. If the problems are tied to user error, analysts focus on training and system optimization to encourage staff members to use the IT solution correctly. If they find a bug in the existing systems, analysts work to correct the issue and may recommend needed system upgrades for both software and hardware.

Other computer analysts work on the design of a totally new system. Once the architecture and design is approved and initial screens are built, analysts oversee the testing of the system. These specialists are often called *quality assurance testers*. They observe end users (people who use the designed system) to make sure the system performs as planned. They also review computer reports to check the accuracy of the data reported. If the new system must "talk" to other systems, analysts ensure that data is flowing between the systems accurately and efficiently. These analysts are often called *network* or *integration specialists*. Any bugs that are discovered are corrected by *programmers* and retested again.

Once a system passes testing or the quality assurance process, computer systems analysts must help train staff members to use the new solution. Some do this through written manuals, online videos, or in-person training. Analysts are tasked with designing a training program, conducting the training, and creating the documentation used during training. Written manuals or guides must be easy to understand and thorough, covering every feature of a system and each workflow. Documentation often includes screenshots taken from the system and corresponding step-by-step instructions customized to the end user's role and responsibilities in the system. A new IT solution is worthless if users do not know how to utilize it—so training is a critical part of analysts' jobs.

Computer analysts spend much of their day in front of a computer, conducting tests, assisting in programming or code writing, documenting "bugs," and writing software manuals. However, they also may spend a good deal of time on their feet, meeting clients and listening to their needs. They may conduct walk throughs of business operations, taking a physical tour of the place of business and meeting end users throughout the process to get an idea of the workflow that needs to be captured within a proposed system.

Most analysts work a typical 40-hour week, but they may work 50 hours or longer a week if facing a tight deadline. They also may work odd hours, for example, if testing integration systems that run or sync up overnight, but the majority of their work is conducted during regular business hours. Although many systems analysts work on-site, some are able to do their jobs by telecommuting from home offices.

Because the computer data of any organization is essentially priceless and critical to its operations, clients put a lot of confidence in computer systems analysts to manage and organize their data. Tight security and confidentiality are in place as the analysts design the new system. For example, they may encounter trade secrets such as a new product design, or confidential data such as employee Social Security numbers, so they must be very careful and conscientious when handling these records. Despite these pressures, the work of computer system analysts can be very rewarding because they make people's jobs easier and create solutions where there had been chaos and disorganization.

REQUIREMENTS

High School

Take as many computer science courses as possible in high school. The Association for Computing Machinery recommends that students take algebra, geometry, trigonometry, calculus, physics, and chemistry. Speech classes will help you become comfortable giving presentations, and English will help you develop your report- and proposal-writing skills.

Postsecondary Training

Most companies require computer systems analysts to have at least a bachelor's degree and relevant work experience. Companies that are offering highly technical positions may require applicants to have a master's degree. Systems analysts who work in business settings typically have degrees in management information systems. Those in scientific or technical settings have degrees in applied mathematics, computer science, engineering, information science, or the physical sciences. The U.S. Department of Labor reports that employers are increasingly seeking applicants with a master's degree in business administration with a concentration in information systems. It will be useful if a systems analyst has knowledge of the particular industry he or she wants to work in. For example, if you want to work in the banking industry, you should have knowledge of finance and electronic financial systems.

Some people with technical skills and training enter this career without earning degrees in the aforementioned majors.

Systems analysts continue to learn throughout their careers by taking seminars, classes, and other educational offerings from hardware and software vendors, employers, colleges and universities, industry associations, and private training institutions.

CERTIFICATION AND LICENSING

Certification, while voluntary, is highly recommended. It is an excellent way to stand out from other job applicants and demonstrate your abilities to prospective employers. Certification is offered by the Institute for Certification of Computing Professionals (www.iccp.org), CompTIA (www.comptia.org), the IEEE Computer Society, and other computer associations.

OTHER REQUIREMENTS

Computer systems analysts need excellent communication skills. They need to be able to explain complicated computer technology to the average person with no technical background and be able to listen closely to managers and employers as they describe what features they want in a system or what problems they are having with a current system. Analysts should be ethical because they may work with a company's trade secrets or a customer's private information. Other important traits include strong technical knowledge, the ability to solve problems and work under deadline pressure, a logical and analytical personality, the ability to multitask, and the ability, as the situation requires, to work independently or with a team of workers on a large project.

EXPLORING

There are many ways to learn more about a career as a computer systems analyst. You can read books and magazines (such as *Computerworld*) about the field, visit the websites of college computer science departments to learn about typical classes and possible career paths, and ask your teacher or school counselor to arrange an information interview with a computer systems analyst. You should also try to land a part-time job in a company that employs computer systems analysts. This will give you a chance to interact with these professionals and see if the career is a good fit for your interests and abilities.

To help young people explore opportunities in computer science, the ACM and other organizations have created a useful website, Computing Degrees and Careers (http://computingcareers.acm.org), that provides a wealth of information about important skills, educational requirements, and career paths; interviews with computer science students and recent graduates; and answers to frequently asked questions about the field. Here are two other useful sites for those interested in learning more about computer careers: Why Choose Computer Science & Engineering? (www.cs.washington.edu/WhyCSE) and Sloan Career Cornerstone Center (http://careercornerstone.org). Finally, The Computing Technology Industry Association has created the CompTIA TechCareer Compass (http://tcc.comptia.org), which helps aspiring computer professionals assess their skills and interests, learn about certification, and plan for their careers.

EMPLOYERS

Approximately 532,200 computer systems analysts are employed in the United States. Analysts may be self-employed, work for an IT consulting firm, or be employed by a large corporation that has its own IT department.

Some analysts are hired on a contract basis by businesses for the duration of a project. Approximately 24 percent of analysts work in the computer systems design and related services industry.

GETTING A JOB

Many computer systems analysts obtain their first jobs as a result of contacts made through college internships or networking events. Others seek assistance in obtaining job leads from college career services offices and newspaper want ads. Additionally, professional associations, such as the Association for Computing Machinery, provide job listings at their websites. See For More Information for a list of organizations. Many computer professionals also seek out job opportunities at job-search websites such as ComputerJobs.com (www.computerjobs.com), Robert Half Technology (www.roberthalf technology.com), Dice (www.dice.com), and Crunchboard (www.crunch-board.com). Those interested in positions with the federal government should visit the U.S. Office of Personnel Management's website, www.usajobs.opm.gov.

ADVANCEMENT

To be eligible for advancement, systems analysts must usually have advanced degrees or considerable experience and a proven track record of improving or developing systems. They may be promoted to the positions of senior or lead analyst, computer and information systems manager, or chief information officer. Others start their own consulting firms. About 6 percent of analysts are self-employed.

EARNINGS

Salaries for computer systems analysts vary by type of employer, geographic region, and the worker's experience, education, and skill level. Median annual salaries for computer systems analysts were $77,080 in 2009, according to the U.S. Department of Labor (USDL). Salaries ranged from less than $47,130 to $119,170 or more. The USDL reports the following mean annual earnings for computer systems analysts by industry: computer and peripheral equipment manufacturing, $94,930; support activities for air transportation, $92,650; computer systems design and related services, $85,460; insurance carriers; $77,010; and state government, $67,720.

According to *Computerworld*'s 2010 Salary Survey, systems analysts earned an average base salary of $73,432 and an additional $3,759 in bonuses. Senior systems analysts earned an average of $85,520, plus $4,713 in bonuses.

Employers offer a variety of benefits, including the following: medical, dental, and life insurance; paid holidays, vacations, and sick days; personal days; 401(k) plans; profit-sharing plans; retirement and pension plans; and educational assistance programs. Self-employed workers must provide their own benefits.

EMPLOYMENT OUTLOOK

Employment for computer systems analysts is expected to grow much faster than the average for all careers through 2018, according to the U.S. Department of Labor (USDL). The career of computer systems analyst was chosen by CareerCast.com as the third-best job in 2010 based on five criteria (income, work environment, stress level, employment outlook, and physical demands of the job).

Demand is growing because companies are increasingly utilizing complex technologies in their daily business operations. The USDL reports that "demand for computer networking, Internet, and intranet functions...and the increasing adoption of the wireless Internet, known as WiFi, and of personal mobile computers...will drive demand for computer systems analysts." Companies are also focusing on computer and information security, and analysts trained in information security will be needed to develop and troubleshoot the systems that contain sensitive information.

FOR MORE INFORMATION

For information on education and careers, visit the association's websites.
Association for
Computing Machinery
2 Penn Plaza, Suite 701
New York, NY 10121-0701
http://computingcareers.acm.org
www.acm.org

For membership information, contact
Association for
Women in Computing
41 Sutter Street, Suite 1006
San Francisco, CA 94104-4905
www.awc-hq.org

For industry news, contact
Association of Information
Technology Professionals
401 North Michigan Avenue, Suite 2400
Chicago, IL 60611-4267
www.aitp.org

For information on high school competitions and women in the computer industry, contact
National Center for Women
and Information Technology
University of Colorado
Campus Box 322 UCB
Boulder, CO 80309-0322
www.ncwit.org

Opportunities are expected to be especially good in the health care industry, as more information technology is used in this fast-growing field.

Interview: Nora Kerr

Nora Kerr is a systems analyst for a software development company in Chicago. She discussed her career with the editors of *Hot Jobs*.

Q. **What is one thing that young people may not know about a career as a computer systems analyst?**

A. In my experience, the one surprising thing is that you do not need to be the stereotypical computer geek to succeed in this job. I work with many of these types, but I have a liberal arts major and just a lot of on-the-job experience working with computer systems. Much of the job is communication and working in teams, so often I feel like the arbiter in the middle of it all, working with highly technical developers, nontechnical end users, and everyone in between.

Q. Can you please briefly describe a day in your life on the job?

A. A typical day really depends on at what point within a project I am currently working. If we are planning for a new Information Technology (IT) solution for our clients, much of my day is meeting with the end users and their bosses, gathering information on their needs and how we can improve upon their processes using technology. This must be very detailed. I ask questions like WHO is entering the data, WHAT are the options for each entry point, WHO can edit these entries, WHERE does this data flow, and HOW do they want to report out this information? Because I work for a large school system, they need to report student statistics that we capture within our systems out to the state, and school funding is tied to these reports. For this reason, gathering accurate requirements is critical.

If we have already launched an IT system, my job turns into a support or quality assurance role, checking for bugs, assisting users with questions on how to use the system, or even training large groups of people.

Q. What are the most important qualities for systems analysts?

A. You have to be detail oriented, a GREAT listener, and be creative in order to be able to translate client requests into what is feasible within a computer system. Communication skills are key to relay these needs to the developers working on the system. The system requirement documents I create can turn out to look like textbooks. The more information I give to the developers, the clearer their job becomes.

Q. What are some of the pros and cons of your job?

A. Pros: I enjoy being able to deliver a solution that makes people's jobs easier and more streamlined. Its exciting to see what technology can do to improve on business processes that may have once been paper dominated.

Cons: Managing client expectations and working with tight deadlines can be challenging. Late or weekend hours come into play during crunch time or if we need to test systems after business hours so as not to disrupt their normal workday.

Q. What advice would you give to aspiring systems analysts?

A. Never assume that just because you are not a computer or math genius you don't have a future in a technology field. Speaking from my own experience, my background in liberal arts really helped me. I advise you to explore different fields and classes, because a well-rounded education is more useful than you might think. Take computer science and advanced math classes but also make sure you are exposing yourself to other areas where applied knowledge will be helpful in this line of work, such as psychology, writing, or even drama to improve public speaking skills.

Also take advantage of internships or summer jobs that may give you a taste of working in an office and examine their current IT systems. Think of ways in which they can be improved or made more efficient.

CONSTRUCTION MANAGERS

OVERVIEW

Construction managers, also known as *project managers, construction superintendents,* and *general contractors,* oversee all aspects of a building project, from inception to completion. They keep the project on schedule, coordinate various tasks with sub-contractors, and hire and fire workers. Besides time management, construction managers are mindful of the cost and quality of the project, which could range from a single-family home or a new high school to skyscrapers and monuments. A growing number of companies require construction managers to have a bachelor's degree; some construction managers still enter the field after gaining years of experience in the industry. Approximately 551,000 construction managers are employed in the United States. Employment for workers in the field is expected to grow faster than the average for all careers through 2018.

THE JOB

Whether building a single-family home, a strip mall, or a 100-story skyscraper, someone must manage all the construction activities in order to complete the project in a timely and cost-effective manner. This is the role of the construction manager.

A construction manager's duties, regardless of the scope of the project, can be divided into different operational areas. Before the project can get off the ground, he or she is involved in the preconstruction planning and administrative support. Meeting with architects, engineers, and the owners of the project, the construction manager assists in preparing a financial estimate of the project and a preliminary construction schedule. He or she may also be asked to voice any issues or questions regarding the project, including owners' expectations, materials used, or architectural or engineering designs. Any conflicts are resolved as a team at this point. Preconstruction goals include developing a project's working budget, finalizing a realistic construction schedule, and creating a pre-purchase log.

Once plans have been refined and finalized, the construction manager can seek necessary permits, solicit bids for sub-contractors, and begin ordering building materials. He or she can also start to interview and hire construction crews. Major construction companies may have the manpower and equipment to see a project from beginning to end, but many smaller companies contract aspects of the project to specialized subcontractors. For example, a cement company may be hired to pour the foundation, a plumbing company to install water pipes or a sprinkler system, a roofing company to construct the roof, an elevator company to install elevators, or even a crane company to lift steel beams or large pieces of material to the upper floors of a skyscraper. Depending on the project's size, the construction manager may hire a *foreman, assistant manager,* or other necessary personnel to help manage the project. The construction manager also has to identify any materials that may be hard to acquire or that may require delivery times that will impact the construction schedule. It is the construction manager's responsibility to ensure that building materials arrive in a timely manner and that subcontractors finish their portions of the project on schedule, otherwise further construction cannot proceed. For example, the frame of a house cannot be put up until the foundation is laid; drywall cannot be put into place until the electrical wiring and gas lines are finished; cabinets cannot be installed if flooring materials have not been delivered. The construction manager also needs to acquire or rent heavy construction equipment such as cranes, mechanical lifts, or other machinery.

Once the materials have been purchased, and the work crew hired, the construction manager supervises the project through each step. He or she continually monitors the crew's productivity and the quality of its work. During various phases of construction, building inspectors inspect certain aspects of the project to make sure its construction complies with government code. Passing inspection is an important responsibility of the construction manager, since it allows the project to continue. For example, if the project's electrical wiring is found to be faulty and not up to code, then the construction manager would have to make sure changes are made before passing inspection. Sometimes, it takes many changes before the project passes inspection. Since delays can cause havoc on the construction schedule, it's important for the project to pass inspection on the first try. When such problems arise, however, construction managers must be able to work around them, perhaps by rescheduling the arrival of materials or work done by subcontractors. Planning changes often come with additional costs. Any scheduling or budgetary modifications must be reported to the project's owners or financial managers. Also, construction managers must be in constant communication with project officials, engineers, architects, and accountants regarding the progress of the project.

Construction managers are also responsible for the safety of their crew and contractors. They often meet with officials from the Occupational Safety and

Health Administration, a federal government agency, to make sure the work environment and materials used are free from dangerous chemicals or other hazards, all equipment is properly maintained and in working order, and crew are wearing adequate protective clothing such as hard hats, work boots, and gloves.

Construction managers also establish wage rates for their crew and may assist the accounting department in working with union rules and rates. When necessary, the construction manager may need to impose disciplinary action or even terminate problem workers.

Full-time construction managers are employed 40 hours a week, but they often work extra hours or on weekends to meet construction deadlines or finish special projects. Also, construction managers are on call to respond to any emergencies that occur during a building project—be it with the materials, inspections, or crew.

Construction managers often maintain an office from which the overall construction project is supervised. These offices are usually well lit and comfortable and serve as a place to meet with vendors and contractors. Construction managers also make field visits, traveling to the jobsite in order to oversee the building's progression. They wear protective clothing such as hardhats, steel-toed boots, and heavy leather gloves when visiting a job site.

Access to a reliable car is important, especially when a construction site is located far from the main office, or when a supervisor is responsible for multiple building projects. When the building project is located out of state, or in some instance, out of the country, construction managers may need to live close to the site.

Construction managers interact with many different vendors, independent contractors, building inspectors, and crew, often addressing small mishaps or delays. They must stay calm and focused, even when dealing with delays in the delivery of materials, labor issues, or changing deadlines.

REQUIREMENTS

HIGH SCHOOL

In high school, take courses in business, mathematics, accounting, finance, and shop. English and speech classes will help you develop your communication skills. Computer science classes will help you to learn how to use databases, software programs, and other technology.

POSTSECONDARY TRAINING

A growing number of companies require construction managers to have a bachelor's degree in construction management, construction science, building science, architecture, or civil engineering. Some construction managers also earn a master's degree in business administration or finance to improve their business and financial acumen. Some construction managers are able to enter the field with an associate's degree or after gaining years of experience in the industry. Degrees in construction management are available at all academic levels. More than 74 construction management programs are accredited by the American Council for Construction Education. Visit the council's website, http://acce-hq.org/accreditedprograms.htm, for a list of accredited two- and four-year programs in construction management. College degree programs in construction management typically include many industry-specific courses (such as site planning, construction methods, construction materials, building codes and standards, inspection procedures, value analysis, and cost estimating), combined with business courses in operations, finance, and marketing. Some colleges offer master's degrees in construction management or construction science. Recipients of these degrees typically work at very large construction firms that oversee multimillion-dollar projects.

CERTIFICATION AND LICENSING

Certification is available from the American Institute of Constructors and the Construction Management Association of America. While not required, becoming certified is an excellent way to show employers that you are a competent worker who has met the high standards of your industry. Contact these organizations for more information on certification.

OTHER REQUIREMENTS

Key traits of successful construction managers include good time-management skills, the ability to multitask and work under deadline pressure, the ability to solve problems, decisiveness, and leadership skills. Construction managers need excellent communication skills because they frequently interact with a wide range of people—from business executives and managers, to architects and engineers, to building inspectors, to tradespeople. Construction managers who are fluent in Spanish will have an extra advantage in the industry because many construction workers speak Spanish as a first language. Finally, good computer skills are necessary to create schedules and cost analyses, as well as to stay in touch with colleagues, suppliers, and contractors.

EXPLORING

The Construction Management Association of America offers a wealth of career resources, including *A Career in Construction Management: Build America's Future as You Build Your Own*. It can be accessed at the association's website, www.cmaanet.org. Other ways to learn more about a career in construction management include reading books and magazines about the field, visiting the websites of college construction management departments, talking with a construction manager about his or her career, landing a part-time or summer job at a construction firm, or managing your friends and resources on a building project (such as a treehouse).

EMPLOYERS

Approximately 551,000 construction managers are employed in the United States. They work for general contractors; specialty contractors such as mechanical, plumbing, and electrical; architectural firms; engineering firms; and government agencies. Many construction managers have their own consulting businesses. In fact, 61 percent of construction managers are self-employed.

Did You Know?

The U.S. Department of Labor reports that 28 percent of construction managers work for specialty trade contractor businesses (heating, plumbing, air-conditioning, and electrical contractors), nonresidential building construction companies, and residential building construction firms.

GETTING A JOB

Construction management graduates break into the industry by working as assistants to project managers, field engineers, cost estimators, or schedulers. It is important to gain experience in the field while in school to demonstrate your knowledge of the field to employers. Some ways to gain practical experience include participating in internships and cooperative education programs, or landing an entry-level job in the construction industry.

Many construction managers obtain their first jobs as a result of contacts made through college internships or networking events. Others seek assistance in obtaining job leads from college career services offices, newspaper want ads, and employment websites. Additionally, the Construction Management Association of America offers job listings at its website, www.cmaanet.org/career-headquarters. Those interested in positions with the federal government should visit the U.S. Office of Personnel Management's website, www.usajobs.opm.gov.

ADVANCEMENT

Construction managers at small firms advance by receiving higher wages or by seeking employment at larger firms that work on more prestigious projects. Managers at large firms receive salary increases and promotion to positions as top-level managers or executives. Some construction managers start their own consulting firms or specialty general contracting companies. Others serve as expert witnesses in legal proceedings.

EARNINGS

Salaries for construction managers vary by type of employer, geographic region, and the worker's experience level and skills. New graduates with a bachelor's degree in construction science or construction management received average starting salary offers of $53,199 in July 2009, according to the National Association of Colleges and Employers.

Median annual salaries for construction managers were $82,330 in 2009, according to the U.S. Department of Labor (USDL). Salaries ranged from less than $49,320 to $151,630 or more. The USDL reports the following mean annual earnings for construction managers by industry: oil and gas extraction, $119,070; building equipment contractors, $99,520; nonresidential building construction, $92,260; foundation, structure, and building exterior contractors, $90,160; and residential building construction, $89,040.

Construction managers usually receive benefits such as health and life insurance, vacation days, sick leave, and a savings and pension plan. Self-employed workers must provide their own benefits.

FOR MORE INFORMATION

For information on accredited educational programs, contact
American Council for Construction Education
1717 North Loop 1604 E, Suite 320
San Antonio, TX 78232-1570
acce@acce-hq.org
www.acce-hq.org

For certification information, contact
American Institute of Constructors
700 North Fairfax Street, Suite 510
Alexandria, VA 22314-2090
www.aicnet.org

For information on K-12 programs, contact
Associated General Contractors of America
2300 Wilson Boulevard, Suite 400
Arlington, VA 22201-5426
www.agc.org

For information on careers and certification, as well as a glossary of construction management-related terms, contact
Construction Management Association of America
7926 Jones Branch Drive, Suite 800
McLean, VA 22102-3303
info@cmaanet.org
www.cmaanet.org

For information about construction careers and education, contact
National Center for Construction Education and Research
3600 NW 43rd Street, Building G
Gainesville, FL 32606-8134
888-622-3720
www.nccer.org

EMPLOYMENT OUTLOOK

Employment in the construction industry is expected to be good over the next decade. In fact, according to the U.S. Department of Labor, employment in the construction industry is projected to increase by 19 percent from 2008 to 2018, as compared to an average of 11 percent for all industries. Opportunities will be best in nonresidential construction. Developments that will increase the need for managers include the construction of residential and commercial structures; the renovation of existing structures; the repair and construction of infrastructure, such as bridges, roads, water and sewer pipes, and energy supply lines; and the trend toward retrofitting existing buildings to make them more energy efficient.

Opportunities will be best for those with at least a bachelor's degree in construction management, construction science, or civil engineering who also have practical experience in the industry. The best jobs will also go to those who stay up to date with constantly changing construction technology, building techniques, and construction materials.

Employment for construction managers is tied to the health of the U.S. economy. When the economy is strong, more funding for construction projects is available, and opportunities are good. When the economy is poor, fewer jobs are available as the private and public sectors reduce funding.

Interview: Allyson M. Gipson

Allyson M. Gipson is a senior business development manager for Chevron Energy Solutions. She discussed her career with the editors of *Hot Jobs*.

Q. How long have you worked in the field? What made you want to enter this career?

A. I have been in the construction industry for about 25 years, and in the energy industry for the past 2.5 years. I initially had an interest in architecture but after interning throughout college, I decided I wanted to be out in the field more often. When I discovered construction management, I found that I was able to combine my love of architecture and building with my organizational and management skills.

Q. What is one thing that young people may not know about a career in construction management?

A. Careers in construction management allow you to be an integral part of the construction of interesting facilities, provide opportunities for travel, and provide interesting challenges. In addition, much of the work is outdoors, which is great for people who want to stay active.

Q. What are some of the pros and cons of your job?

A. Pros: interesting projects, tangible results of your work, always something new, overcoming challenges, meeting new people
Cons: always must be in a problem-solving mode, can be assigned to projects you don't enjoy while waiting for more interesting ones, and dealing with regulatory agencies can be a challenge

Q. Have you faced any special challenges as a female working in a male-dominated field? If so, how did you deal with these challenges?

A. One challenge was that I wanted the opportunity to gain experience in the trades and no one would hire me and allow me to learn because I'm female. I believe this has changed a lot since I was just entering into the industry, but I wanted to learn carpentry in particular and never got the chance. Another challenge is that, as a woman, men on the job sometimes doubt that you know what you're doing. I made sure to have more education than most (I have two architecture degrees and a law degree), and I found mentors to learn from. I took on a lot of tasks that others didn't want to do so that I could learn.

Q. What advice would you give to young people—especially young women—who are interested in becoming construction managers?

A. The best advice I can give is to understand that you have to work your way up in the industry—no one is going to hire you in a highly responsible position until you get experience at the more junior levels of the industry. Continue to educate yourself; our industry is constantly changing and improving so you have to stay current. Find a mentor who you respect and admire and learn from them. Ask questions, volunteer to help them in any way you can. Learn as much about the trades as you can— it will help you find solutions to challenges that arise. Get your hands dirty—volunteer for Habitat for Humanity or other organizations that give you practical building experience. Get management experience any way you can; internships—either paid or unpaid—will allow you to learn more about the industry and help you build your résumé.

Interview: Christine J. Flaherty

Christine J. Flaherty, CCM, LEED AP is the director of business development at STV, Inc., a full-service planning, architecture, engineering, and construction management firm that provides services nationwide. She discussed her career with the editors of *Hot Jobs*.

Q. What made you want to enter this career?

A. I have always worked in the field of construction and project management. From college, I was always intrigued with learning how to build projects and being out in the field. I found a firm that gave me those opportunities. My father is an engineer and I earned my engineering degree. He was definitely my most influential mentor in looking at engineering, aside from my Advanced Placement physics teacher in high school.

Q. What is one thing that young people may not know about a career in construction management?

A. Young people don't realize the exciting and dynamic nature of what it's like to work on a project. From working with people from all walks of life with diverse, unique, and important skill sets to contributing to the construction of complex structures and infrastructure that all of us use every day, it is a very rewarding job. There is always something new to learn on each construction project—they are each unique, as are the project team members.

Q. What are the most important qualities for construction managers?

A. Interpersonal skills are important. Being able to work collaboratively on teams and communicate effectively and efficiently all contribute to an individual's success. In addition, it is important to realize that hard work and a curious and tenacious attitude all remain important characteristics to achieve success. From a professional qualifications standpoint, young professionals need to have a bachelor's degree in architecture/engineering or construction management at a minimum, and in the long term, they should plan on pursuing a master's, either in engineering, architecture, construction engineering, or business, depending on the area of focus. Finally, wait a few years before investing time and money on a master's degree. You want to make sure you are investing in the career that you are best suited for and most interested in. Also, if you wait to determine what master's program you would like to pursue, you may have the opportunity for the firm you work for to sponsor your master's education, if it supports the long-term career plans you have established with the firm where you work. A master's degree is expensive, so you need to consider it as an investment that is well thought out. I would recommend going for your master's at least after three years' experience and before you hit 10 years.

Q. What are some of the pros and cons of your job?

A. Pros: Having a variety of tasks to work on every day. Working with highly knowledgeable people from all walks of life. I have enjoyed learning from the foreman and women in the field as well as the senior project managers, executives, owners, and lawyers who I have worked with and for. All of them have specific tasks on a project to successfully and safely complete a project, and you are in a team environment every day.

Cons: This career is not for someone who wants to start work late in the day or work less than eight-hour days. Often this job requires many hours above and beyond the 9-5 lifestyle. When you are part of a project, the mission is complete the project first and foremost. Fast-tracking projects and pushing jobs requires the hard work of many often times long hours, but for the many people who love their jobs, this is a minor aspect about being a construction manager.

Q. Have you faced any special challenges as a female working in a male-dominated field? If so, how did you deal with these challenges?

A. I've actually found that ageism is a harder stereotype to deal with than sexism. The older generations feel that without experience, a young person doesn't have much to offer, yet the younger generation, when given mentorship and good training, can make a great contribution to firms.

As a female working in the industry, there have been times when you get the sense that you are being treated or observed "differently," but you have to ignore that and perform your job, and eventually you earn the respect from those you work with because they see how you are contributing. One word of advice for young women entering this industry—always remember that you are representing yourself and your company in a professional environment, even if a casual business environment in the field. As such, it is always sound advice to dress in a manner that is appropriate to going to work, not school. Short skirts, tight-fitting shirts, and clothes that distract people will not help you earn respect in the work environment. I know this first hand because I learned this early on in my career. If you are uncertain if that outfit will be OK at work, than the answer probably is no.

Q. What advice would you give to young people—especially young women—who are interested in becoming construction managers?

A. This is an excellent industry to work in. Always ask questions and look for mentors to learn from any and all areas of the business where you are interested. As a woman, you may have to work harder to earn the respect of your peers or supervisors, but that hard work and tenacity will pay off in the long run. Also, do not think that you are alone in your endeavor in this career. There are many women in this industry, many, many talented, bright, and aggressive women who are successful in their own right. Seek them out to mentor you when you may have difficulties. Also, please remember that this is a team-oriented industry; your success does not have to be at the expense of others. Honesty and integrity are critical and important values to hold onto in this business. You are only as good as your word, and honesty is THE most important value to hold onto. As an offshoot of honesty, be true to yourself in your career—use your own style of work and do not think that you have to behave the same way as others do to get results (i.e., don't feel like you have to yell at contractors to get results, there are other ways to accomplish the goals you are trying to achieve).

COST ESTIMATORS

OVERVIEW

Cost estimators are employed by the construction and manufacturing industries to forecast the cost of a proposed product, construction project, manufacturing process, or other endeavor. By carefully analyzing all components that make up a project or proposed process, they deliver a total cost for the company so managers can decide if the project is a good idea economically. At least some postsecondary training is required to land a job in the field; increasingly employers are seeking cost estimators with bachelor's degrees. Approximately 217,800 cost estimators are employed in the United States. Good job opportunities are expected for workers in the field through 2018.

THE JOB

The majority of cost estimators work in the construction industry. Construction estimators study blueprints and specifications to create cost estimates for projects. They also visit proposed project sites to study the building conditions and determine if there are any special issues that might affect the estimate. For example, they must account for the nearest utility lines or sewers and add these factors into their cost projections. If the land is dense with trees, bushes, or other vegetation, they need to factor the cost of clearing the land into their estimate. Cost estimators also take into account the proposed building materials (analyzing quality, quantity, type, and cost of the materials that will be used), the type of equipment proposed to be used to construct the building, the size of and rates paid to labor crews, and the computer hardware and software required. They also calculate taxes and insurance costs. After these and other details have been added together, estimators add a certain percentage to the estimate to cover unforeseen or emergency expenses and to ensure that the construction company will make a profit.

Estimators may specialize in residential or commercial project estimation. Construction companies often employ more than one cost estimator, with each worker specializing in a particular area of construction. For example, they may hire an *electrical cost estimator*, a *concrete or flooring cost estimator*, and a *drywall estimator*.

Cost estimators also work in the manufacturing industry. They are hired to estimate the cost of producing a new product or changing a manufacturing process, and to analyze its profitability. They must consider the quality of material to be used, tools and equipment needed to produce the products, labor costs, and other associated costs.

Some cost estimators with specialized knowledge are known as *cost engineers*. These estimators specialize in minimizing costs of a project using what is called Total Cost Management (TCM). TCM is a process by which the estimator uses his or her professional and technical expertise to plan and control resources, costs, profitability, and risk. Cost engineers typically specialize based on industry (such as construction, manufacturing, or information technology) or production type (such as buildings or software).

Cost estimators just starting out often work on smaller components of a project and then report their findings to a lead estimator who reviews them and adds them to the final pricing of the overall project. Estimators in a *lead* or *head estimator* role must have management skills to be able to lead cost estimation teams and juggle other administrative tasks such as payroll, vacation scheduling, and performance reviews. Some lead estimators may be expected to coach or mentor estimating personnel just starting out in the field.

Cost estimators use a variety of techniques to determine their projections, including statistical modeling, time-phase charts, learning-curve analysis, and cost-estimating relationships. Time-phase charts show the time required for tool design and fabrication, troubleshooting and correcting all problems, manufacturing parts, assembly, and testing. Learning curves graphically represent the rate at which the labor force employed on a project becomes more efficient. As the project moves on, the performance of workers improves with practice. These statistical graphs are also commonly called "cost reduction" curves, because many issues that can creep up during the life cycle of a project, such as staffing changes, redesigns, shortages of parts, and lack of operator skills, generally diminish over time. Much of this analysis of charts and curves is done with the help of high-tech computer software, so estimators must be adept at and comfortable using computers.

Once an estimate has been delivered and if a project does go through, some estimators are maintained on the project to monitor completion and prepare cost summaries.

Cost estimators typically work in offices with standard hours of operation. Those who are employed in the construction industry often keep earlier hours—getting to the office or construction sites as early as 5:00 or 6:00 A.M. Some travel is necessary to review proposed building sites or processes.

A career as a cost estimator can sometimes be stressful. In many cases, the success or failure of the contractor depends on the estimator. If he or she underestimates costs, the contractor will lose money. On the other hand, if the estimator presents an inflated cost, the proposed bid for the project will most likely be rejected.

REQUIREMENTS

HIGH SCHOOL

In high school, take courses in accounting, mathematics, business, economics, and computer science. English and speech courses will help you to develop your communication skills, which you will use frequently as a cost estimator to write reports and interact with coworkers. Take shop and drafting courses to learn how to read blueprints and other technical documents.

POSTSECONDARY TRAINING

At least some postsecondary training is required to land a job in the field. Employers in the construction and manufacturing industries are increasingly seeking cost estimators with bachelor's degrees.

Cost estimators in the construction industry have degrees in construction management, building science, or construction science. Courses in cost estimating are included in these degree programs. In addition to formal education, cost estimators should gain experience through participation in internships or cooperative education programs, or entry-level work in the industry.

Cost estimators in the manufacturing industry typically have degrees in engineering, mathematics, statistics, physical science, operations research, accounting, finance, business, economics, or a related subject.

According to the U.S. Department of Labor, "many colleges and universities include cost estimating as part of bachelor's and associate degree curriculums in civil engineering, industrial engineering, information systems development, and construction management or construction engineering technology. In addition, cost estimating is often part of master's degree programs in construction science or construction management."

Cost estimators also receive long-term, on-the-job training because each company has its own protocol regarding cost estimation techniques. Professional cost-estimating associations—such as the American Society of Professional Estimators, the Association for the Advancement of Cost Engineering, and the Society of Cost Estimating and Analysis—also offer continuing education programs.

CERTIFICATION AND LICENSING

The American Society of Professional Estimators, the Association for the Advancement of Cost Engineering, and the Society of Cost Estimating and Analysis offer voluntary certification to cost estimators. Contact these organizations for more information.

OTHER REQUIREMENTS

Cost estimators should have excellent mathematical ability, an analytical nature, the ability to multitask, confidence, and strong interpersonal skills to work well with management and colleagues. They should also be computer-savvy and be familiar with cost estimation software, including commercial and building information modeling software (which is used frequently in the construction industry). Estimators must have excellent communication skills to effectively negotiate prices with subcontractors, vendors, and their client. Often the people they work with have widely differing goals, interests, and points of view, so estimators must be able to take into account these issues while still doing their jobs. They also might be asked to report their findings to management during project meetings in a presentation-style format. They need to be able to translate highly technical findings into straight talk regarding pricing and recommended courses of action.

EXPLORING

Read books and magazines about cost estimating. Visit the websites of professional cost estimating associations and college programs that offer degrees or classes in the field. Talk with a cost estimator about his or her career. Try to land a part-time or summer job at a construction firm or a factory to get a taste of what a career in these industries is like. Join business clubs at school.

EMPLOYERS

Approximately 217,800 cost estimators work in the United States. The construction industry employs nearly 60 percent of all cost estimators, and approximately 15 percent work for manufacturers. The remaining percentage are employed in a variety of industries.

GETTING A JOB

Many cost estimators obtain their first jobs as a result of contacts made through college internships, career fairs, and networking events. Others seek assistance in obtaining job leads from college career services offices, newspaper want ads, and employment websites. Additionally, professional associations, such as the American Society of Professional Estimators, provide job listings at their websites. See For More Information for a list of organizations. Those interested in positions with the federal government should visit the U.S. Office of Personnel Management's website, www.usajobs.opm.gov.

Did You Know?

The U.S. Department of Labor reports that salaries for cost estimators are highest in 1) the District of Columbia, 2) Massachusetts, 3) Alaska, 4) California, and 5) Nevada.

ADVANCEMENT

Cost estimators advance by earning higher salaries, being assigned managerial duties, and working on larger or more prestigious projects. Some become construction project managers or managers of industrial engineering departments at factories. Others start their own consulting firms.

EARNINGS

Salaries for cost estimators vary by type of employer, geographic region, and the worker's experience level and skills. Median annual salaries for cost estimators were $57,300 in 2009, according to the U.S. Department of Labor

(USDL). Salaries ranged from less than $33,560 to $95,190 or more. The USDL reports the following mean annual earnings for cost estimators by industry: natural gas distribution, $77,160; architectural, engineering, and related services, $71,140; nonresidential building construction, $68,410; building equipment contractors, $64,540; building finishing contractors, $60,740; foundation, structure, and building exterior contractors, $60,270; and residential building construction, $59,430.

Cost estimators usually receive benefits such as health and life insurance, vacation days, sick leave, and a savings and pension plan. Self-employed workers must provide their own benefits.

FOR MORE INFORMATION

For information on society-spon-sored educational programs and cer-tification, contact
**American Society
of Professional Estimators**
2525 Perimeter Place Drive, Suite 103
Nashville, TN 37214-3674
888-EST-MATE
SBO@aspenational.org
www.aspenational.org

For information on career paths in cost estimation and certification, contact
**Association for the Advancement
of Cost Engineering International**
209 Prairie Avenue, Suite 100
Morgantown, WV 26501-5934
800-858-2678
info@aacei.org
www.aacei.org

For information on certification and a glossary of cost estimating terms, visit the society's website.
**Society of Cost
Estimating and Analysis**
527 Maple Avenue East, Suite 301
Vienna, VA 22180-4753
703-938-5090
scea@sceaonline.net
www.sceaonline.net

EMPLOYMENT OUTLOOK

Employment for cost estimators is projected to grow much faster than the average for all careers through 2018, according to the U.S. Department of Labor. The construc-tion industry, which is expected to grow by 19 percent during this time span, will provide the most job open-ings for cost estimators. Factors that are fueling demand for cost estima-tors in the construction industry include increasing population (which is creating demand for construction projects of all types, including infras-tructure such as highways, bridges, and subway systems) and the grow-ing complexity of construction pro-jects (which is prompting demand for estimators with specialized skills). Opportunities will be best for those with at least a bachelor's degree, certi-fication, and industry experience.

Employment for cost estimators in the construction industry is tied to the health of the U.S. economy. When the economy is strong, more funding for construction projects is available, and opportunities are good. When the economy is poor, fewer jobs are avail-able as the private and public sectors reduce funding.

Interview: Marcene N. Taylor

Marcene N. Taylor, CPE, LEED AP is a cost estimator and the owner of
MARCENE TAYLOR INC. in Boise, Idaho. She has worked in the field
since 1996. Marcene discussed her career with the editors of *Hot Jobs*.

Q. What made you want to enter this career?

A. I just started my own firm, consulting to owners and design professionals
during the planning stages of construction. Prior to opening my company, I have worked for both cost consulting firms and an architecture firm.

I did not have any idea that this career existed while I was going to
college. I worked doing administrative and accounting work and happened to get a job for Davis Langdon answering their phones and typing
their estimates. After I was there about six months, I was offered an
apprenticeship to learn how to estimate. I think it is fascinating and quite
creative to estimate costs of buildings without a lot of detail to measure.

**Q. What is one thing that young people may not know about a career as
a cost estimator?**

A. Estimators play a critical role in the design and construction of any project. They are usually the one person on the team who has touched every
part of the project during the planning stage, and they have thought
about all the nuances of the construction. Estimators are go-to players for
architects, engineers, project managers, and owners.

Q. What are the most important qualities for people in your career?

A. Estimators need to be detail-oriented as well as willing to see the big picture—it is a job that requires a mixture of creativity and science. They
need to be adept at using numbers/math and have good computer skills.
Estimators also need to be diplomatic, good leaders, and team players.

Q. What are some of the pros and cons of your job?

A. Pros include great opportunities for career advancement, opportunities to
continue to learn and work on a variety of job types, and opportunities to
live and work anywhere in the country. In addition, you have the opportunity to work in construction, but work in an office as opposed to being
in the field—so it may be easier on your body long term.

Cons include times of high stress and long hours when estimates and
bids are due. Also, if working for a contractor, job opportunities may be
dependent on the construction climate in your area.

Q. Any advice for aspiring estimators? What's the best way to land a job?

A. Learn all that you can about a variety of aspects of design and construction and building types. There isn't a degree course in estimating, so you
will have to learn on the job. Ask questions and pay attention to what is
going on around you—be willing to be mentored. The people who are
the best teachers are the ones who have been estimating for a long time.

The best way to find a job is to express interest in estimating. Many people don't think that estimating is an exciting career choice and only choose it
as a pathway to get out onto construction sites as a project manager or supervisor. In addition, join a professional organization such as the American
Society of Professional Estimators and network with others in the field.

COUNSELORS

OVERVIEW

Counselors work with children, adolescents, adults, or families that have a variety of issues, such as mental health disorders, alcohol and drug addiction, disability or employment needs, school problems, and college and career counseling needs, as well as those affected by abuse or other trauma. A minimum of a master's degree in counseling is required to work in the field. There are approximately 665,500 counselors employed in the United States. Employment for counselors is expected to be strong through 2018.

THE JOB

The work responsibilities of counselors depend on their specialty and the people whom they serve. The following paragraphs detail the most popular specialties in counseling.

SCHOOL COUNSELORS

School counselors at all academic levels focus on preventive and developmental counseling to enhance students' personal, social, and academic growth and to provide students with the life skills needed to deal with problems before they worsen.

Counselors work with students one-on-one, in small groups, or as an entire class. They often work as part of a team to develop and implement strategies to help students succeed. This team includes parents, teachers, school administrators, school psychologists, school nurses, social workers, and medical professionals.

Types of school counselors are broken down by the ages of the children they serve. *Elementary school counselors* work with younger children and observe them in the classroom and during play to evaluate their strengths, problems, or special needs. They help young students develop the knowledge, attitudes, and skills necessary to become healthy, competent, and confident learners.

High school counselors advise older students regarding college majors, the college application process, obtaining scholarships and financial aid,

---

FAST FACTS

High School Subjects
English
Psychology
Sociology

Personal Skills
Active listening
Communication
Helping

Minimum Education Level
Master's degree

Salary Range
$20,000 to $45,000 to $84,000+

Employment Outlook
Varies by specialty

O*NET-SOC
21-1011.00, 21-1012.00,
21-1013.00, 21-1014.00,
21-1015.00, 21-1019.00

GOE
12.02.02, 12.03.01

DOT
045

NOC
4143

researching colleges, universities, or vocational schools, and seeking out internship programs. They also help students develop job search skills, such as résumé writing and interviewing techniques.

High school counselors understand and respond to the challenges presented by today's diverse student population. As high school is often the defining moment when students begin to discover what the future holds for them, these years are critical in a child's development. However, these years are also filled with academic stress, peer pressure, and social angst. High school counselors help students navigate through these years by helping them to build self-esteem, confidence and social values, and by ensuring that they realize their full academic potential.

College counselors provide advice to students regarding potential career paths, résumé and cover letter writing, interviewing skills, and other important skills that will help students become successful in life. They also provide counseling for personal issues such as depression, drug and alcohol abuse, physical abuse, bullying, or other personal challenges.

CAREER COUNSELORS

Career counselors, also called *vocational* or *employment counselors,* focus on helping individuals make career decisions. They evaluate an individual's education, training, work experience, personal interests, skills, and personality traits to help him or her make career decisions. They also help people improve their job search skills and assist them in locating and applying for jobs. They are employed at high schools, colleges and universities, and local and state employment agencies. Some career counselors work in private practice.

MENTAL HEALTH COUNSELORS

Mental health counselors work with individuals, families, and groups to identify and treat mental and emotional disorders and promote mental health. They help address issues such as depression, stress, anxiety, suicidal impulses, low self-esteem, addiction and substance abuse, trauma, and grief. In order to best treat the individual, they may collaborate with other mental health specialists and counselors, such as psychiatrists, psychologists, clinical social workers, and school counselors.

Substance abuse and *behavioral disorder counselors* help people who have problems with dependence and addictions that have rendered their lives unhealthy or unmanageable. Sources of addiction can include alcohol, drugs, food, gambling, video games, or sex. These counselors also help individuals with eating disorders or those who voluntarily harm themselves via such acts as cutting. Counseling is done on an individual or group basis. During these sessions, counselors work to identify and address the addictions and develop recovery programs that encourage healthy behaviors and provide coping strategies. Counselors also work with a patient's family members or loved ones who are also affected by the addiction or disorder.

MARRIAGE AND FAMILY COUNSELORS

Marriage and family counselors treat a wide range of serious clinical problems including depression, marital problems, anxiety, psychological problems, and child-parent issues. These therapists differ from other counselors in one key way: instead of focusing on an individual's issues, marriage and family therapists focus on a group dynamic such as a couple or an entire family unit and the interactions that occur within that unit. They meet with each member individually but spend most of their time working with the couple or group as a whole. They focus on modifying people's perceptions of each other and behaviors toward one another and encourage increased communication and understanding. They may ask questions about family roles, rules, and expectations, as these patterns may be the cause of the problem and therefore need to be a part of the treatment plan. Marriage and family counselors may refer individuals to other psychiatric resources for additional assistance.

REHABILITATION COUNSELORS

Rehabilitation counselors help people living with disabilities deal with any associated personal, social, or employment challenges. They work with people with both physical and emotional disabilities resulting from birth defects, illness, accidents, or other causes. Rehabilitation counselors collaborate with the individual's families or loved ones, physicians, psychologists, employers, and physical, occupational, and speech therapists to determine the client's strengths and weaknesses and develop a rehabilitation plan for their client. They arrange training to help clients develop job or life skills or even help them find a job. Their main goal is to help their clients live happy and independent lives.

GENETIC COUNSELORS

Families with genetic disorders such as Down syndrome, PKU deficiency, hemophilia, or a history of physical defects such as cleft palate or short stature often seek medical advice to help them understand these anomalies and determine the chance of recurrence in future generations. Professionals who specialize in this field are known as *genetic counselors*. They work as part of a medical team to provide testing and give informational support to families at higher risk for these genetic disorders or inherited birth defects.

Genetic counselors investigate genetic issues by conducting extensive interviews with families and researching the medical histories of past generations. They may conduct genetic testing in order to interpret and analyze inheritance patterns and risks of recurrence. They present different options and scenarios based upon their findings. Genetic counselors provide education to help families better understand their risks, give advice on how to best live with these conditions, and refer families to government agencies or nonprofit organizations that focus on a particular disorder.

Counselors work in schools, hospitals, community centers, nursing homes, or other treatment centers. While the specific work environment will vary depending on the type of counseling in which the therapist specializes, counselors typically work indoors in an office setting, seeing clients by appointment. School counselors may work in a classroom setting, but most also have an office within the school for one-on-one or small group appointments. Some counselors travel out in the community to provide services, such as providing door-to-door wellness checks on the elderly.

Counselors spend much of their time dealing with hurt, afflicted, or unhappy people, so they cannot let what they hear or see bother them personally or take anything that is said to them to heart. Finally, because of client/patient confidentiality, anything that is said during a session must remain private, unless the client admits to a crime such as child or elder abuse or is in danger of hurting himself or herself or another person.

REQUIREMENTS

HIGH SCHOOL

In high school, take courses in psychology, English, and speech. If you plan to work as a mental health, rehabilitation, or genetic counselor, take as many science classes as possible, including biology, chemistry, and anatomy and physiology.

POSTSECONDARY TRAINING

You will need a master's degree to become a licensed counselor, which is typically one of the job requirements set by employers. Contact the professional associations (listed in For More Information) in your specialty of interest for detailed information about educational requirements.

CERTIFICATION AND LICENSING

Certification and licensing requirements vary greatly based on whether the counselor works for a private or public employer and by state law (although most states have laws requiring counselors to have some form of licensure). Contact professional associations in your specialty of interest for detailed information about certification and licensing requirements.

Some counselors choose to become certified by the National Board for Certified Counselors (NBCC, www.nbcc.org). This organization awards a general practice credential of national certified counselor. According to the U.S. Department of Labor, "this national certification is voluntary and is distinct from state licensing. However, in some states, those who pass the national exam are exempt from taking a state certification exam." The NBCC also offers specialty certifications in clinical mental health, addiction, and school counseling

OTHER REQUIREMENTS

Key traits of all counselors include empathy, a strong desire to help others, good listening skills, the ability to communicate well both orally and in writing, strong ethics, the ability to work independently or as part of a team, and physical and mental energy to deal with sometimes stressful and demanding situations (as well as heartbreaking stories). In order to be successful in the field, genetic counselors should possess a curiosity and passion for science, as well as patience for the extensive research and experiments necessary for this field.

EXPLORING

There are many ways to learn more about a career as a counselor. You can read books and magazines about the field, visit the websites of college counseling programs to learn about typical classes and possible career paths, and talk to career and guidance counselors at your school about their careers (or ask them to help arrange information interviews with counselors who do not work in academic settings). Professional associations can also provide information about the field. You should also try to volunteer or land a part-time job in a counseling office. This will give you a chance to interact with counselors and see if the career is a good fit for your interests and abilities.

EMPLOYERS

The U.S. Department of Labor reports the following employment statistics for counselors by specialty: educational, vocational, and school counselors, 275,800; rehabilitation counselors, 129,500; mental health counselors, 113,300; substance abuse and behavioral disorder counselors, 86,100; counselors, all other, 33,400; and marriage and family therapists, 27,300. Counselors work in community agencies, hospitals, schools, nursing homes, and treatment centers. An increasing number of counselors are working in private practice.

GETTING A JOB

Many counselors obtain their first jobs as a result of contacts made through college internships or networking events. Others seek assistance in obtaining job leads from college career services offices, newspaper want ads, and employment websites. Additionally, professional associations, such as the American Counseling Association (ACA), provide job listings at their websites. The ACA also provides helpful articles on writing résumés, acing job interviews, and other career-oriented topics. See For More Information for a list of organizations. Those interested in positions with the federal government should visit the U.S. Office of Personnel Management's website, www.usajobs.opm.gov.

ADVANCEMENT

Advancement for counselors varies by specialty. School counselors, for example, can become counseling department directors. After earning a doctorate degree, they can become school administrators or counseling psychologists. Some counselors choose to work for their state's department of education or work as supervisors or administrators. Others go into private practice or become college professors.

EARNINGS

The U.S. Department of Labor reports the following mean annual earnings for counselors by specialty: school counselors, $52,550; marriage and family counselors, $46,920; mental health counselors, $38,010; substance abuse and behavioral disorder counselors, $37,700; and rehabilitation counselors, $31,210. Counselors not otherwise classified (including genetic counselors) earned mean annual salaries of $41,320. Salaries for all counselors ranged from less than $20,440 to $84,080 or more.

Employers offer a variety of benefits, including the following: medical, dental, and life insurance; paid holidays, vacations, and sick days; personal days; 401(k) plans; profit-sharing plans; retirement and pension plans; and educational assistance programs. Self-employed workers must provide their own benefits.

Colleges Hiring More Mental-Health Professionals

College mental-health centers are seeing an increase in student traffic, according to *The Philadelphia Inquirer*. As cultural stigmas regarding mental illness decrease, students are seeking help for a variety of routine life challenges (such as roommate conflicts, relationship troubles, academic difficulties, etc.). Students are also reporting more serious mental-health issues than in past years. Approximately 15 percent of college students in spring 2008 reported that they had been diagnosed with depression, according to the American College Health Association. This is an increase of 5 percent since 2000. The number of students who have contemplated suicide has also increased on some campuses.

The *Inquirer* reports that the hiring of mental-health professionals (such as counselors, psychologists, psychiatrists, social workers, and substance-abuse specialists) is increasing on college campuses as mental-health centers try to meet growing student demand for services. Look for this growth to continue—if budgets allow—as more students enroll in college and the number of students seeking mental-health assistance continues to rise.

EMPLOYMENT OUTLOOK

Employment for counselors in all fields should be favorable through 2018, according to the U.S. Department of Labor. There will be more jobs available (especially in rural areas) than there are people graduating with degrees in counseling. Much-faster-than-average employment growth is expected for substance abuse and behavioral disorder counselors and mental health counselors. Faster-than-average growth is expected for educational, vocational, and school counselors; marriage and family therapists; and rehabilitation counselors.

Employment for educational, vocational, and school counselors will increase as more people seek advice regarding college and career life planning. Demand is also increasing for school counselors because they are being asked to take on new counseling responsibilities such as crisis and preventive counseling. Budget cuts at schools may limit employment growth for these counselors, although this may be ameliorated by federal grants and subsidies.

Mental health counselors will enjoy good employment prospects because there is growing demand for mental health services and increasing insurance reimbursements for the services of counselors (which are causing them to be sought after by health care providers as cost-effective alternatives to psychiatrists and psychologists).

There is less stigma regarding marital and family problems today, which is prompting more people to seek out the services of marriage and family therapists.

The increasing number of elderly people (who typically become disabled or injured at a higher average rate than other demographic groups) will create good employment prospects for rehabilitation counselors. Growth will also occur as more elderly people are treated for mental health-related disabilities.

Due to evolving technology used to detect diseases, medical advances in treatment, and increased public awareness, employment opportunities for genetic counselors will continue to grow. Their expertise will be in demand in clinical, educational, and administrative settings. Jobs will also be plentiful for those interested in working in private genetic counseling practices or consulting agencies.

FOR MORE INFORMATION

For information on marriage and family therapy, contact
American Association for Marriage and Family Therapy
112 South Alfred Street
Alexandria, VA 22314-3061
www.aamft.org

For information on certification and accredited graduate programs, contact
American Board of Genetic Counseling
PO Box 14216
Lenexa, KS 66285-4216
www.abgc.net

For information on certification and the job search, contact
American Counseling Association
5999 Stevenson Avenue
Alexandria, VA 22304-3304
www.counseling.org

For information on mental health counseling, contact
American Mental Health Counselors Association
801 North Fairfax Street, Suite 304
Alexandria, VA 22314-1775
www.amhca.org

For information about rehabilitation counseling, contact
American Rehabilitation and Counseling Association
www.arcaweb.org

For information on careers, certification, state school counseling association websites, and publications, contact

American School Counselor Association
1101 King Street, Suite 625
Alexandria, VA 22314-2957
www.schoolcounselor.org

For information on educational programs and to read *Training and Careers in Human Genetics* and *Solving the Puzzle: Careers in Genetics,* visit
American Society of Human Genetics
9650 Rockville Pike
Bethesda, MD 20814-3998
www.ashg.org

For information on certification, contact
Commission on Rehabilitation Counselor Certification
1699 East Woodfield Road, Suite 300
Schaumburg, IL 60173-4957
www.crccertification.com

For information on accredited programs, contact
Council for Accreditation of Counseling and Related Educational Programs
American Counseling Association
1001 North Fairfax Street, Suite 510
Alexandria, VA 22314-1587
703-535-5990
www.cacrep.org

For information on approved programs, contact
Council on Rehabilitation Education
1699 East Woodfield Road, Suite 300
Schaumburg, IL 60173-4957
847-944-1345
www.core-rehab.org

For information about college admission counseling and to read the *State of College Admission, Steps to College Newsletter,* and other publications, visit the association's website.
National Association for College Admission Counseling
1050 North Highland Street, Suite 400
Arlington, VA 22201-2197
www.nacacnet.org

For information on rehabilitation counseling, contact the following organizations
National Clearinghouse of Rehabilitation Training Materials
Utah State University
6524 Old Main Hill
Logan, UT 84322-6524
http://ncrtm.org

National Rehabilitation Association
633 South Washington Street
Alexandria, VA 22314-4109
www.nationalrehab.org

National Rehabilitation Counseling Association
PO Box 4480
Manassas, VA 20108-4480
info@nrca-net.org
http://nrca-net.org

For detailed information about careers in genetic counseling, contact
National Society of Genetic Counselors
401 North Michigan Avenue, 22nd Floor
Chicago, IL 60611-4245
nsgc@nsgc.org
www.nsgc.org

Interview: Dotti Dixon Schmeling

Dr. Dotti Dixon Schmeling is a school counselor in Bismarck, North Dakota. She discussed her career with the editors of *Hot Jobs*.

Q. What is one thing that young people may not know about a career in counseling?

A. I believe that young people only see what their experiences in dealing with a school or community counselor have been, and they fail to understand the complexities beyond their face-to-face experiences, as they relate to a career in counseling. Consequently, if a student has dealt with a counselor on a very limited basis, their understanding might be less than a student who has utilized a counselor's services to a greater degree. The behind-the-scenes issues might include some of the following things: length of time required to complete a counseling degree (master's degree); the consultation process of counselors; curriculum responsibilities; and ethical issues.

Q. If you could do anything different in preparing for your career in college/high school, what would it be?

A. If I had lived in a larger city with more curriculum opportunities, I might have taken a foreign language in high school, and I would have looked for internship possibilities related to the counseling field.

Q. What are the most important qualities for counselors?

A. Personal qualities: Honesty; empathetic; caring; self-motivated; goal oriented; social consciousness; energetic. Professional qualities: educated in a quality program; intellect; knowledgeable ethnically; leadership; able to build relationships; collaborative; visionary.

Q. What are some of the pros and cons of your job?

A. The pros of my position include being able to implement a comprehensive school counseling program in my school, so that all students have services available to them. I have not been given additional responsibilities that interfere with my ability to be a counselor.

   The biggest hurdle is that we do not have enough staff to adequately deliver the program to each student, so there are times when we have had to be more reactive than proactive. Hopefully, this will be resolved soon, as the legislature has mandated that the counselor/student ratio be no more than 1/300 in grades seven-12 in our state. If this were to happen, the program could be delivered to all students as we would have numbers of between 250-300 students to each counselor.

Q. Any advice for young people? What are the best ways to find a job?

A. I would advise that students work in their school counseling office during high school if possible; get a broad education specializing in psychology, sociology, philosophy, math, and at least one foreign language; and take every available internship/field experience that is possible during grades nine-16. I do believe that if a student is interested in being a school counselor, they need to work in an educational environment to gain valuable experience in that location. It is also important that the counselor experience a variety of jobs in many different career fields, so they have an understanding of careers first hand as they communicate with their students. Finally, someone interested in the field should be aware that the profession takes an emotional toll, so it is important that the candidate have strong emotional and mental health in order to thrive in the profession.

Interview: Lindsey Bowman

Lindsey Bowman is a counselor at West Fargo High School in West Fargo, North Dakota. She discussed her career with the editors of *Hot Jobs*.

Q. How long have you worked in the field? What made you want to become a school counselor?

A. I have completed four years as a professional school counselor. There were many things that helped me choose this field as a career. My high school counselor was definitely a big factor. She helped me through so many rough times, and I still keep in touch with her. It's a great relationship I built with her and I hope to do the same with my students. I also really like the age range of students I work with. Being a teenager is never easy and I want to help my students get through that however I can.

Q. What are the most important qualities for people in your career?

A. Effective school counselors have a variety of qualities and each uses those qualities in different ways. But the most common qualities we all share are compassion, empathy, organization, and genuine concern for the well-being of the students we serve. It also helps to be flexible, people-oriented, good at multi-tasking, and capable of handling stress.

Q. What are some of the pros and cons of your job?

A. The best part of my job is the students I work with. They make my job worthwhile, and there is nothing better than hearing from them after they have graduated and moved on to bigger and better things! Many times it can feel like a thankless job because most people do not know what school counselors really do. But when you can see the change in your students as they progress through high school and when you get a simple "thank you" at graduation you know you have done your job. It is definitely a stressful career with a lot of responsibility. You work with a range of people—from students, to parents, to teachers, to administrators. You just have to remember you are there in support of the students, and sometimes supporting them can put you in difficult positions. But it is always worth it to see them succeed thanks to your help.

Q. What advice would you give to aspiring counselors?

A. Get as much experience working with the age group you plan to before your first counseling job. Be sure to take care of yourself and live a healthy, stress-free lifestyle because your day-to-day responsibilities can be wearing. The students you work with will depend on you, so be sure you are fresh and ready every morning to assist them as best as you can.

Q. What are the best ways to find a job?

A. The best ways to find a job in school counseling are through the college you are getting your degree from or the webpages for the districts you are interested in working in.

Interview: Lindsi Bennett

Lindsi Bennett works as a career counselor at Idaho State University's Career Center. She has a master of arts in counseling, is a licensed professional counselor in Idaho, and is a national certified counselor. She began full-time work as a counselor in August 2004. Lindsi discussed her career with the editors of *Hot Jobs*.

Q. What made you want to enter this career?

A. I loved my psychology classes in high school and college and also received positive feedback from my family and instructors. Even so, I was rather aimless about a career direction until I graduated college and worked a temporary job for a year. Two months into my temp job, I looked at grad schools and various programs related to psychology. The counseling programs sounded like the best fit for me. Once I was in the University of North Dakota's counseling program, I enjoyed my classes and also the practical experiences like practicum and internship, and realized I wanted to do some kind of counseling in a university setting, so I applied for positions in university counseling centers and career centers.

Q. What is one thing that young people may not know about a career in mental health/career counseling?

A. I imagine most do not know how rewarding and fulfilling it is to help clients uncover things about themselves that they can use to inform a wise career or life decision. It is important to be a good listener, be accepting of people, think of things from various angles, and keep client's names and information confidential. It is essential to keep client information confidential! Also, career counseling is seldom solely about career;

life issues influence career issues and vice versa. Career is a life issue, so career counseling and mental health counseling have a lot of overlap.

Q. Can you briefly describe a typical day on the job?

A. The hours in my office are 8-5 August through May, and 7:30-4 during the summer. In the morning, I take a look at my schedule to see what appointments, presentations, or meetings I have. Then I check and answer some emails and also do any necessary preparation for classes or presentations in the gaps between scheduled items. During the Fall and Spring semesters, it is possible that I have eight different things on my schedule (most are scheduled for one hour). During the Summer, it is more common to have two or three appointments and spend the rest of the day working on projects that there is not time for during the Fall and Spring. In terms of appointments, I see clients for career counseling, résumé reviews, and practice interviews; I provide supervision to one or two student interns from the Idaho State University Counseling Department who see clients in our office; and I spend one day a week at a satellite campus 50 miles away where I teach a Career and Life Planning class and provide career and mental health counseling to individuals and couples.

Q. What do you like most and least about your career?

A. I enjoy meeting lots of great people, learning with them about themselves and careers, supporting them, and discussing how they make decisions and solve problems. It doesn't happen often, but when it does, I love hearing back from a client who has changed their life or career for the better and seeing how much more at peace they seem.

I don't enjoy paperwork (writing notes after sessions, filling out forms to get reimbursed for any work-related travel, etc.), but fortunately most of my time is not spent on paperwork, and I can at least see the value and necessity of writing case notes after a session to document what was covered.

Q. What advice would you offer counseling majors as they graduate and look for jobs? What's the best way to get a job?

A. Get related experience, and build and use your network. I think the two should go hand-in-hand. Your competition in the job search will all have similar degrees/credentials to you; you need to set yourself apart by getting experience and then presenting that experience in such a way that impresses employers. And as you are gaining experience, build relationships with professionals in your field. Show them that you are good at what you do so that they will want to hire you, tell you about openings they hear of, or at least serve as a really positive reference for you. Also, be intentional and proactive in your job search, and start applying before you think you need to.

Q. What is the employment outlook for counselors?

A. According to the *Occupational Outlook Handbook,* all areas of counseling are expected to grow faster than average in the United States in the 2008-2018 period due to more positions than trained graduates in the field, especially in rural areas. If you are someone who likes listening to and helping people, have good boundaries and are comfortable with ambiguity, and are willing to go to graduate school, this may be a fun and rewarding career for you.

DENTAL HYGIENISTS

OVERVIEW

Dental hygienists perform prophylaxis procedures on patients (preventive care that helps a patient avoid gum disease and cavities), take oral x-rays, administer local anesthetics, and remove sutures and dressings. They perform administrative duties such as charting and/or taking oral and medical histories of patients. Dental hygienists also educate patients about the importance of oral preventive care. A minimum of an associate's degree or certificate is required to work as a dental hygienist. Approximately 174,100 dental hygienists are employed in the United States. Employment in this field is expected to grow much faster than the average for all careers through 2018.

FAST FACTS

High School Subjects
Biology
Health

Personal Skills
Helping
Technical

Minimum Education Level
Associate's degree

Salary Range
$44,000 to $67,000 to $92,000+

Employment Outlook
Much faster than the average

O*NET-SOC
29-2021.00

GOE
14.03.01

DOT
078

NOC
3222

THE JOB

Dental hygienists are licensed dental professionals who are responsible for many of the routine duties once performed by dentists—which leaves dentists free to complete more complicated and invasive procedures.

At the beginning of the appointment, the dental hygienist first assesses the patient. He or she reviews the patient's medical and oral history, takes x-rays, and conducts a clinical exam. Then he or she examines the condition of the patient's teeth as well as the periodontal area. Dental hygienists report their findings to the dentist, who then conducts a follow-up exam for a final diagnosis of any dental problems.

If the patient is there for a routine cleaning, the dental hygienist can perform the prophylaxis. This involves the removal of any tartar (hardened mineralized plaque) and stains from the surface of the teeth. Dental hygienists use various hand instruments and power-driven dental instruments to help them during the process. If the patient suffers from periodontal disease, the dental hygienist may administer a local anesthetic before continuing on with scaling (removing plaque and other stains) or root planing (more involved cleaning that focuses on the roots) to help curb the disease. The dental hygienist may also finish the session with an application of fluoride, which prevents tooth decay.

Dental hygienists may also be specially trained to remove sutures or change dressings for patients who have had oral surgery or other invasive procedures. They may also assist the dentist by creating teeth molds in preparation for denture pieces, tooth caps, or implants. They may help the dentist when providing ultrasonic teeth whitening by prepping the gum line with wax or other protective coverings.

Dental hygienists also teach patients about good oral health. They instruct the patient about the proper techniques to use when brushing and flossing teeth. They may use a model of upper or lower teeth to demonstrate these techniques. If the patient complains of tooth sensitivity, the dental hygienist may recommend a special toothpaste or rinse to help alleviate this problem.

Depending on the size and scope of the dental office, dental hygienists may have additional duties such as charting and keeping track of and ordering necessary medical supplies.

Full-time dental hygienists work about 40 hours a week. Some evening and weekend shifts are required to accommodate patients' schedules. Dental hygienists wear professional attire, often a lab coat. Comfortable shoes are a must, since dental hygienists are on their feet for much of the day, or walking from exam room to exam room. They also wear latex gloves, masks, and other protective equipment when working with patients.

Dental hygienists work in clean, comfortable, well-lit offices. They often sit on stools when performing procedures in order to better reach the patient. Dental hygienists are at high risk of developing carpal tunnel syndrome— nerve damage to the hand caused by the use of small tools in repetitive movements. Dental hygienists often use special braces and perform stretching exercises to reduce the risk of developing carpal tunnel syndrome.

At times, dental hygienists' work schedules can be quite hectic, especially when handling a heavy patient load. They can also fall behind schedule due to a difficult case or a patient who is especially nervous or jittery. They also may work at more than one office—sometimes even in the course of a single workday. If the dental hygienist is employed at more than one facility, he or she needs a reliable means of transportation in order to travel from one office to another.

REQUIREMENTS

HIGH SCHOOL

Take courses in biology, chemistry, psychology, math, and health. Speech classes will help you develop your communication skills, which you will use often when interacting with patients, dentists, dental assistants, and other hygienists.

POSTSECONDARY TRAINING

A minimum of an associate's degree or certificate is required to work as a dental hygienist. More than 310 dental hygiene programs are accredited by the

Commission on Dental Accreditation. Visit www.ada.org/267.aspx for a list of accredited programs. Most programs award an associate's degree, but some offer certificates, bachelor's degrees, and master's degrees. According to the American Dental Hygienists' Association (ADHA), a typical associate's degree program offers courses in the basic sciences (anatomy, physiology, pathology, general chemistry, biochemistry, microbiology, pathology, nutrition, and pharmacology), the liberal arts (English, speech, sociology, and psychology), dental science courses (dental anatomy, head and neck anatomy, oral pathology, radiography, oral embryology and histology, periodontology, and pain control and dental materials), and dental hygiene science courses (patient management, clinical dental hygiene, oral health education/preventive counseling, community dental health, and medical and dental emergencies). Students also participate in preclinical and clinical experiences in which they work directly with patients under the close supervision of dental educators. The average associate's degree program requires 86 credit hours, according to the ADHA. Dental hygienists who plan to work in research, clinical practice, or teaching typically have at least a bachelor's degree.

Did You Know?

According to the American Dental Hygienists' Association, the typical dental hygiene educational program requires 86 credit hours for an associate degree and 122 credit hours for a bachelor's degree.

CERTIFICATION AND LICENSING

All states require dental hygienists to be licensed. According to the U.S. Department of Labor, "nearly all states require candidates to graduate from an accredited dental hygiene school and pass both a written and clinical examination. The American Dental Association's Joint Commission on National Dental Examinations administers the written examination, which is accepted by all States and the District of Columbia. State or regional testing agencies administer the clinical examination. In addition, most states require an examination on the legal aspects of dental hygiene practice."

OTHER REQUIREMENTS

To be a successful dental hygienist, you should have excellent communication and interpersonal skills, since you will spend the majority of your workday interacting with patients, dentists, and dental assistants. You should have good manual dexterity in order to skillfully use dental instruments to conduct prophylaxis procedures. Other important traits include attention to detail, punctuality, cleanliness, and patience and compassion to deal with patients who may be fearful of undergoing dental procedures.

EXPLORING

There are many ways to learn more about a career as a dental hygienist and dentistry as a whole. You can read books and magazines about the field, visit the websites of college dental hygiene programs to learn about typical classes and possible career paths, and ask your health teacher or school counselor to arrange an information interview with a dental hygienist. Professional associations can also provide information about the field. Both the American Dental Association (www.ada.org) and the American Dental Hygienists' Association (www.adha.org/careerinfo) provide a wealth of information about dental hygiene education and careers at their websites. You should also try to land a part-time job in a dental office. This will give you a chance to interact with dental hygienists and see if the career is a good fit for your interests and abilities.

Good Advice

Caryn Loftis Solie, RDH, the president of the American Dental Hygienists' Association, offers the following advice to young people who are interested in becoming dental hygienists:

"Contact the American Dental Hygienists' Association to find local dental hygienists to meet and have the opportunity to observe dental hygienists working in various settings. Take every opportunity to expand your knowledge base in science studies but also incorporate speech, interpersonal communications, and psychology."

EMPLOYERS

Approximately 174,100 dental hygienists are employed in the United States, with nearly all working in dental offices. Others work for employment services and in physicians' offices, hospitals, nursing homes, prisons, schools, and public health clinics. Some dental hygienists work for companies that sell dental-related equipment and supplies. Opportunities are also available in the U.S. military. About 50 percent of dental hygienists work part time.

GETTING A JOB

Many dental hygienists obtain their first jobs as a result of contacts made through college internships or networking events. Others seek assistance in obtaining job leads from college career services offices, newspaper want ads, employment websites, and dental auxiliary placement services (which charge a fee for their services). Additionally, professional dental associations, such as the American Dental Association, provide job listings at their web sites. See For More Information for a list of organizations. The American Dental Hygienists' Association offers tips on career planning and résumé writing at its website, www.adha.org/careerinfo/dhcareers.htm. Those interested in positions with the federal government should visit the U.S. Office of Personnel Management's website, www.usajobs.opm.gov.

FOR MORE INFORMATION

For information on education and careers, contact
American Dental Association
211 East Chicago Avenue
Chicago, IL 60611-2678
312-440-2500
publicinfo@ada.org
www.ada.org

For information on education, contact
American Dental Education Association
1400 K Street, NW, Suite 1100
Washington, DC 20005-2415
202-289-7201
adea@adea.org
www.adea.org

For comprehensive information about a career as a dental hygienist, contact
American Dental Hygienists' Association
444 North Michigan Avenue, Suite 3400
Chicago, IL 60611-3980
312-440-8900
mail@adha.net
www.adha.org

ADVANCEMENT

Dental hygienists advance by receiving salary increases or by working at larger practices. Some hygienists pursue advanced education and become dentists. Others pursue bachelor's or master's degrees in dental hygiene and work as college educators or public health researchers and educators.

EARNINGS

Salaries for dental hygienists vary by type of employer, geographic region, and the worker's experience level and skills. Median annual salaries for dental hygienists were $67,340 in 2009, according to the U.S. Department of Labor (USDL). Salaries ranged from less than $44,900 to $92,860 or more. The USDL reports the following mean annual earnings for dental hygienists by industry: offices of dentists, $68,160; employment services, $68,150; outpatient care centers, $68,100; offices of physicians, $61,740; and general medical and surgical hospitals, $57,570.

Approximately 50 percent of dental hygienists received fringe benefits in 2009, according to a survey by the American Dental Hygienists' Association. Sick leave, paid vacation, and retirement plans were the most commonly cited benefits.

EMPLOYMENT OUTLOOK

Employment for dental hygienists is expected to grow much faster than the average for all careers through 2018, according to the U.S. Department of Labor. It is one of the fastest-growing careers in the United States, with growth of 36 percent expected from 2008 to 2018. Demand will increase for dental hygienists as a result of the growth of the U.S. population, the increasing focus on preventive dental care, and a growing reliance on hygienists to perform duties that were previously handled by dentists. Competition for jobs will vary by geographic region. In some areas, there is an overabundance of hygienists, which will make finding a job more difficult.

Interview: Caryn Loftis Solie

Caryn Loftis Solie, RDH is a dental hygienist and the president of the American Dental Hygienists' Association. She discussed her career with the editors of *Hot Jobs*.

Q. What made you want to enter this career?

A.   I was inspired by a dental hygienist I met when I worked part-time in a dental office while in high school. Her ability to provide a valuable service to her patients, have diversity in her duties, and earn a reasonable income impressed me. She was very instrumental in my decision to become a dental hygienist.

Q. What is one thing that young people may not know about a career in dental hygiene?

A.   Dental hygienists may work in a variety of settings. Many dental hygienists provide care in a private dental office, but opportunities are also available to work in hospitals, community health centers, nursing homes, schools, prisons, and mobile clinics. Dental hygienists work in public health settings as caregivers, but also as administrators. Dental hygienists are educators in dental and dental hygiene schools. Many dental manufacturers and companies hire dental hygienists as researchers, and utilize dental hygienists in product development, sales and marketing, as education specialists, and as executives.

Q. What are the most important qualities for people in your career?

A.   It is important to be outgoing, to genuinely like people and want to help them. Being a good communicator and motivator is very important. As in any profession the qualities of hard work, dedication, and a willingness to always be learning new things are critical to your success.

Q. What are some of the pros and cons of your job?

A.   Pros: The gratification you have in knowing you have improved someone's health and well being is tremendous. You meet many interesting people from all walks of life and each encounter gives you more knowledge. You are continually learning as science and technology make advances.

Cons: The 50 state regulations that vary in what duties a dental hygienist can perform often can be limiting to your job satisfaction. Those same regulations may impede one in easily moving from state to state.

Q. Can you tell me about the American Dental Hygienists' Association? How important is association membership to career success?

A.   The American Dental Hygienists Association is the organization that represents the profession of dental hygiene on the national level. Each state has a chapter and there are local chapters in most communities as well. The association works to advance the profession as a whole and to provide education and support for dental hygienists. Membership in the association is a personal choice. I found that being a member and taking the opportunities to be an active member gave me more personal confidence, improved my critical thinking and public speaking skills, and opened up new venues of employment.

FINANCIAL PLANNERS

OVERVIEW

Financial planners, also known as financial advisors and personal financial advisors, provide people and organizations with expertise and advice on business, personal, and family finances. Although most planners offer advice on a wide range of topics, some specialize in areas such as retirement and estate planning or divorce settlements. Financial planners must have at least a bachelor's degree in accounting, business, economics, finance, law, or mathematics to work in the field. Approximately 208,400 financial planners are employed in the United States. Employment in the field is expected to grow much faster than the average for all careers through 2018.

FAST FACTS

High School Subjects
Business
Mathematics

Personal Skills
Communication
Helping
Management

Minimum Education Level
Bachelor's degree

Salary Range
$33,000 to $68,000 to $215,000+

Employment Outlook
Much faster than the average

O*NET-SOC
13-2052.00, 41-3031.01, 41-3031.02

GOE
12.03.01

DOT
250

NOC
1114

THE JOB

Individuals, families, and businesses depend on financial planners to advise them on wise economic decisions. Individuals hire these professionals for objective third-party advice to help them address emotional disruptions in their lives, such as the loss of a job, a critical illness that will incur large medical costs, a death of a spouse who was a breadwinner for the family, or the financial challenges caused by a divorce. Planners also assist with happier events in people's lives, such as getting married, buying or selling a house, adopting or having a baby, funding a college education, or planning for retirement.

Financial planners first meet with their clients and discuss their clients' financial goals or concerns. They discuss an expected time frame for results and, if relevant, how clients feel about aggressive (riskier) versus conservative (safer) investments. Generally, if a client is trying to meet an immediate financial need, a riskier investment might be needed to obtain the greatest financial gain in a shorter amount of time. Conversely, if a client is trying to meet a long-term goal such as establishing a retirement plan, the financial advisor may recommend safer investments that typically pay off gradually, but consistently, over time.

A financial planner consults with clients. Employment for financial planners is expected to grow by 30 percent through 2018, according to the U.S. Department of Labor. (Jupiterimages/Thinkstock)

In order to best advise their clients, financial planners must study the whole picture. For example, purchasing a particular investment might help a client pay off his or her mortgage faster in the short term, but it might delay his or her retirement savings in the long term. By viewing each financial decision as part of a whole, financial planners examine the short- and long-term effects on their clients' determined life goals.

Much of the job consists of preparing financial plans for clients. Written plans presented to clients may be referred to as retirement plans or estate plans. To write them, planners first gather as much information as possible about the individual, business, or family's financial data, including tax returns, investments, and insurance policies. They then analyze the data and make recommendations on changes in saving and investment strategies to assist clients in achieving their financial goals and making the most money in the long term. In order to succeed in their job, financial planners need to be knowledgeable about issues relating to taxes, retirement, insurance, real estate planning, and more. A good financial planner will work with other professionals, such as stockbrokers, accountants, and insurance agents, to coordinate their efforts with a client's overall financial needs.

Once a financial plan has been mapped out and agreed upon, planners assist in implementing the proposed investments, strategies, or other changes. Depending on the situation, the planner may actually carry out the plan or coordinate the process among the client and his or her stockbrokers, insurance agents, or attorneys.

Finally, once the plan is in place, financial planners must monitor the client's progress towards his or her goals. Since the economic market is always in flux, the planner may have to make modifications to recommendations or revise investment strategies to ensure that goals are met. Similar to economic changes, a client's life goals may change, and the financial planner must stay in line with the client's fluctuating needs.

Private bankers or *wealth managers* are specialized financial planners who manage finances for very wealthy people who have a large amount of money to invest. They typically directly manage their employer's finances and work with a team of lawyers, accountants, financial analysts, and other professionals.

Financial planners must be well versed in the various planning software tools that are available, such as Excel and Quicken. They use these programs to do their jobs and may even instruct clients in their use.

Some financial planners conduct public speaking arrangements, advising large groups of people on investment strategies. These may be in a traditional seminar arrangement or, with the popularity of the Internet, may even be presented as an online webinar.

Financial advisors usually work in offices and keep standard business hours. However, to accommodate working families, planners often consult with their clients during evenings or weekends. Consultations are often personal in nature, so face-to-face meetings are preferred. As a result, considerable amounts of travel may be involved. Planners typically set their own schedules, which allows for a lot of freedom and flexibility in their work hours. Busy periods often occur during tax preparation seasons (April for annual filers, as well as four times a year for quarterly filers), but since financial planners assist in any type of life or business decision, their busy periods can extend year-round.

REQUIREMENTS

High School

Take a college-preparatory course load in high school, which includes classes in mathematics, business, computer science, speech, English, and psychology.

Postsecondary Training

You will need at least a bachelor's degree in accounting, business, economics, finance, law, or mathematics to work in the field. Many financial planners also earn a master's degree in finance or business administration and obtain certification to demonstrate their financial acumen to potential employers.

Certification and Licensing

Many financial planners pursue voluntary certification from the CFP Board (www.cfp.net), Fi360 (www.fi360.com), The American College (www.theamericancollege.edu), and the Investment Management Consultants Association (www.imca.org). Contact these organizations for more information.

Licensing to sell stocks and insurance is required at the state and federal levels, but requirements vary. Information on state licensing for registered investment advisors is available from the North American Securities Administrator Association (www.nasaa.org).

OTHER REQUIREMENTS

Because they have direct interaction with clients or large businesses, financial planners must have excellent interpersonal and communication skills. They also view and analyze confidential financial data and, as a result, must be discreet and professional as well as highly ethical. Other important traits include strong math and analytical skills, good sales ability, and excellent organizational and research skills.

EXPLORING

There are many ways to learn more about a career as a financial planner. You can read books and magazines about the field and ask your teacher or school counselor to arrange an information interview with a financial planner. Professional associations can also provide information about the field. You should also try to land a part-time job with a financial investment firm or bank. This will give you a chance to interact with financial planners and see if the career is a good fit for your interests and abilities.

Books to Read

Holmberg, Joshua. *The Teen's Guide to Personal Finance: Basic Concepts in Personal Finance That Every Teen Should Know.* Bloomington, Ind.: iUniverse, 2008.

Jones, Nancy Langdon. *So You Want to Be a Financial Planner: Your Guide to a New Career.* 5th ed. Sunnyvale, Calif.: AdvisorPress, 2009.

Napolitano, John P. *The Complete Idiot's Guide to Success as a Personal Financial Planner.* New York: Alpha, 2007.

EMPLOYERS

Approximately 208,400 financial planners are employed in the United States. Opportunities are available throughout the U.S., but many planners work in California, Florida, and New York. They work independently or for banks, insurance carriers, financial investment firms, and securities and commodity brokers. Approximately 29 percent of financial planners are self-employed.

GETTING A JOB

Many financial planners obtain their first jobs as a result of contacts made through college internships or networking events. Others seek assistance in obtaining job leads from college career services offices, newspaper want ads, and employment websites. Additionally, professional associations, such as the Financial Planning Association and the National Association of Personal Financial Advisors, provide job and internship listings at their websites. See For More Information for contact information.

ADVANCEMENT

Financial planners who are self-employed advance by building a larger clientele who have a higher amount of wealth to invest. Those who work for financial planning firms advance by receiving pay raises and becoming managers. They may also leave their employer to start their own financial consulting businesses.

EARNINGS

Earnings for financial planners vary by type of employer, geographic region, and the worker's experience level and skills. Median annual earnings for financial planners who were not self-employed were $68,200 in 2009, according to the U.S. Department of Labor. Salaries ranged from less than $33,790 to $116,580 or more. Certified financial planners earned a median annual gross income of $215,345 in 2009, according to the College of Financial Planning's *2009 Survey of Trends in the Financial Planning Industry*. Financial planners earn their income by charging hourly consulting fees, receiving commissions for financial products that they sell, or charging a fee based on a percentage of their clients' assets that are under management.

Financial planners usually receive benefits such as health and life insurance, vacation days, sick leave, and a savings and pension plan. Self-employed workers must provide their own benefits.

EMPLOYMENT OUTLOOK

Employment for financial planners is expected to grow much faster than the average for all careers through 2018, according to the U.S. Department of Labor. Despite this prediction, new workers will experience strong competition for jobs as a result of the strong interest in this high-paying career. Those with certification and advanced education will have the best job prospects.

Interview: Carolyn McClanahan

Carolyn McClanahan, M.D., CFP is a financial planner at Life Planning Partners, Inc. (www.lifeplanningpartners.com) in Jacksonville, Florida. She has been quoted in *The Wall Street Journal, Money, Kiplinger's,* and *Smart Money* and has appeared on CNBC and been interviewed on NPR. She discussed her career with the editors of *Hot Jobs.*

Q. What made you want to enter this career?

A. I've always enjoyed learning about finances—investing, insurance, budgeting, and taxes. In my previous profession as a doctor, we were taught nothing about finance so I tried to find a "financial planner." Back when I started, people who called themselves "financial planners" mostly did just investments. I went back to school to learn about financial planning for fun and realized how much I enjoyed the subject. There was a huge need for people doing comprehensive financial planning instead of just investments, so I decided to enter the field. I love what I do, and it is one of the best decisions I have ever made.

Q. Can you tell us about Life Planning Partners?

A. Life Planning Partners, Inc. is a financial life planning firm. We help people form the goals on what they want out of life, then simplify and arrange their finances to match their goals, and monitor their plan on an ongoing basis to help them keep track of their goals.

Q. What are some of the pros and cons of your job?

A. The great part is helping people craft their dreams and helping them realize they can do what they need to reach those dreams. It is also rewarding to help people who haven't had good planning by helping them get everything together so they know things will be fine when bad events happen in life. The cons are when people are unrealistic with themselves and we have to rein them in to align their finances with their goals.

Q. What are the most important qualities for financial planners?

A. The most important quality by far is the ability to actively listen and ask good questions to understand who your client is and what they want to accomplish. The relationship is about them, and a planner has to develop the ability to help without judging. A planner must be very open, kind, and caring when asking clients tough questions. Technical skills include computer literacy, being great with numbers, and paying attention to detail.

Q. Any advice for young people? What's the best way to land a job?

A. Volunteer to work for a comprehensive fee-only financial planner for the summer. Major in financial planning, and consider obtaining a minor in counseling or communication. The best way to find a job is to be involved, volunteer for National Association of Personal Financial Advisors or Financial Planning Association events, attend conferences, and network.

Q. What has been one of the most rewarding experiences in your career and why?

A. One of my favorite parts of the job is helping people who haven't been taught good financial skills, so they depend on a spouse or other people to help them. When they are left alone, like when a spouse dies, I love educating them about finances and how they can manage their lives. In one case, I had a widow whose husband had invested in one stock, and all their money was in that one stock. She had enough money, but if that stock didn't do well, she could have lost everything. I convinced her to sell the stock and invest in safer assets. This was right before a major stock market crash, so she was very thankful.

Interview: Michael A. Branham

Michael A. Branham, CFP is a financial planner at Cornerstone Wealth Advisors, Inc. in Edina, Minnesota. He discussed his career with the editors of *Hot Jobs*.

Q. What made you want to enter this career?

A. I wish I could tell you that when asked as a child that "financial planner" was what I "wanted to be when I grew up." That, of course, would be a lie. In fact, I embarrassingly stumbled on my career near the end of my college life while trying to find a job that could feed my young family. However, I quickly realized the impact sound financial advice can have on the lives of those with which I worked. It became clear to me that I had an opportunity to really help people and work with them towards the achievement of their life's goals. There is a great deal of personal satisfaction in working with people in a manner that makes a difference in their lives, and the lives of their families.

Q. What is one thing that young people may not know about a career in financial planning?

A. No matter your education, there is much more to being an effective financial planner than the knowledge you can learn from a book or in a classroom. Only experience and the willingness to listen and learn will prepare you to sit with clients and deliver advice. In our office we talk about the three facets of "being" a financial planner—knowledge, the application of that knowledge, and the ability to communicate. While you may be able to learn the requisite knowledge through a degree program or a continuing education class, applying that knowledge and developing an effective communication style takes time and practice. Be patient!

Q. What do you like most about your job?

A. My job affords me the opportunity to work with people every day, and to face new and exciting challenges on a regular basis. Clients have a unique way of finding new ways to challenge our abilities, thought processes, and skills as their lives unfold. Some of the work is mundane, but in general it is intellectually stimulating and personally rewarding.

Q. What advice would you give to aspiring financial planners?

A. Be patient and humble. Recognize that regardless of how much you know, there is much more to learn. Understand that no matter how talented you are, there are others on whom you can rely on for advice, information, and personal development. Develop your ability to listen intently, and always keep the best interest of your clients paramount in the advice that you give.

Q. What are the best ways to find a job?

A. The first task is to assess your skills, abilities, and desires for your career. Do you want to work towards being a senior planner or firm owner? Are you comfortable working in a support role throughout your career? You should tailor your search accordingly. From there, networking and involvement in professional associations and communities is essential.

Q. What has been one (or more) of the most rewarding experiences in your career and why?

A. Rewarding experiences come daily in this career, and sometimes the reward is bittersweet. We once helped a mother of two, dying of cancer, get her affairs in order and ensure that the children she was about to orphan were taken care of for life. Though incredibly difficult and emotional, this kind of effort helps to bring some comfort to those at death's door, and illustrates what is really important in the lives of our clients!

Interview: Aaron S. Coates

Aaron S. Coates, CFP, CIMA is a financial planner at Valeo Financial Advisors, LLC in Indianapolis, Indiana. He discussed his career with the editors of *Hot Jobs*.

Q. What made you want to enter this career?

A. It combines my two varied skills in relational counseling and math/logic/problem solving.

Q. What is one thing that young people may not know about a career in financial planning?

A. That it is nothing like being a broker and selling securities. It is much more like counseling mixed with engineering.

Q. What are your main responsibilities as a financial planner?

A. I help people define their life goals, segment off the financial part and map out a process to reach them; identify any serious mental, or emotional roadblocks obstructing their ability to align their finances and their values (or their subconscious and conscious finances); discover any opportunities they may be missing to more productively grow or enjoy their wealth; and discover any opportunities to more productively steward their wealth for the betterment of their legacy. This may include better definition around charitable giving, but typically involves creating learning environments for children who have not had opportunities to grow in the area of financial wisdom.

Q. What advice would you give to young people who are interested in the field? What are the best ways to find a job?

A. Find a mentor. Get involved in professional organizations early. Attend one of the few well-respected programs in the country (i.e., Texas Tech University) and learn everything you can.

MANAGEMENT ANALYSTS

OVERVIEW

Management analysts, often referred to as *management consultants* in private industry, help companies and organizations improve business processes by minimizing costs and maximizing production and profits. They work independently or for large consulting firms with thousands of other analysts. Management analysts need at least a bachelor's degree in management consulting, accounting, business, computer and information science, economics, engineering, management, marketing, or statistics to work in the field. Some private-sector employers require a master's degree in one of these disciplines or specialized knowledge. Approximately 746,900 management analysts are employed in the United States. Employment is expected to grow much faster than the average for all careers through 2018.

FAST FACTS

High School Subjects
Business
Computer science
Speech

Personal Skills
Communication
Complex problem solving
Judgment and decision making
Leadership

Minimum Education Level
Bachelor's degree

Salary Range
$42,000 to $75,000 to $134,000+

Employment Outlook
Much faster than the average

O*NET-SOC
13-1111.00

GOE
13.02.04

DOT
161

NOC
1122

THE JOB

In today's challenging economy, companies need the advice of experts to stay financially "lean and mean." Management analysts are these experts, advising organizations, ranging from large corporations to small local companies, on how to stay competitive. Analysts are tasked with helping their clients operate with the optimal number and allocation of resources. They analyze business processes and structure to look for waste or redundant systems.

Management analysts may specialize in either a certain element of business, such as benefits and payroll, quality assurance, or communications, or in an industry, such as finance, manufacturing, or food service. Analysts tackle issues ranging from poor customer service to analyzing the market potential of a new product line.

Depending on the size of the organization and the scope of the issue at hand, management analysts may work alone or in a large team of consultants.

Regardless of their specialty, analysts approach their jobs in the same way. They are presented by management with a problem. Analysts then gather as much information about the organization as possible, interviewing employees—from new hires to long-time executives—to get their take on business processes and goals. They also study company documents such as tax returns, balance sheets, executive summaries, annual reports, mission statements, and other communications. They may even talk to business clients and end users to get their opinion on the organization's products or services. Before they make their recommendations and document their findings, management analysts have to take into account the type of industry the organization is operating in and any limitations or opportunities that creates. They also consider the organizational culture and its stated goals. Finally, they have to account for current economic conditions and consumer buying trends.

After considering these factors, management analysts develop a plan of attack for the organization. This is typically written out as a prepared document for the company to keep for reference. The analyst also may be asked to orally present his or her findings to executives or the organization.

Most analysts are hired on a contract basis, and job opportunities are put out to bid. This means the company requests proposals from consultants and consulting firms. Sometimes hundreds of analysts compete for the same job, so they need to be able to put together a solid proposal to even get a foot in the door of a company. This proposal includes past references, cost and scope estimates, and a drafted project plan with deadlines for completion. The company then selects the proposal that best suits its needs. Once a plan is selected, analysts may be kept on the job to implement the plan. In this regard, analysts ensure that stated goals are carried out and that the organization's staff is comfortable and clear with the process or structural changes.

Management analysts work in office settings or out of their homes if they are self-employed. They usually spend at least half their time traveling out to client sites, meeting with staff and observing operations. The remainder of their time is spent in front of a computer, writing up business plans and recommendations.

Depending on the timeline for their projects, analysts may work at least a traditional 40-hour workweek, but if facing a deadline, they may have to put in considerable overtime to complete an assignment.

This career can be stressful as a result of unhappy clients who have unattainable and unrealistic expectations and too-tight deadlines, and because of the constant need to advertise one's services and secure new business opportunities. Self-employed consultants in particular face pressure to build their client base and find new work. However, most analysts find it very rewarding to be able to help organizations improve or to solve major operational or structural challenges.

REQUIREMENTS

HIGH SCHOOL

Take a college preparatory course load in high school that includes classes in accounting, business, computer science, economics, mathematics, psychol-

Best Undergraduate Business Programs

Bloomberg BusinessWeek compiles an annual list of the best undergraduate business programs in the United States. Here were the top 7 in 2010. Visit www.businessweek.com for a complete list.

1. University of Notre Dame (Mendoza, http://business.nd.edu)

2. University of Virginia (McIntire, www.commerce.virginia.edu)

3. Massachusetts Institute of Technology (Sloan, http://mitsloan.mit.edu)

4. University of Pennsylvania (Wharton, www.wharton.upenn.edu)

5. Cornell University (www.cornell.edu)

6. University of California-Berkeley (Haas, www.haas.berkeley.edu)

7. Emory University (Goizueta, http://goizueta.emory.edu)

ogy, and statistics. English and speech classes will help you to develop strong communication skills, which are very important in this career.

POSTSECONDARY TRAINING

Management analysts need at least a bachelor's degree in management consulting, accounting, business, computer and information science, economics, engineering, management, marketing, or statistics to work in the field. Some private-sector employers require a master's degree in one of these disciplines or specialized expertise. Most analysts also have years of experience in information technology, accounting, management, human resources, or other business specialties.

After they are hired, management analysts participate in formal company training programs. They also must continue to update their skills and knowledge throughout their careers by attending seminars and educational conferences and by pursuing other educational opportunities.

CERTIFICATION AND LICENSING

Voluntary certification is provided by the Institute of Management Consultants USA, Inc. Contact the organization for more information.

OTHER REQUIREMENTS

In order to succeed in their work, analysts and consultants must be confident, enterprising, good listeners, strong communicators, and able to work both independently and as a member of a team when the situation arises. They are presented with seemingly overwhelming problems and must be able to break a complex issue down into manageable pieces. They need to be able to objectively analyze the situation, apply business logic and standards, and develop a solution for their employer. Management analysts have to be able to "sell" their developed plan, so they should be comfortable with public speaking and making presentations. They also must be "salesmen" if they are self-employed and are bidding for projects. Analysts are part problem solver, part project manager, and part teacher. They must enjoy overcoming obstacles and applying business policies and logic to issues at hand.

EXPLORING

There are not many direct ways to gain experience as a management analyst, but you can learn about the general field of business by participating in a variety of activities. If your high school has a business club, be sure to join it and take on leadership responsibilities. You should also consider joining Junior Achievement (www.ja.org) and Business Professionals of America (www.bpa.org), membership organizations for high school students who are interested in business careers. You can also learn more about the business world by reading books, magazines (*Forbes, Fortune,* and *Bloomberg Businessweek),* and newspapers (*Wall Street Journal)* about business and checking out the websites of college business programs. *Bloomberg Businessweek* and *U.S. News & World Report* publish annual lists of the best college business programs in the United States. Finally, ask a school counselor or business teacher to arrange an information interview with a management analyst or business executive.

EMPLOYERS

Approximately 746,900 management analysts are employed in the United States. They work throughout the U.S., but most are employed in large metropolitan areas with a large number of businesses and government agencies (especially with the U.S. Department of Defense at the federal level). Approximately 26 percent of management analysts are self-employed. This is three times the average for all occupations. Many management analysts start their own firms because, unlike in many other industries, start-up and business overhead costs for analysts are low.

GETTING A JOB

The position of management analyst is not typically an entry-level job. It takes years of experience and education to be trusted to provide consulting services to a large corporation or government agency that has a multibillion-dollar budget. After they gain this education and experience, aspiring analysts obtain their first jobs via word-of-mouth, through networking contacts made at industry events, and by placing advertisements in industry trade publications and business-related newspapers and magazines.

Additionally, professional associations, such as the Association of Internal Management Consultants and the American Management Association, provide job listings at their websites. See For More Information for a list of organizations. Those interested in positions with the federal government should visit the U.S. Office of Personnel Management's website, www.usajobs.opm.gov.

ADVANCEMENT

Management analysts with considerable experience and expertise advance by taking on larger projects, being assigned managerial duties for consulting teams, or even being asked to become partners or work in other top-level positions at their employer. Analysts may decide to start their own consulting firms. Some analysts become college professors; others write books about the field and appear as media experts on television and radio.

EARNINGS

Salaries for management analysts vary by type of employer, geographic region, and the worker's education, experience, and skill level Median annual salaries for management analysts and consultants were $75,250 in 2009, according to the U.S. Department of Labor (USDL). Salaries ranged from less than $42,550 to $134,820 or more. The USDL reports the following mean annual earnings for management analysts and consultants by industry: management, scientific, and technical consulting services, $97,100; computer systems design and related services, $91,040; federal government, $84,280; management of companies and enterprises, $82,030; and state government, $56,340.

Employers offer a variety of benefits, including the following: medical, dental, and life insurance; paid holidays, vacations, and sick days; personal days; 401(k) plans; profit-sharing plans; retirement and pension plans; and educational assistance programs. Travel expenses are also typically reimbursed by employers. Self-employed workers must provide their own benefits.

EMPLOYMENT OUTLOOK

Employment for management analysts is expected to grow much faster than the average for all careers through 2018, according to the U.S. Department of Labor (USDL). Despite this pre-

FOR MORE INFORMATION

For job listings and information on educational training, scholarships for high school and college students, and careers, contact
American Institute of Certified Public Accountants
1211 Avenue of the Americas
New York, NY 10036-8775
212-596-6200
www.aicpa.org

For information on jobs and management training, contact
American Management Association
1601 Broadway
New York, NY 10019-7434
877-566-9441
customerservice@amanet.org
www.amanet.org

For information about internal management consulting, contact
Association of Internal Management Consultants
824 Caribbean Court
Marco Island, FL 34145-3422
info@aimc.org
www.aimc.org

For job listings, contact
Association of Management Consulting Firms
370 Lexington Avenue, Suite 2209
New York, NY 10017-6573
info@amcf.org
www.amcf.org

For information on certification and to read management blogs, visit the institute's website.
Institute of Management Consultants USA
2025 M Street, NW, Suite 800
Washington, DC 20036-3309
office@imcusa.org
www.imcusa.org

diction, there will be very strong competition for jobs, since many people want to enter this rewarding and high-paying field. The USDL reports that "job growth is projected in very large consulting firms with international expertise and in smaller consulting firms that specialize in specific areas, such as biotechnology, health care, information technology, human resources, engineering, and marketing." Other areas of growth include green technology and energy efficiency. Analysts with advanced degrees, specialized knowledge, and a proven track record of helping companies save money and improve employee performance will have the best job prospects.

Interview: Laurie Taylor

Laurie Taylor is the founder and president of FlashPoint! Solutions (www.igniteyourbiz.com) in Westminster, Colorado. She discussed her career with the editors of *Hot Jobs*.

Q. How long have you worked in the field? What made you want to enter this career?

A. Overall, 23 years. Consulting is a second career for me. I received a degree in parks and recreation and a master's degree in public administration and progressed through my career rather quickly upon graduation in 1973. I started many of the first recreation programs in Colorado, as leisure-time activities were a booming industry in the early 70s. I ran one of the largest and one of the first recreation centers in Colorado at the young age of 24. I was active in the Colorado Parks and Recreation Association, chaired many committees, and took a turn as president. I also started the first magazine for that association. Fourteen years into that career, I was suddenly fired from a job I had held for six years as the superintendent of recreation for a small community north of Denver, Colorado.

So in 1986, I was left without a job, without a career, and without any self esteem. In fact, over a period of six months, I lost my job, lost my dad, and got divorced.

I ended up helping start, manage, and ultimately grow a $12 million marketing communications company, taking it from two people to more than 120 people. Back in 1987, I ran into a good friend who had also left a position and we decided to join forces and see what we could do to put food on our tables. From that very shaky start, I became a reluctant entrepreneur. So I wasn't looking to become a consultant, but as so often happens, sometimes life throws us curve balls and you have to be able to handle the curveballs as well as the fastballs.

Through my experiences with managing and running that business for 14 years, I learned a lot about managing people, processes, and profit. My business partner was the 'what' person and I was the 'how' person. We continued to apply new skills to our business to meet the needs of our clients. Many times as we were growing that business we 'simply didn't know what we didn't know'.

Our strong values drove us to hire and keep great people and our belief that we needed to stay ahead of our clients' needs kept clients coming back for our services. I loved the challenges of growing a business and, today, my company, FlashPoint! is all about helping companies find solutions that will ignite their business.

Q. Can you tell us about FlashPoint!?

A. I started FlashPoint! in 2006. Along with my experiences of running and managing a growing enterprise, I also worked for five years with James Fischer, author of the book, *Navigating the Growth Curve*. James' research on fast-growing companies turned into a business model referred to as the 7 Stages of Entrepreneurial Growth. The model can predict how growth will impact a company, help a leader adapt to the needs of his or her company as it grows, and helps a CEO focus on the right things at the right time. James and I started Origin Institute and for five years brought the concepts of this model to hundreds of companies all over the U.S. and Canada. I left Origin and started FlashPoint! to become a nationally recognized speaker and consultant, using my own experiences and the 7 Stages of Growth as my platform to help businesses succeed.

My services include:

✔ Online programs for business owners with fewer than 19 employees that help them build a foundation for growth. I help them create profit plans, understand cash flow management, and get them focused on key indicators that track and predict growth.

✔ Training programs for other business consultants who would like to differentiate themselves in their field. I train qualified consultants on the 7 Stages of Growth material as a licensed program. Consultants can then deliver two revenue-producing programs to their clients—all with the intent of helping more businesses succeed and stay ahead of their growth curve.

✔ Presentations to business audiences on critical business issues with interactive assessments so audience members walk away with critical insights into their top business challenges and ideas on how to make changes.

✔ Consultative programs for business owners with 20-500 employees that focus the CEO and the management teams on their past, current, and future stages of growth so they can be proactive in planning for growth.

Q. What do you like most and least about your career?

A. What do I like most? I love the freedom running my own company provides. Freedom to create my own programs, freedom to connect with people I like and respect, freedom to create my own destiny, freedom to follow my own dreams. I love working with business owners. I am naturally curious about how businesses run, the challenges business owners face daily, and the creative way they go about addressing those challenges. It's my personal belief that small business owners are the drive train of our economy. The stats about how many people small businesses hire, how much innovation they bring, how critical they are in pumping revenue into any local environment tell me that it is the small business owner who is the hero and heroine of our world economy.

What do I like least? Nothing really. Are there continual challenges when you are a solo-preneur (my choice—I use outsourced support staff, but do not plan on adding full-time employees). Yes. You have to be very clear about what you want from your business and have a clear vision of where you want to go. Some days are longer than others. However, I am passionate about what I do. I believe in the value I bring to my clients. And I absolutely love helping business owners succeed. So for me, since doing what I do is my choice, I deal with the good and the bad because it's mine and I love knowing I am in charge of everything I do everyday.

Q. What are the most important personal and professional qualities for consultants?

A. I'm not sure the qualities are different. I think personal and professional qualities include:

✔ Integrity: doing what you say you will do.

✔ Curiosity: a genuine interest in what people do, how they do it, and why.

✔ Tenacity: the drive to keep going even on tough days because you believe in what you are doing.

✔ Continual learning: in order to provide the most effective solutions for your clients, you can't rest on your laurels, ever.

✔ Empathy: the ability to feel what others feel and to understand the world they live in vs. the one you live in. It's all about the client, not you.

✔ Commitment to growth: because no matter what external issues impact our businesses, if you aren't growing you are dying so you have to find areas within your business that you know can be improved.

Q. What advice would you give to aspiring management analysts? What are the best ways to enter the field/build one's business?

A. Talk to consultants. Call them up. Tell them what you are doing. They will talk with you. Find out about their business. Be curious. Ask a lot of questions. Offer to do an internship for a business owner. If you have technical skills, you could be very valuable on site while learning the business. You may not be able to get in front of clients right away, but you can provide valuable service to a business. Be creative. Be aggressive. Be yourself. Remember that starting a business, in my opinion, is the easy part. Running a business with a sustainable profit is the challenge. Know that you have to HAVE money to make money. And while many a business has ramped up with no capital, that isn't the best way to start any business. Find out how much it takes to run a consulting business. Figure out early on how to differentiate yourself as this is a very crowded industry and getting more crowded every day. Know your strengths. Know your weaknesses. Be truthful about what you want out of a business. If you are looking for a walk in the park, go work for someone else. There is nothing easy about running your own business. Nothing. So know what you want and set a path to achieve it by working hard, having strong values, and bringing solutions that solve problems to your clients.

Q. What has been one (or more) of the most rewarding experiences in your career and why?

A. Training a CEO advisory group, facilitators who work directly with CEOs all over the world, on the 7 Stages of Growth and watching how quickly the concepts were embraced. Seeing that the concepts of this work resonate with these CEOs five to seven years after first hearing about it. A standing ovation after my first paid speaking experience. Staying connected to clients for years, creating long-lasting relationships, watching CEOs I've worked with continue to excel. Launching my Growth Curve Specialist program, where the concepts of the 7 Stages of Growth are now in Canada and London, as well as the United States.

Interview: Josette Goldberg

Josette Goldberg is the president of Goldberg Executive Coaching (www.goldbergexecutivecoaching.com), a Chicago-based executive coaching and leadership development firm. She discussed her career with the editors of *Hot Jobs*.

Q. How long have you worked in the field?

A. Between human resources and having my own coaching business: 25 years.

Q. What made you want to enter this career?

A. I was in the finance department at Balcor/American Express. They needed someone to convert their finance system and personnel system into one integrated system (now known as human resources information systems, or HRIS). I converted the two systems as a payroll manager. I was promoted to a compensation/HRIS manager. Within four years, I moved up through the organization to become the first female officer of the company in 1991.

Q. Can you please tell us about your business?

A. I am the president of Goldberg Executive Coaching, a Chicago-based executive coaching and leadership development specializing in taking already successful business leaders and their teams to the next level of performance. Typical client engagements include executive assessment and coaching, strategic planning, high potential/succession planning, and team transformation and alignment. The firm focuses on aligning priorities, systematically developing goals and action plans, and inspiring leaders' passion for excellence. Our persuasive and collaborative style supports rapid resolution of business issues and productive relationships. We have demonstrated success in assisting our clients meet their financial and operational goals by focusing on analysis, planning, and execution.

Q. What type of services do you provide?

A. Program Development; Executive/Leadership Mentor Programs; High Potential Development Programs/Succession Planning; Team Transformation Programs; On Boarding of New Leadership; Team Integration Workshops for Newly Hired or Promoted Leaders and Their Teams; Assessments: electronic or, in some cases through interview (360° Assessment, Forte Communication and Interpersonal Style Assessments, Hiring Assessments, Developmental Assessments, Sale or Customer Service Assessments, Team Assessments, Engagement Surveys); Workshops, which can include follow-up coaching (individual or team); Executive coaching [Developmental (weekly or bi-weekly); High Potential or Succession Plan]; Human Resources Organizational Effectiveness Consulting (Strategic Planning Meetings, 90-Day Goals (may be accompanied by accountability coaching), Organizational Design, Roles and Responsibilities)

Q. What do you like most and least about your career?

A. I love that I have been fortunate enough to have a lot of great mentors who stretched my comfort zone and gave me opportunities to grow. I also love that I can now do what I am most passionate about, developing leadership and teams, as a living. The part of my job that I like the least is when I work with someone who is unwilling to be open to the process and to grow (this does not happen often).

Q. What are the most important personal and professional qualities for executive coaches?

A. Professionalism, direct communication style, compassion, and willingness to work in a field where it is truly "all about the client". Coaches are not working directly with problem-solving concrete matters. They work with people. The most exciting part for the coach is the ability to work with others to positively influence organizations to achieve greater results. Coaches challenge leaders to understand every aspect of their company, evaluate what makes them and their organization unique, and leverage the talents of each individual team member. A top-down approach to coaching has a cascading affect on the entire organization. When employees see their leaders re-energized and armed with the fundamentals of leadership, teamwork, and personal effectiveness, the whole company and its bottom line grows.

Q. What advice would you give to young people who are interested in the field?

A. I tell young people to do the best they can in their current role, keep their eyes open for new opportunities, and take advantage of any stretch or challenging assignments.

Q. What are the best ways to enter the field/build one's business?

A. A great way to enter the field is through learning and development and organization development. My background is much more eclectic. I came up through finance and always took a business approach, with human resources as a specialty. This business approach is what allows you to assist clients grow their businesses. If individuals want to build their business, they need to understand that it takes about a 2.5:1 ratio of business development/client servicing to coaching. Therefore, to have 20 hours of client work (what you are passionate about) takes about a 70-hour workweek.

Q. What have been some of your most rewarding experiences in your career and why?

A. My most rewarding experiences have been when a very bright executive or high-potential executive are "stuck" or derailing and helping them break through to the next level. I also find taking top executives and helping them to influence, motivate, and inspire their organization in a way that drives business results rewarding. Last, I find it rewarding to work with teams and being able to assess their strengths and missing attributes, followed by either organizing or developing the team in a different way to drive greater business results.

MARKETING RESEARCH ANALYSTS

OVERVIEW

Marketing research analysts gather information about products and services for businesses and government agencies. They identify the wants and needs of consumers by conducting research, interviews, surveys, and focus groups. They interpret this data and recommend needed changes, including how the product is manufactured or priced or how the service is presented to the public or other buyers. A bachelor's degree in marketing or a related subject is the minimum educational requirement to enter the field; technical positions usually require a master's degree. Approximately 249,800 marketing research analysts are employed in the United States. Employment in the field is expected to grow much faster than the average for all careers through 2018.

FAST FACTS

High School Subjects
Business
Mathematics

Personal Skills
Communication
Critical thinking

Minimum Education Level
Bachelor's degree

Salary Range
$34,000 to $61,000 to $111,000+

Employment Outlook
Much faster than the average

O*NET-SOC
19-3021.00

GOE
13.02.04

DOT
050

NOC
4163

THE JOB

Let's think about laundry detergent. Its main purpose is to clean clothes, but apart from that, how does a manufacturer get its product to stand out in the crowded detergent aisle and into your shopping cart? It relies heavily on the work of marketing research analysts and the suggestions they make—add more whitening or stain-fighting power, add floral scents, create an easier dispensing spout, or make the formula more environmentally friendly.

Marketing research analysts are concerned with the sales potential of a product or service. When working with a new client or prepping for the launch of a new product, marketing research analysts consider the target consumers. What are their preferences? What are their needs? Who are they, and what are their buying habits? This data is collected using a variety of methods, including past or relevant sales records, telephone interviews, door-to-door interviews, Internet surveys, and booths or focus groups. Consumer attitudes vary by geographic region. What people want on the

East Coast often may differ from the preferences of Midwesterners, so many times different focus groups must be surveyed according to region.

When organizing a focus group, marketing research analysts gather a number of like-minded people to test the product or service. They identify each member according to their age, sex, family income, ethnic group, or other criteria. If the product in question is a particular brand of mascara, for example, members of the focus group will be given the product to use for a number of weeks. After the allotted time, focus group members are asked to provide their opinions on the product. Marketing research analysts gather and compile the data and report their findings to the manufacturer. Among their considerations include available shades, wand control, condition of lashes after prolonged use, ease of mascara removal, and even the attractiveness of the mascara's bottle. Manufacturers may feel the need to tweak the mascara's formula or container design to meet the expectations of the focus group, which would translate into the needs and satisfaction of consumers as a whole.

Books to Read

Ferguson Publishing Company. *Careers in Focus: Advertising & Marketing.* 2nd Edition. New York: Ferguson Publishing Company, 2009.

Goodman, Jennifer. *Vault Career Guide to Marketing and Brand Management.* New York: Vault Inc., 2006.

Stair, Lila B. *Careers in Marketing.* 4th ed. New York: McGraw-Hill, 2008.

Marketing research analysts also identify potential rival companies in a particular region. For example, if working with a food item such as barbeque sauce, they gather data on companies with a similar product. Marketing research analysts collect information and create a report regarding the taste, bottling, sales, promotional techniques, and other issues associated with the rival brands. Their research can help companies with brand A to better produce their product according to the tastes of consumers—sweeter or spicier flavors, pourable formula, or even a more attractive bottle or label. Marketing research may even suggest a promotional tie-in with the new product in order to gain favorable consumer opinion.

Companies may also have marketing research analysts measure the effectiveness of the product's marketing or advertising strategies. Again, working with collected data or past sales figures, marketing research analysts may find that advertising in daily newspapers or mainstream magazines may not be beneficial for a product such as, say, high-end denim jeans. They may suggest targeting women's fashion magazines or publications with a style or living focus. They may suggest advertising placement on the Internet for certain products or services.

Marketing research analysts also forecast trends in sales or track changes in consumer preferences or buying behaviors. They do this by keeping track of current sales figures, making note of any regions with high sales or those whose sales are sluggish. Depending on the data, marketing research analysts suggest changes in the advertising campaign, or in the worst-case sales scenario, pulling out of that particular market. Besides focus groups, surveys, sales reports, and collected data, marketing research analysts use information from industry trade magazines, government reports, and financial publications.

Verbal skills are a must for marketing research analysts, who spend a great deal of time interviewing people—whether in the field, in focus groups, or via the phone. They often meet with company executives to present their findings and make marketing recommendations. Depending on the size and scope of the project, marketing research analysts may supervise a team that is responsible for inputting data or compiling survey results.

Full-time marketing research analysts work about 40 hours per week, though they may work extra hours in order to meet important deadlines. They often have a set schedule every week. They work primarily indoors, in clean, comfortable, and well-lit offices.

Marketing research analysts spend a good part of their day in social interaction. They must often meet with clients to discuss goals, run focus groups, or work on projects with coworkers. However, marketing research analysts must also spend time in front of their computers analyzing market data or conducting additional research.

REQUIREMENTS

HIGH SCHOOL

Useful high school courses include business, computer science, economics, English, mathematics, psychology, sociology, speech, and statistics.

POSTSECONDARY TRAINING

A bachelor's degree in marketing or a related subject is the minimum educational requirement to enter the field. Typical courses include business, computer science, consumer behavior, economics, marketing, mathematics, psychology, research methods, sampling theory, sociology, statistics, and survey design and methodology. Marketing research analysts in technical positions usually need a master's degree in business administration, communications, marketing, statistics, or other closely related disciplines.

CERTIFICATION AND LICENSING

The American Marketing Association and the Marketing Research Association offer voluntary certification to marketing research analysts. Contact these organizations for more information.

OTHER REQUIREMENTS

Good communication skills are important for success in this career, since marketing research analysts often consult with coworkers and clients via telephone, via email, or in person. It's also important for analysts to always act in a professional manner—whether with clients or in front of a focus group. Other important traits include strong quantitative skills, the ability to work as a member of a team, attention to detail, patience, persistence, excellent organizational skills, and a willingness to continue to learn throughout your career.

EXPLORING

There are many ways to learn more about a career as a marketing research analyst. You can read books and magazines about the field, visit the websites of college marketing programs to learn about typical classes and possible career paths, and ask your teacher or school counselor to arrange an information interview with a marketing research analyst. Another good way to explore this field is by conducting research for school clubs or other organizations. By trying your hand at actual research gathering and analysis, you will get a good idea of whether this career is a good match for your interests and skill set. Professional associations can also provide information about the field. The Council of American Survey Research Organizations, for example, offers a website called Careers Outside the Box-Survey Research: A Fun, Exciting, Rewarding Career (www.casro.org/careers), which provides information on education and careers in the field. You should also try to land a part-time job or an internship at a marketing research firm. This will give you a chance to interact with marketing research analysts.

EMPLOYERS

Approximately 249,800 marketing research analysts are employed in the United States. The U.S. Department of Labor reports that the largest employers of marketing research analysts are "management, scientific, and technical consulting services; management of companies and enterprises; computer systems design and related services; insurance carriers; and other professional, scientific, and technical services—which includes marketing research and public opinion polling." Approximately 7 percent of marketing research analysts are self-employed.

GETTING A JOB

Many marketing research analysts obtain their first jobs as a result of contacts made through college internships or networking events. Others seek assistance in obtaining job leads from college career services offices, newspaper want ads, and employment websites. Additionally, professional associations, such as the American Marketing Association and the American Association of Advertising Agencies, provide job listings at their websites. See For More Information for a list of organizations.

ADVANCEMENT

In addition to receiving pay raises, marketing research analysts can become marketing research managers or top executives at companies. They can start their own marketing research firms or enter academia and work as professors.

EARNINGS

Salaries for marketing research analysts vary by type of employer, geographic region, and the worker's education, experience, and skill level. Median annual salaries for marketing research analysts were $61,580 in 2009, according to the U.S. Department of Labor (USDL). Salaries ranged from less than $34,260 to $111,900 or more. The USDL reports the following mean annual earnings for marketing research analysts by industry: computer and peripheral equipment manufacturing, $101,210; software publishers, $97,960; federal government, $90,010; computer systems design and related services, $81,040; and management, scientific, and technical consulting services, $64,360.

Marketing research analysts usually receive benefits such as health and life insurance, vacation days, sick leave, and a savings and pension plan. Self-employed workers must provide their own benefits.

EMPLOYMENT OUTLOOK

Employment for marketing research analysts is expected to grow much faster than the average for all careers through 2018, according to the U.S. Department of Labor. There is growing demand for marketing research analysts as businesses seek to gain an extra edge when competing for customers and trying to gauge customer satisfaction and likes and dislikes. The growing global nature of U.S. businesses is also creating demand for analysts to study foreign markets. In this instance, analysts with knowledge of foreign cultures and languages will have the best job prospects.

Opportunities will be best for those with certification, strong

FOR MORE INFORMATION

For profiles of advertising workers, visit the foundation's website.
Advertising Educational Foundation
220 East 42nd Street, Suite 3300
New York, NY 10017-5813
www.aded.org

For information on graduate education, contact
American Association for Public Opinion Research
111 Deer Lake Road, Suite 100
Deerfield, IL 60015-4943
www.aapor.org

Marketing Research Association
110 National Drive, 2nd Floor
Glastonbury, CT 06033-4372
www.mra-net.org

For industry information, contact
American Advertising Federation
1101 Vermont Avenue, NW, Suite 500
Washington, DC 20005-6306
www.aaf.org

American Association of Advertising Agencies
405 Lexington Avenue, 18th Floor
New York, NY 10174-1801
www.aaaa.org

For information on careers, contact
American Marketing Association
311 South Wacker Drive, Suite 5800
Chicago, IL 60606-6629
www.marketingpower.com

For information on public opinion research and internships, contact
Council of American Survey Research Organizations
170 North Country Road, Suite 4
Port Jefferson, NY 11777-2606
www.casro.org

quantitative skills, and a master's or Ph.D. degree in marketing or a related field. Consulting firms and marketing research firms that offer marketing research services to companies will offer the best job prospects. Companies are outsourcing marketing research to save money.

Interview: Kristin Branch

Kristin Branch is the Director of the A.C. Nielsen Center for Marketing Research (www.bus.wisc.edu/nielsencenter) at the University of Wisconsin-Madison's Wisconsin School of Business. She discussed her career and the field of marketing research with the editors of *Hot Jobs*.

Q. Can you tell us about your professional background and interests?

A. Academically, I started with a curiosity in psychology. I loved thinking I could learn about how and why people thought the things they did. However, I quickly refocused on studying marketing, as it balanced my human behavior interests with business. Both my undergraduate and MBA studies are in marketing. After years working in marketing and brand management, I wanted to come back to the University of Wisconsin to help students find and prepare for their career passion. From my profession as a 'user' of research, I love helping students know the importance of applying insights into business.

Q. What is one thing people may not know about a career in the field?

A. Honestly, many young people don't even know about marketing research or that it could be an exciting and rewarding career path. Many people casually know about marketing—thinking of advertising and maybe branded products. But for the marketing-interested person who has a slant to wanting to know why a consumer behaves the way they do, what marketing strategies will work best, and understanding the benefits of being able to track the success of various marketing activities—that is when we love to introduce a marketing research career to them. He or she is often delighted to find this career, which mixes marketing strategy and analytical curiosity.

Q. Can you please tell us about the A.C. Nielsen Center and your program?

A. The A.C. Nielsen Center for Marketing Research at the Wisconsin School of Business is the country's leading full-time MBA program that offers specialized course work and corporate interaction in marketing research. The two-year, full-time MBA program combines the core MBA classes for the strategic full business exposure one would expect from a MBA program, but also requires seven specific marketing research classes ranging from Quantitative Models in Marketing to Developing Breakthrough New Products. Each semester, the students also take a Current Topics class that focuses on demonstrating how marketing research is applied in the current workplace by having industry leaders come in to work with the students and demonstrate a specific area of expertise. Last semester's topics included shopper insights through loyalty programs and marketing research through social media.

   The elite program only accepts 10-15 students each year, as the Center focuses on highly individualized attention to both learning and career coaching to prepare their students for post-MBA careers. The Center was founded in 1990 after a generous gift from the A.C. Nielsen family.

Q. What types of students pursue study in your program?

A. There are many specific qualities we look for when selecting students for our program:

✔ A natural sense of curiosity. A researcher needs to enjoy digging deeper to find the discovery that lays below the surface. Whether it is a qualitative insight formed after hours of observation or a quantitative analysis of piles of data, a researcher often enjoys discovering the insight from the consumer.

✔ A desire to impact business. One of the cornerstones of our program is that our students not only learn how to do marketing research but they learn how to apply the insights into the marketing and business strategy. This application is what our corporate partners tell us is really essential for the upcoming research talent.

✔ Integrity. As a researcher is often the keeper of consumer truth for the company, we look for the indicators of high personal integrity to both be that protector of truth, but we have noticed it also equates to a love of discovery that goes hand-in-hand with our first point of curiosity.

✔ Intelligence combined with a hard work ethic. Marketing research is not a light subject. The sophisticated statistics and quantitative methods we teach are not easily grasped. We believe the combination of intelligence and work ethic is what it takes to do well both in this program, but also in the workplace.

Q. What advice would you offer marketing research majors as they graduate and look for jobs? What's the best way to land a job?

A. When we are working with our students on how to find their first post-MBA job, as well as how to manage their career moving forward, we start with encouraging them to discover what part of the industry really excites them most. If someone is really excited about the application of insights in business, we encourage them to look into consumer packaged goods manufacturers for the brand-team consumer insights position. If one finds the quantitative analysis thrilling we encourage them to round out their coursework with electives in advanced modeling or statistics. Then we help them find specialized research provider firms that are really exploring advanced analytics methods. We believe that if a student can focus on what they are most excited about, they are more successful in interviewing, especially with the academic training they receive in our program.

Q. What is the employment outlook for marketing research professionals?

A. We are delighted to say that the career outlook for marketing researchers looks quite bright. We see more and more companies plan a long-term strategy around how their consumers behave and developing innovations around consumers. This is exactly what talented marketing researchers provide. So even throughout the recession we continued to see opportunities for all levels of marketing researchers and now as the economy picks up, the job opportunities are everywhere. It is an exciting time to be in this field.

MEDICAL SCIENTISTS

OVERVIEW

Medical scientists work to enhance and prolong human life by conducting research on human diseases and conditions. Their research has resulted in advances in the diagnosis, treatment, and prevention of many diseases and conditions. Medical scientists need a Ph.D. in a biological science; some scientists also have medical degrees. Approximately 109,400 medical scientists work in the United States. Employment in the field is expected to be good through 2018.

THE JOB

The invention of the airplane has made even the remotest reaches of the world accessible. One can fly from the United States to Africa in the better part of a day. However, that new freedom comes with a price. Infectious diseases can also travel the globe via airplane, bringing illnesses such as malaria or yellow fever to populations that have not experienced these diseases in decades. Thankfully we have vaccines for many of these diseases, which has stopped their large-scale spread. We can thank medical scientists for these and other discoveries that help protect our health.

Most medical scientists specialize in a particular discipline. For example, *pharmacologists* study the effects of drugs on biological systems; *cytologic scientists* study cellular materials; *histologic scientists* study tissue structure; and *medical microbiologists* work to identify the microorganisms that cause disease or can be used to fight illness. *Epidemiologists* investigate the causes and spread of disease and try to prevent or control disease outbreaks. *Research epidemiol-*

FAST FACTS

High School Subjects
Biology
Chemistry
Mathematics

Personal Skills
Communication
Complex problem solving
Critical thinking
Scientific
Technical

Minimum Education Level
Doctorate degree (medical scientists, except epidemiologists)
Master's degree (epidemiologists)

Salary Range
$41,000 to $74,000 to $138,000+

Employment Outlook
Much faster than the average (medical scientists, except epidemiologists)
Faster than the average (epidemiologists)

O*NET-SOC
19-1041.00, 19-1042.00

GOE
02.03.01

DOT
041

NOC
2121, 3111

ogists study diseases in the field and in medical laboratories to find ways to prevent future outbreaks. *Applied epidemiologists* respond to disease outbreaks. They find out what caused the outbreak and suggest ways to contain it. They typically work for state health agencies. *Infectious disease specialists* help physicians and public health workers identify diseases that are difficult to diagnose, are accompanied by a high fever, or do not respond to treatment.

Most medical scientists work in laboratories, preparing samples to study cell structure or studying bacteria or other organisms. They may examine tissues, cells, or microorganisms, often using an electron microscope. Some analyze changes in cells that signal health problems. Medical scientists must understand the behavior of a healthy cell to help diagnose a sick or dying cell. Similarly, they take note of the effects of certain treatments on cells to fine-tune drugs. Medical scientists also try to find ways to prevent health problems. For example, they may study the link between radiation from x-rays and cancer or between alcoholism and liver disease.

Once they finish collecting data, medical scientists use statistical modeling software and other computer-based technologies to analyze their findings. Then they write reports or articles about their findings. Depending on where they work, scientists may also make presentations on their research or write articles for publication in scientific journals.

In hospitals and medical offices, medical scientists conduct tests on blood and tissue samples to diagnosis illnesses. They send their results to *physicians,* who then decide on treatment options. Some medical scientists are also physicians. These individuals interact with patients directly. They administer new or experimental drug treatments to patients, closely monitoring their health during trials. They adjust dosage levels to minimize potential negative side effects or increase levels to maximize the medicine's effectiveness.

Some medical scientists work for pharmaceutical companies. They work to create new drugs or improve on existing ones that are manufactured by their employer. The downside to working in business is these scientists are sometimes limited to the business goals of their company.

A field that has taken off in recent years is biomedical research. *Biomedical scientists* study genetics and DNA to pinpoint the functions of each link and their relationship to well-being or illnesses. Biomedical breakthroughs have made it possible to manufacture human substances such as insulin that have improved the lives of millions diagnosed with diabetes. Biomedical scientists hope to apply this same approach to discover the genetic causes of cancers, Alzheimer's disease, and Parkinson's disease, among other diseases.

Medical scientists also do a lot of writing for their job, either mapping out their research approach before they begin their lab work or writing about their end results. They prepare their findings for publication or simply to share with their colleagues and other scientists. Many scientists depend on grant money to conduct their work, so much of their time is spent writing detailed proposals to continue or increase their funding sources. The National Institutes of Health administers many of these grants, and competition for funding is intense. The better that medical scientists can convey the goals of their proposed study, the better their chances of securing a grant.

Medical scientists also do a considerable amount of reading. In order to enhance their own work, they must understand the discoveries and failures that came before them. The field of medical science changes every day, so they must stay on top of the latest breakthroughs.

Most scientists work in laboratories, hunched over a microscope, research article, or computer. Eyestrain and physical stress involved in being stationary for many hours at a time is part of the job. The stereotype of a lone scientist in a dark and dingy lab is not usually accurate. Medical scientists often work with teams of scientists, research subjects, engineers, doctors, and other medical professionals in their work. Because their work can expose them to infectious diseases, medical scientists must follow strict guidelines in the handling of hazardous materials. They often wear a white lab coat and may also wear goggles, gloves, and face masks or respirators depending on their work.

A medical scientist studies a sample in a laboratory. (Thinkstock)

Since research funding is often obtained through the awarding of grant money, scientists face the stress of deadlines for applying or, once they receive a grant, reporting results to the grantor agency. Medical scientists typically work standard 9 to 5 hours, but weekend and evening hours may be required when working on certain experiments or projects. The U.S. Department of Labor reports that research and development professionals worked an average of 36.8 hours per week in 2008—approximately 3.2 hours more than workers in all private industries.

REQUIREMENTS

HIGH SCHOOL

Take as many health, biology, anatomy and physiology, mathematics, biology, chemistry, physics, English, and speech classes in high school as you can.

POSTSECONDARY TRAINING

Medical scientists need a Ph.D. in a biological science; some scientists also have medical degrees. A growing number of new graduates also complete postdoctoral work in the laboratory of a senior researcher. Epidemiologists need at least a master's degree in public health, although some employers require a doctorate or a medical degree.

To prepare for graduate study, you should earn a bachelor's degree in a biological science. Biology-related degrees are offered by thousands of colleges and universities throughout the United States.

Once students have earned their bachelor's degrees, the U.S. Department of Labor reports that "there are two main paths for prospective medical scientists. They can enroll in a university Ph.D. program in the biological sciences; these programs typically take about six years of study, and students specialize in one particular field, such as genetics, pathology, or bioinformatics. They can also enroll in a joint M.D.-Ph.D. program at a medical college; these programs typically take seven to eight years of study, where students learn both the clinical skills needed to be a physician and the research skills needed to be a scientist." Visit www.aamc.org/students/considering/exploring_medical/research/mdphd to learn more about M.D.-Ph.D. dual degree training.

The American Society for Pharmacology and Experimental Therapeutics offers a list of graduate-level pharmacology training programs at its website, www.aspet.org/training_programs.

CERTIFICATION AND LICENSING

The American Board of Clinical Pharmacology (www.abcp.net) offers voluntary board certification to pharmaceutical scientists. The Certification Board of Infection Control and Epidemiology (www.cbic.org), a subgroup of the Association for Professionals in Infection Control and Epidemiology, offers voluntary certification to epidemiologists. Contact these organizations for more information.

The USDL reports that "medical scientists who administer drug or gene therapy to human patients, or who otherwise interact medically with patients—drawing blood, excising tissue, or performing other invasive procedures—must be licensed physicians." To become licensed, physicians must pass a licensing examination, graduate from an accredited medical school, and complete one to seven years of graduate medical education.

OTHER REQUIREMENTS

Medical scientists should have strong scientific and research skills. They must be extremely focused in order to conduct meticulous, time-consuming research that may or may not result in ground-breaking discoveries. Medical scientists need to be excellent communicators. They frequently convey their findings to colleagues, the press, and the general public in both oral and written format. They also need to have good writing skills in order to craft grant proposals that help them obtain funding for their research. Other important traits include strong organizational skills, the ability to work independently or as part of a team, and an interest in continuing to learn and stay abreast of industry developments throughout their careers.

EXPLORING

There are many ways to learn more about a career as a medical scientist. You can read books and magazines about medical scientific research and visit the websites of college programs that offer degrees in pharmacology, genetics, biology, biotechnology, biomedical science, and related fields, and you can ask your teacher or school counselor to arrange an information interview with a medical scientist. Professional associations can also provide information about the field. For example, the American Association of Pharmaceutical Scientists offers videos and interviews with scientists at its website, www.aaps.org/features/10Questions. The American Society for Pharmacology and Experimental Therapeutics provide a wealth of information on pharmacology and careers at its website, www.aspet.org. The Infectious Diseases Society of America offers *A World of Opportunities: Career Paths in Infectious Diseases and HIV Medicine* at its website, www.idsociety.org. The Association of American Medical Colleges offers information about a career in biomedical research at its website, www.aamc.org/students.

EMPLOYERS

Approximately 109,400 medical scientists are employed in the United States. Medical scientists work for universities, government agencies, medical offices, nonprofit research organizations, and hospitals, and in the private sector for pharmaceutical companies. The U.S. Department of Labor reports that "about 31 percent of medical scientists were employed in scientific research and development services firms; another 27 percent were employed in educational services; 13 percent were employed in pharmaceutical and medicine manufacturing; and 10 percent were employed in hospitals." Although opportunities are available throughout the United States, more than half of all research and development workers are employed in seven states: California, Illinois, Maryland, Massachusetts, New Jersey, New York, and Pennsylvania.

GETTING A JOB

Many medical scientists obtain their first jobs as a result of contacts made through postdoctoral positions. Others seek assistance in obtaining job leads from college career services offices, networking events, career fairs, newspaper want ads, and employment websites. Additionally, professional associations, such as the American Association of Pharmaceutical Scientists and the American Society for Pharmacology and Experimental Therapeutics, provide job listings at their websites. See For More Information for a list of organizations. Those interested in positions with the federal government should visit the U.S. Office of Personnel Management's website, www.usajobs.opm.gov.

ADVANCEMENT

Medical scientists advance by receiving higher pay, by working on research projects that are more prestigious or offer larger budgets, by taking on managerial duties, or by becoming college professors and receiving tenure.

EARNINGS

Salaries for medical scientists vary by type of employer, geographic region, and the worker's experience, education, and skill level. Median annual salaries for medical scientists were $74,590 in 2009, according to the U.S. Department of Labor (USDL). Salaries ranged from less than $41,320 to $138,840 or more. The USDL reports the following mean annual earnings for medical scientists by industry: management, scientific, and technical consulting services, $113,250; federal government, $111,810; medical and diagnostic laboratories, $107,490; management of companies and enterprises, $104,400; scientific research and development services, $92,130; pharmaceutical and medicine manufacturing, $91,720; general medical and surgical hospitals, $76,520; and colleges, universities, and professional schools, $65,040. Salaries for epidemiologists ranged from less than $40,860 to $92,610 or more in 2009.

Medical scientists usually receive benefits such as health and life insurance, vacation days, sick leave, and a savings and pension plan. Self-employed scientists must provide their own benefits.

EMPLOYMENT OUTLOOK

Employment for medical scientists-except epidemiologists is expected to grow much faster than the average for all careers through 2018, according to the U.S. Department of Labor. Employment for epidemiologists is expected to grow faster than the average during this same time span. The growth of the biotechnology industry has fueled employment opportunities for medical scientists and will continue to do so in the next decade. Other factors that are influencing the strong employment outlook are the increasing number of people age 65 and older, which is creating demand for more drugs and therapies; the expansion in research related to illnesses such as cancer and avian flu, as well as treatment issues such as antibiotic resistance; and the increasing ease of travel and the growing world population, which will increase the chances of epidemics and pandemics and other global health outbreaks. Medical scientists who have both a Ph.D. and an M.D. will experience the best job prospects.

FOR MORE INFORMATION

To learn more about pharmacology, contact
American Association of Pharmaceutical Scientists
2107 Wilson Boulevard, Suite 700
Arlington, VA 22201-3046
703-243-2800
www.aapspharmaceutica.com

For information on undergraduate and graduate programs in pharmacology and careers in the field, visit the society's website.
American Society for Pharmacology and Experimental Therapeutics
9650 Rockville Pike
Bethesda, MD 20814-3995
301-634-7135
info@aspet.org
www.aspet.org

For information on careers, contact
American Society for Microbiology
1752 N Street, NW
Washington, DC 20036-2904
202-737-3600
www.asm.org

For information about the benefits of biotechnology research, visit the BIO website.
Biotechnology Industry Organization (BIO)
1201 Maryland Avenue, SW, Suite 900
Washington, DC 20024-6129
202-962-9200
info@bio.org
www.bio.org

For information on biotechnology careers and industry facts, visit the institute's website.
Biotechnology Institute
2000 North 14th Street, Suite 700
Arlington, VA 22201-2500
703-248-8681
info@biotechinstitute.org
www.biotechinstitute.org

The federation consists of 23 scientific societies with more than 100,000 researcher-members throughout the world. Visit its website for more information.
Federation of American Societies for Experimental Biology
9650 Rockville Pike
Bethesda, MD 20814-3999
301-634-7000
info@faseb.org
www.faseb.org

For detailed information about biotechnology, visit the center's website.
National Center for Biotechnology Information
National Library of Medicine
Building 38A
Bethesda, MD 20894
info@ncbi.nlm.nih.gov
www.ncbi.nlm.nih.gov

For information on pharmaceutical and biotechnology research, contact
Pharmaceutical Research and Manufacturers of America
950 F Street, NW, Suite 300
Washington, DC 20004-1440
202-835-3400
www.phrma.org

For information on epidemiology, contact the following organizations and government agencies
Association for Professionals in Infection Control and Epidemiology
1275 K Street, NW, Suite 1000
Washington, DC 20005-4006
202-789-1890
apicinfo@apic.org
www.apic.org

Centers for Disease Control and Prevention
1600 Clifton Road, NE
Atlanta, GA 30333-4018
800-232-4636
cdcinfo@cdc.gov
www.cdc.gov/phtrain/epidemiology.html

Council of State and Territorial Epidemiologists
2872 Woodstock Boulevard, Suite 303
Atlanta, GA 30341-4015
770-458-3811
www.cste.org/dnn

Epidemic Intelligence Service
Centers for Disease Control and Prevention
1600 Clifton Road, NE, Mailstop E-92
Atlanta, GA 30333-4018
404-498-6110
EIS@cdc.gov
www.cdc.gov/eis/index.html

Infectious Diseases Society of America
1300 Wilson Boulevard, Suite 300
Arlington, VA 22209-2332
info@idsociety.org
www.idsociety.org

PARALEGALS

OVERVIEW

Paralegals, also known as *legal assistants,* provide support to lawyers. One of their primary duties is to help lawyers prepare for trials, hearings, closings, or corporate meetings, but they may also be responsible for conducting legal preparatory work such as research and writing drafts. The most popular method of educational preparation for a career as a paralegal is an associate's degree. Approximately 263,800 paralegals are employed in the United States. Employment for paralegals is expected to grow much faster than the average for all careers through 2018.

THE JOB

Paralegals are trained and certified to help lawyers with much of their work. They may be viewed by some as merely legal aides, but many paralegals conduct their work independently and, in today's legal offices, have many of the same responsibilities as lawyers. However, paralegals are prohibited by law from giving legal advice, setting legal fees, or presenting a case in court. Paralegals work in a variety of legal specialties such as bankruptcy, corporate law, criminal law, employee benefits, family law, immigration, intellectual property, labor law, litigation, personal injury, and real estate.

Paralegals conduct research; maintain general contact with clients; and draft and revise contracts, depositions, closings, or agreements. Paralegals have other additional duties or functions depending on their area of specialization.

Paralegals working for large corporations or independent law firms may be involved in litigation. When assigned a case, paralegals may have general duties such as maintaining a database of current court rulings or reviewing past legal periodicals and all material relevant to the case or area of law. They may also maintain a litigation docket, calendar, or tickler system to help keep track of important deadlines, meetings, or court appearances.

FAST FACTS

High School Subjects
Computer science
English
Government

Personal Skills
Communication
Following instructions
Judgment and decision making
Time management

Minimum Education Level
Some postsecondary training

Salary Range
$20,000 to $55,000 to $80,000+

Employment Outlook
Much faster than the average

O*NET-SOC
23-2011.00

GOE
04.04.02

DOT
119

NOC
4211

Paralegals prepare legal documents and conduct research or any necessary investigation before bringing a lawsuit to trial. Tasks at this stage include preparing the client's background information, interviewing witnesses, and examining public records that are relevant to the lawsuit. They are responsible for locating and hiring expert witnesses, if necessary. If the case goes to trial, paralegals coordinate the deposition schedule with the client and attorneys, including the opposing counsel. They also help in reviewing and assembling all documents to be used in the depositions, including drafting an outline of all examination and cross-examination questions used in court. Paralegals are often available to help prepare witnesses for a deposition, including discussing courtroom etiquette with the client and witnesses. They also work with graphic designers and multimedia artists to coordinate exhibits, videos, animations, or any computer presentations used as trial evidence. Post-trial, paralegals may draft a notice of appeals or documents regarding satisfaction of judgment.

Paralegals specializing in immigration law also have similar general duties as those working in litigation. They are responsible for maintaining a tickler file to keep track of deadlines for filing extensions, petitions, and applications with U.S. Citizenship and Immigration Services (USCIS) or the U.S. Department of Labor (USDL). Oftentimes, they must draft letters and affidavits, or organize required documents supporting these applications and petitions. Some documents—such as foreign birth records, military service records, or police records—may be difficult to obtain. All documents must be certified as valid. *Immigration law paralegals* are often responsible for coordinating the translation of foreign documents or determining the equivalency of foreign degrees. Some may be responsible for preparing the client for interviews with officials from the USCIS, or perhaps outlining immigrant and nonimmigrant visa alternatives. Another important duty is acting as a liaison between the USCIS, USDL, and the law firm.

Some paralegals specialize in tax law. Their additional duties in this area include maintaining records and drafting returns for corporate income tax and annual and quarterly employer returns, as well as completing applications for tax-exempt organizations, charitable organizations, or private foundations. They gather information for audits and tax reviews and maintain federal and state tax form files and publications. Paralegals may also research current tax laws and recent tax court decisions, especially if these laws are applicable to current cases.

Paralegals employed in a real estate office, or mortgage and title office, specialize in real estate law. They may use a lawyer's notes or perhaps an interview transcript to draft a purchase agreement or make necessary revisions to an existing agreement. They pay special attention to details such as dates and any contingencies listed in the contracts. *Real estate paralegals* may conduct title searches and check the property's legal description against a map and county records. In preparation for a real estate closing, paralegals review insurance agreements and contracts, prorate property taxes and utilities, and adjust closing figures. They create a final closing checklist and folders. If necessary, paralegals may accompany lawyers to real estate closings.

Paralegals have additional administrative duties, regardless of their specialty. Depending on the size of the office, paralegals may be responsible for office management, especially the supervision of legal secretaries and other paralegals. They maintain financial office records and coordinate in-house training sessions, seminars, or continuing educational classes. Some paralegals also act as their firm's notary public.

The work environment for paralegals depends on the firm or company and its specialty, though most paralegals work in comfortable, well-lit offices or law libraries. The office atmosphere is professional in manner of dress and conduct. At times paralegals may be required to assist lawyers while at court, especially if assigned to a major or high-profile case.

Paralegals work a standard 40-hour workweek, with time off on weekends and holidays. However, paralegals should expect to work longer hours, especially during the busy season, in order to prepare for an important case or to meet a deadline. Travel is sometimes necessary to complete an investigation, to conduct additional research, or to interview witnesses.

REQUIREMENTS

HIGH SCHOOL

Take a wide range of subjects in high school to prepare for college. These include government, computer science, social studies, and foreign languages, especially Latin and Spanish. English and speech classes will help you to develop your communication skills.

POSTSECONDARY TRAINING

The most popular method of educational preparation for a career as a paralegal is an associate's degree in paralegal studies. Some people enter the field after earning a bachelor's degree in another field and a certificate in paralegal studies. A few schools offer bachelor's and master's degrees in paralegal studies. Some employers provide on-the-job training to legal secretaries or promising college graduates who do not have legal experience.

More than 1,000 postsecondary programs offer formal paralegal training programs. Approximately 260 paralegal programs are approved by the American Bar Association (ABA). Visit the ABA website, www.abanet.org/legalservices/paralegals/directory/home.html, for a list of approved programs. The American Association for Paralegal Education also offers a list of programs at its website, www.aafpe.org/m_search.

CERTIFICATION AND LICENSING

Certification, while voluntary, is highly recommended. It is an excellent way to stand out from other job applicants and demonstrate your mastery of paralegal duties to prospective employers. Certification is offered by the National Association of Legal Assistants, the American Alliance of Paralegals, the National Federation of Paralegal Associations, and NALS...the association for legal professionals. Contact these organizations for more information.

OTHER REQUIREMENTS

Paralegals may be responsible for multiple cases at a time, or they may be assigned to work with a group of lawyers. It is important for paralegals to be well organized in such situations and to be able to juggle a variety of tasks, deadlines, and personalities. They also need excellent oral and written communication skills. Paralegals are in steady contact with lawyers, other paralegals, legal secretaries, court workers, law librarians, and others throughout their workday. Other important traits include excellent research and investigative skills, an understanding of legal terminology and procedures, a mastery of legal databases and computer programs, and a willingness to continue to learn in order to upgrade their skills throughout their careers.

EXPLORING

There are many ways to learn more about a career as a paralegal. You can read books and magazines (such as the National Federation of Paralegal Associations' *The National Paralegal Reporter*) about the field, visit the websites of college paralegal studies programs to learn about typical classes and possible career paths, and ask your teacher or school counselor to arrange an information interview with a paralegal. Professional associations can also provide information about the field. The National Association of Legal Assistants and NALS...the association for legal professionals provide a wealth of information on paralegal education and careers at their websites (see For More Information). You should also try to land a part-time or summer job in a law office. This will give you a chance to interact with paralegals and see if the career is a good fit for your interests and abilities.

EMPLOYERS

Approximately 263,800 paralegals are employed in the United States, according to the U.S. Department of Labor. Seventy-one percent work for private law firms. Paralegals are employed by law firms, federal government agencies [such as the Justice Department (the largest federal employer), Federal Trade Commission, Social Security Administration, Treasury Department, Internal Revenue Service, and Interior Department], state and local agencies, corporate legal departments, and other organizations that provide legal services. An increasing number of insurance companies, real estate and title insurance firms, and banks are hiring paralegals. Some paralegals start their own freelance businesses and offer their services on a contract basis.

GETTING A JOB

Many paralegals obtain their first jobs as a result of contacts made through college internships or networking events. Others seek assistance in obtaining job leads from college career services offices, newspaper want ads, and employment websites. Additionally, professional associations, such as the National Federation of Paralegal Associations and NALS...the association for legal professionals, provide job listings at their websites. See For More Information for a list of organizations. Those interested in positions with the federal government should visit the U.S. Office of Personnel Management's website, www.usajobs.opm.gov.

ADVANCEMENT

There are many advancement avenues for skilled paralegals. In addition to pay raises, paralegals may be asked to manage other paralegals, legal secretaries, and other workers. Some may move to more prestigious law firms and take on more demanding duties. Others may decide to attend law school and become lawyers, or earn a master's degree in education and become paralegal studies professors.

EARNINGS

Salaries for paralegals vary by type of employer, geographic region, and the worker's education, experience, and skill level. Paralegals earned salaries that ranged from less than $29,800 to $75,700 or more in 2009, according to the U.S. Department of Labor (USDL). They earned median annual salaries of $46,980. Paralegals employed in the legal services industry (the largest employer of paralegals) earned mean annual salaries of $48,460. The USDL reports the following mean annual earnings for paralegals by government level: federal, $62,570; state, $44,160; and local, $50,480.

According to the National Association of Legal Assistants' *2010 National Utilization and Compensation Survey Report,* paralegals earned an average of $55,281 in total compensation ($52,188 in salary and $3,093 in bonuses). Salaries ranged from less than $20,000 to $80,000 or more.

Employers offer a variety of benefits, which may include the following: medical, dental, and life insurance; paid holidays, vacations, and sick days; personal days; 401(k) plans; profit-sharing plans; retirement and pension plans; bonuses (as compensation for working long hours); free legal representation; a leased car/mileage; and educational assistance programs. Self-employed workers must provide their own benefits.

EMPLOYMENT OUTLOOK

Employment for paralegals is expected to grow much faster than the average for all occupations through 2018, according to the U.S. Department of Labor (USDL). Because paralegals are able to perform many of the same tasks as lawyers, but do not command a lawyer's salary, it makes economic sense for employers to hire paralegals to share in the legal workload. Many law firms, government agencies, and, especially, corporations, are moving in this direction. Additionally, the growing U.S. population will require more legal services. The USDL predicts that this growth will create especially strong opportunities for paralegals in criminal law, elder law, environmental law, health care law, intellectual property law, and international law. Other promising areas include real estate, bankruptcy, medical malpractice, product liability, and community legal service programs.

Despite the prediction for strong growth, there will be considerable competition for jobs. Many people are attracted to the field because it offers good pay and only an associate's degree is required to enter the field. Paralegals with advanced education, experience, and industry certifications will have the best job prospects.

FOR MORE INFORMATION

For certification information, contact
American Alliance of Paralegals
4001 Kennett Pike, Suite 134-146
Wilmington, DE 19807-2315
www.aapipara.org

For a database of paralegal studies programs and advice on choosing a program, visit the association's website.
**American Association
for Paralegal Education**
19 Mantua Road
Mt. Royal, NJ 08061-1006
www.aafpe.org

For information about careers in the legal field, contact
American Bar Association
Standing Committee on Paralegals
321 North Clark Street
Chicago, IL 60610-7598
www.abanet.org/legalservices/paralegals

For information on careers, contact
Association of Legal Administrators
75 Tri-State International, Suite 222
Lincolnshire, IL 60069-4435
www.alanet.org

For information on careers and certification, contact
**NALS...the association
for legal professionals**
8159 East 41st Street
Tulsa, OK 74145-3313
www.nals.org

For information about education, careers, earnings, and certification, contact
**National Association
of Legal Assistants**
1516 South Boston Avenue, Suite 200
Tulsa, OK 74119-4013
www.nala.org

For detailed information about paralegal education and careers, contact
**National Federation
of Paralegal Associations**
PO Box 2016
Edmonds, WA 98020-9516
www.paralegals.org

For information on paralegal schools, contact
National Paralegal Association
PO Box 406
Solebury, PA 18963-0406
www.nationalparalegal.org

Interview: Mianne Besser

Mianne Besser is the immediate past-president of the Rocky Mountain Paralegal Association (RMPA), current RMPA board advisor and primary representative to the National Federation of Paralegal Associations, Inc., and is employed as a senior litigation paralegal at Otten Johnson Robinson Neff + Ragonetti in Denver, Colorado. She has worked as a paralegal for 14 years. Mianne discussed her career with the editors of *Hot Jobs*.

Q. What made you want to become a paralegal?

A. I always had a distinct love, if you will, for the law and I always wanted to be a lawyer. When the opportunity presented itself to make a career change, I wanted to enter law school and obtain my juris doctorate, but having children who would attend college, a husband who had a career of his own, as well as balancing the needs of the family, I felt it was inappropriate to burden the family with an unplanned college expense as well as the possibility of not being able to be fully present in the lives of my family. Taking into account my needs and those of my family and balancing these issues, I decided that becoming a paralegal would satisfy the want and need to have a career in law. Plus, becoming a paralegal would help me decide if I really wanted to be a lawyer.

Q.   What is one thing people may not know about a career in the field?

A.   We, as paralegals, can actually do a great deal of what attorneys do—in so far as document preparation, talking with clients, dealing with opposing counsel, drafting complaints and discovery, conversing with counsel, in-house or opposing counsel. However, we cannot represent clients in the courtroom; also, we cannot sign legal documents. Paralegals are not issued a license by the state bar association where they live. While I can do many of the tasks performed by attorneys, I am careful to identify myself as a paralegal. While there has been a misconception, perhaps, that we are glorified secretaries or just push papers, that is not the case at all.

Q.   Do you do any legal research for cases?

A.   I do conduct legal research, but not all paralegals are assigned such a task—it is really dependent on the type of law firm. Some firms and/or attorneys will have paralegals conduct research; others prefer to have new associate attorneys do the research as a way to familiarize them with cases and case law.

   Another aspect of a paralegal's role as part of the legal team is that since we are able to do so many different things (in terms of helping with a case) we are able to keep legal costs down for a client. That is a great component of being part of the legal team. We are able to do so much of the work and help people who may not have the resources for more expensive services. While we are able to provide legal assistance to our clients, we are always working under the auspices of an attorney. It is considered unethical for a paralegal to work with a client without being supervised by an attorney.

Q.   What are some of the most important qualities for paralegals?

A.   Personal: You have to be cheerful in every way. It's important to have a good attitude. Of course you can't have a good day everyday—it's just not possible—but you also can't let a bad day alter your ability to do good work. It's important, when working with your client and team, opposing counsel or opposing paralegal, to put a good face on and carry forward with the tasks at hand. You also need to be a self-starter. When looking at a case, you need to able to say, "What's the next thing?" Another personal trait, and perhaps also an important professional trait, is that you need good writing skills and good language abilities. This is especially important when dealing with people on the telephone.

   Professional: You need to have the ability to think "outside the box." There are some set ways to go about completing a particular task, such as obtaining a document, and it may be this way for almost every case. But you will get that one case where you can't finish by falling back on something that's rote. You are going to have to find a different way to complete the task, tracking down the documents, or locating the witness(es). You also need confidence to do your job, and that is something that comes from within. You should present yourself well and dress accordingly. Your firm's office culture will help cultivate your professional dress within the office. It is important to note that some firms do offer a "casual/dress down Friday," but that is not always the case. Again, it's the culture of the firm, the attorneys themselves, that will dictate the dress code for the entire office.

Q. What are the pros and cons of your job?

A. Pros. I would have to say unraveling the mystery of any case is the biggest pro. For example, it's identifying what "it" is—whether a document or witness or something else—that is going to push your case forward. Or perhaps reaffirm your client's position. Or shed light on the possible position of your opponent. How do you find this? How do you go about solving this mystery? How do you go about finding this "smoking gun?" And absolutely, the "what" will differ from case to case.

I have spent the majority of my career working on personal injury cases. So where I am now, working on corporate law/real estate law, is a complete shift for me. My challenges now are a little different from those previously experienced. Nonetheless, I attack them the same. Some of the resources I used while working in personal injury law can be applied for real estate and corporate practice.

It's also important to establish relationships with other people in the legal community. This is a definite pro. By building relationships with paralegals from your firm, co-counsel, or the paralegal community within your city (maybe even on a national level) it becomes possible to gain resources and assistance.

I also feel the ability to exercise independent thought is very important. While I discuss cases with other members of my legal team, I am not necessarily told what to do. When faced with a task related to moving the case forward, I contribute ideas on how to accomplish tasks better. For example, I was working with a lawyer who wanted me to create a notebook of a particularly large volume of materials for his reference. I felt the time and effort, not to mention the resources, would not be justified to print out the thousands of pages that would eventually comprise the notebook, as well as being cost-prohibitive to the client. I proposed, instead, to create an electronic notebook for him. I explained to this attorney the benefits of this alternative and he agreed to the suggestion.

There are also the great mix of personalities you come across, whether in your own firm, or those of opposing counsel. I feel it is important to establish good relationships with paralegals from opposing counsel. This way things can get done for both sides and move the case forward, even if lawyers from opposing sides don't get along.

Cons. The law environment can be very stressful, especially when you are gearing up to go to trial. Trial can be a very nervous time; people's nerves can be frayed. Clients can be easily become upset. Your typical 8-to-5 day can easily change to a 7-to-midnight—or later—day. This schedule can last from two to three weeks until you actually walk into trial. So you can imagine there can be a lot of stress, however, you must be able to manage this with professionalism as well as completing your work efficiently and effectively.

Also, at some firms, there is a requirement for paralegals to have billable hours—these are hours billed to a particular case/client. Your firm, should they use a billable hours standard, will give a paralegal his/her annual target and you will have to meet or exceed this target in order to justify your firm's need to keep you on staff.

The legal environment is also very deadline driven—that can be a pro and a con. If the court sets a particular date for a case—you better have your attorney and/or client prepared. Judges suffer no fools, and no paralegal wants his/her attorney to be ill-prepared when facing the judge. Some people love deadlines and thrive under pressure; others struggle working within the confines of a deadline.

Q.   What advice would you give to aspiring paralegals?

A.   It's important to have the abilities to finish a bachelor's program, though there are some associate's programs available for this field.

Regarding high school classes and activities: I would recommend that students enroll in business law classes. It is also important to take any classes to help develop your writing and verbal skills, such as speech class, English, and keyboarding. There can be a great deal of writing with this job; if you're not creating your own work product, you are often times proofreading work that your attorney has prepared. It's important to have good writing skills. I can't tell you how many times you hear of a paralegal missing an error during proofreading and lawyers being very unhappy as a result. Some activities to join include debate team or any club that can help you build confidence in speaking.

Q.   What are some good ways to find a job?

A.   The bar association of your community can be a wealth of information regarding volunteer opportunities within the legal field. The same holds true for shadowing opportunities. It's also important, when finding what specialty of law to pursue, to discover your passions. If you are all about the injustice of domestic violence, you may be a good fit to work in family law or victim's rights. If a student wants to investigate more about becoming a paralegal, I would advise them to check out paralegal magazines as well as law websites. There is a wealth of information out there regarding this field. I would also suggest contacting the local paralegal associations in the community. Paralegals, like attorneys, appreciate opportunities to give back to the community.

Q.   Do employment outlooks vary by specialty?

A.   Yes. As an example, due to the economy, real estate has been relatively unchanged for a few months; however, personal injury cases do not seem to be affected by the economy. In some states, there is an increase in individuals representing themselves ("pro se") for divorce cases. Presently, immigration is a hot topic throughout the country, so there may be a rise in the number of attorneys going into this specialty, creating demand for paralegals familiar with immigration law.

Q.   Can you tell us about your freelance business?

A.   I was a freelance paralegal, that is, I worked for myself (but always worked under the supervision of an attorney) and I hope to be one again sometime soon. When you have your own business, you have to be prepared to do it all—market yourself and your skills. My clients included sole-practitioner attorneys who needed extra support staff because they did not have a paralegal or secretary on staff. Some larger firms, government agencies, or corporate entities may also hire freelance paralegals for short-term projects. It's helpful to have some previous relationships with these clients in order for them to turn to your services.

PHARMACISTS

OVERVIEW

Pharmacists are health care professionals who provide pharmaceutical care. They take medicinal requests written by a medical provider, evaluate the appropriateness of the requests, and dispense medicine to the patient. They also spend a considerable amount of time counseling patients regarding the proper use of medicine or medical supplies, and advising them of any possible adverse side effects. A doctor of pharmacy (Pharm.D.) degree is required to practice as a pharmacist. Approximately 269,900 pharmacists are employed in the United States. Job opportunities in the field are expected to be excellent through 2018.

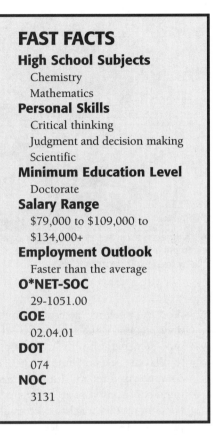

FAST FACTS

High School Subjects
Chemistry
Mathematics

Personal Skills
Critical thinking
Judgment and decision making
Scientific

Minimum Education Level
Doctorate

Salary Range
$79,000 to $109,000 to $134,000+

Employment Outlook
Faster than the average

O*NET-SOC
29-1051.00

GOE
02.04.01

DOT
074

NOC
3131

THE JOB

Pharmacists do more than just count pills. At retail pharmacies, they evaluate the type of medicine prescribed by your doctor, make sure the dosage is correct, check for any incompatibility with existing prescriptions, and warn you about any adverse effects. Sometimes they may contact the doctor, especially with new prescriptions, to verify the type of medicine and dosage, to suggest a generic equivalent, or to get more information from the provider. Pharmacists may compound—combine or change from a solid form to a liquid form—ingredients or medicines to create the desired prescription. This practice is rarely done today, since many medicines are now delivered in their final form by the manufacturer. However, pharmacists may add flavorings, such as fruit or bubblegum, to some juvenile medicines to make them more palatable. Most pharmacists work in community settings, such as a retail drugstore, or in a health care facility, such as a hospital or clinic.

Pharmacists are often a source of valuable health care information. They provide advice on prescription drugs and over-the-counter medications. Many people rely on their expertise regarding a variety of health care products—from the most effective eye drops to help irritated eyes to the most potent topical allergy creams. Pharmacists also provide information on other

A pharmacist accepts payment from a customer. Employment for pharmacists is expected to grow by 17 percent through 2018, according to the U.S. Department of Labor. (Getty Images/Thinkstock)

products such as medical equipment or home health care supplies. Since they recognize the importance of total well-being, many pharmacists also provide general health advice about diet, nutrition, exercise, as well as ways to alleviate stress. Some of their duties are administrative. They maintain computerized records for customers/patients in order to avoid possible drug interactions, as well as complete insurance documents to submit for reimbursement. Pharmacists keep track of all medicine, vaccines, and other supplies, and they place orders when necessary. Some pharmacists are trained to administer vaccinations. Depending on the size of the pharmacy, they may supervise the work of pharmacy technicians, assistants, and interns. In large pharmacy departments, they manage the work of other pharmacists.

Pharmacists who are employed at hospitals or clinics often team up with other health care professionals to monitor patients' drug therapies. They may interpret medical lab results in order to design and implement the proper treatment plan, such as a nuclear medicine course or intravenous nutrition support. Often changes must be made in the type of medicine given or the dosage before obtaining the desired results. There are many pharmaceutical specialties, including the following:

Nuclear pharmacists, along with other members of a nuclear medicine team, use radioactive drugs for diagnosis and therapy of different diseases. Their duties include procuring, compounding, testing, administering, and monitoring the use of radioactive drugs such as isotopes that are used for cardiac stress tests or radioactive iodine that is used to treat certain cancers.

Nutrition support pharmacists help critically ill patients receive nutrition either by gastric tubes, by nasogastric-feeding tubes, or through intravenous feedings. They design or modify nutrition plans for patients and help them maintain optimal nutrition.

Oncology pharmacists work with *oncologists* (cancer doctors) to help design, implement, and monitor pharmacotherapeutic plans, and they make changes as needed.

Pharmacotherapists are responsible for the safe, proper, and economical use of various drugs for patient care. While they work as part of a medical professional team, they are often the primary source of drug information.

Working in consultation with other health care professionals, *psychiatric pharmacists* design and implement treatment plans for patients who have psychiatric illnesses. They make patient assessments, monitor their response to a type of drug, and identify drug-related reactions.

Managing health care information electronically and using information technology and computers is becoming an important part of pharmacy care. According to the American Society of Health-System Pharmacists, *pharmacist informaticists* "use and integrate data, information, knowledge, technology, and automation in the medication-use process for the purposes of improving health outcomes." They design and promote systems and approaches such as electronic medical records, e-prescribing, computerized prescriber order entry, bar code dispensing and administration systems, and automated dispensing cabinets.

Consulting pharmacists provide distributive, administrative, and clinical services to people in nursing facilities, prisons, psychiatric facilities, and adult day-care facilities, as well as those in their own homes. *Senior care pharmacists* are specialized consulting pharmacists who work at nursing facilities, hospices, and other long-term care facilities. They provide and oversee the implementation of drug therapy regimens for the elderly.

In addition to working at hospitals, clinics, and privately owned and chain pharmacies, pharmacists work in other settings. One example is a pharmaceutical manufacturing company. In this capacity, pharmacists conduct research to develop new drugs and test them before they are offered to the public. For example, pharmacists employed at Pfizer Inc. may be in charge of a research and development trial for a new drug to control hypertension. Working with a study group, they adjust dosages and keep track of changes in blood pressure, or any negative side effects. Once the drug passes all testing—which can take many years—pharmacists may help create and launch a marketing campaign for the new drug.

Some pharmacists choose to work for insurance companies. They are responsible for developing patient cost analysis studies, or they may help develop a new drug benefits package. Another career path is in the field of education. Pharmacists teach at colleges and universities or conduct in-service seminars and certification classes for pharmacists. Some pharmacists pursue legal training to become patent attorneys or pharmaceutical law consultants. There are also opportunities in marketing and sales.

Full-time pharmacists work about 40 hours a week, with some evening, weekend, and holiday hours required. Approximately 12 percent of pharmacists work 50 hours or more a week. Some pharmacies are open 24 hours a day; pharmacists employed at such facilities should expect to work some overnight shifts. Approximately 19 percent of pharmacists work part-time.

Pharmacists wear professional attire, often including a lab coat. Comfortable shoes are a must, since they spend the majority of their work-day standing or walking to different areas of the pharmacy. Pharmacists wear gloves, masks, and other protective equipment when working with sterile products or potentially hazardous chemicals.

Attention to detail is a must for this job. Pharmacists are careful when mixing or dispensing medicine, in order to avoid costly, and potentially harmful, mistakes. Customers rely on pharmacists for advice regarding when and how to take medications, as well as potential side effects. Many times, pharmacists speak with physicians or nurses regarding a patient's prescription, either to verify a new prescription or to consult regarding generic forms of the medication. It is important for pharmacists to stay abreast of any new pharmaceutical developments as well as any changes in Medicare, Medicaid, or health insurance coverage for prescription drugs.

Some pharmacists provide consultations to different health facilities, such as nursing homes or rehabilitation centers. In such cases, a reliable means of transportation is needed in order to travel from one facility to another.

REQUIREMENTS

HIGH SCHOOL

You should take a college-preparatory track in high school that includes class-es in mathematics (especially calculus and statistics) and science (especially anatomy, biology, chemistry, and physics). Additionally, you should take English and speech classes because developing good communication skills is key to success in the field. If you plan to work as a retail pharmacist or own your own drugstore, you should take business and accounting courses. Finally, taking one or more foreign languages (especially Spanish) will help you effectively interact with people who do not speak English as a first language.

POSTSECONDARY TRAINING

A doctor of pharmacy (Pharm.D.) degree is required to practice as a pharmacist. The six-year doctor of pharmacy (Pharm.D.1), the degree most commonly offered by pharmacy programs, trains pharmacists to help patients monitor chronic illnesses, to administer immunizations, and to host public education activities. There is also a postbaccalaureate degree offered—a Pharm.D.2. The American Association of Colleges of Pharmacy offers a director of pharmacy training programs at its website, www.aacp.org/RESOURCES/STUDENT/Pages/SchoolLocator.aspx.

Pharmacists who own their own businesses might augment their training in pharmaceutical science by earning a master's degree in business administration. Others earn degrees in public administration or public health.

CERTIFICATION AND LICENSING

The Board of Pharmacy Specialties, which was created by the American Pharmacists Association, offers voluntary certification in the following areas: nuclear pharmacy, nutrition support pharmacy, oncology pharmacy, pharmacotherapy, psychiatric pharmacy, and ambulatory care. The Commission for Certification in Geriatric Pharmacy also provides certification. Contact these organizations for more information about certification requirements.

All states and the District of Columbia, as well as Guam, Puerto Rico, and the U.S. Virgin Islands, require pharmacists to be licensed. Licensing requirements include earning a Pharm.D. degree from a college of pharmacy that has been approved by the Accreditation Council for Pharmacy Education and passing a series of examinations. The North American Pharmacist Licensure Exam (NAPLEX) is required by all states, U.S. territories, and the District of Columbia. The Multistate Pharmacy Jurisprudence Exam (MPJE) is required by 44 states and the District of Columbia. States and territories that do not require the MPJE have their own pharmacy law exams. The NAPLEX and MPJE are offered by the National Association of Boards of Pharmacy.

OTHER REQUIREMENTS

To be a successful pharmacist, you should have excellent communication and interpersonal skills, be very attentive to detail, have a desire to help others live healthier lives, be conscientious, have scientific aptitude, and be willing to continue to learn throughout your career.

EXPLORING

There are many ways to learn more about a career as a pharmacist. You can read books and magazines about the field, visit the websites of college pharmacy programs to learn about typical classes and possible career paths, and ask your teacher or school counselor to arrange an information interview with a pharmacist. Professional associations also provide information about the field at their websites. For example, the Academy of Managed Care Pharmacy offers *Mapping Your Career in Managed Care Pharmacy* (www.amcp.org/mapping_your_career/contributors.cfm); the American Association of Colleges of Pharmacy offers information on pharmacy specialties (www.aacp.org), the National Association of Chain Drug Stores offers *Consider Pharmacy as a Career* (www.nacds.org/wmspage.cfm?parm1=6579), and the National Community Pharmacists Association offers the *Independent Pharmacy Career Guide* (www.ncpanet.org/index.php/independent-pharmacy-career-guide). Additionally, you should try to land a part-time job at a retail pharmacy. This will give you a chance to interact with pharmacists and see if the career is a good match for your interests and abilities.

EMPLOYERS

Approximately 269,900 pharmacists are employed in the United States. Sixty-five percent work at retail pharmacies, and 22 percent are employed in hospitals. Other employers include mail-order and Internet pharmacies, pharmaceutical wholesalers, pharmaceutical manufacturers, insurance companies, offices of physicians, government agencies (including the Food & Drug Administration, Departments of Defense and Veterans Affairs, Indian Health Service, and Public Health Service), and colleges and universities.

GETTING A JOB

Many pharmacists obtain their first jobs as a result of contacts made through college internships, residency programs, or fellowships. Others seek assistance in obtaining job leads from college career services offices, newspaper want ads, and employment websites (such as RX Career Center, www.rxcareercenter.com). Additionally, professional associations, such as the American Pharmacists Association and the American Society of Health-System Pharmacists, provide job listings at their websites. See For More Information for a list of organizations. Those interested in positions with the federal government should visit the U.S. Office of Personnel Management's website, www.usajobs.opm.gov.

ADVANCEMENT

Advancement options for pharmacists vary by employment setting. Pharmacists in retail pharmacies may be promoted to the positions of pharmacy supervisor or store manager. Others become district, regional, or corporate managers. Hospital pharmacists can become supervisors or administrators. Some pharmacists go into business for themselves and open their own pharmacies. Others become professors at colleges and universities.

EARNINGS

Salaries for pharmacists vary by type of employer, geographic region, and the worker's experience level and skills. Median annual salaries for pharmacists were $109,180 in 2009, according to the U.S. Department of Labor (USDL). Salaries ranged from less than $79,270 to $134,290 or more. The USDL reports the following mean annual earnings for pharmacists by industry: health and personal care stores, $107,810; general medical and surgical hospitals, $106,210; grocery stores, $105,640; and department stores, $105,120.

Employers offer a variety of benefits, including the following: medical, dental, and life insurance; paid holidays, vacations, and sick days; personal days; 401(k) plans; profit-sharing plans; retirement and pension plans; and educational assistance programs. Self-employed workers must provide their own benefits.

EMPLOYMENT OUTLOOK

Employment for pharmacists is expected to grow faster than the average for all careers through 2018, according to the U.S. Department of Labor (USDL). Factors that are fueling demand include the growing elderly population (whose members traditionally need more prescriptions than other demographic groups), continuing scientific advances (which are creating more pharmaceutical treatment options), and the growing number of people who are becoming eligible for prescription drug coverage as a result of health care reform. The relatively small number of training programs for pharmacists is also contributing to the shortage of workers in the field.

FOR MORE INFORMATION

Visit the academy's website to read *Mapping Your Career in Managed Care Pharmacy*.
**Academy of
Managed Care Pharmacy**
100 North Pitt Street, Suite 400
Alexandria, VA 22314-3141
800-827-2627
www.amcp.org

To learn more about pharmacy education, contact
**Accreditation Council
for Pharmacy Education**
20 North Clark Street, Suite 2500
Chicago, IL 60602-5109
312-664-3575
info@acpe-accredit.org
www.acpe-accredit.org

For information on postsecondary training, contact
**American Association
of Colleges of Pharmacy**
1727 King Street
Alexandria, VA 22314-2700
703-739-2330
mail@aacp.org
www.aacp.org

For information on education, careers, and licensing, contact
American Pharmacists Association
2215 Constitution Avenue, NW
Washington, DC 20037-2907
202-628-4410
www.pharmacist.com

For information on careers and certification, contact
**American Society
of Consultant Pharmacists**
1321 Duke Street
Alexandria, VA 22314-3563
info@ascp.com
http://ascp.com

For information on careers, contact
**American Society
of Health-System Pharmacists**
7272 Wisconsin Avenue
Bethesda, MD 20814-4820
301-657-3000
www.ashp.org

For more information about pharmacy specialties, contact
Board of Pharmacy Specialties
2215 Constitution Avenue, NW
Washington, DC 20037-2907
202-429-7591
bps@aphanet.org
www.bpsweb.org

For information on state boards of pharmacy, contact
**National Association
of Boards of Pharmacy**
1600 Feehanville Drive
Mount Prospect, IL 60056-6014
847-391-4406
www.nabp.net

For information about pharmacy education and careers, contact
**National Association
of Chain Drug Stores**
413 North Lee Street
Alexandria, VA 22314-2301
703-549-3001
www.nacds.org

Visit the association's website to read the *Independent Pharmacy Career Guide*.
**National Community
Pharmacists Association**
100 Daingerfield Road
Alexandria, VA 22314-6302
800-544-7447
info@ncpanet.org
www.ncpanet.org

The USDL predicts that there will be rapid employment growth at medical care establishments (such as doctors' offices, outpatient care centers, and nursing care facilities) and mail-order pharmacies. Growth will also occur at hospitals, drugstores, mass retailers, and grocery stores because pharmacists in these settings still dispense the majority of prescriptions. Pharmacists in these settings are also beginning to administer vaccinations and offer other patient care services.

The duties of pharmacists have changed in recent years. Pharmacists are spending less time dispensing drugs and more time "advising patients on drug therapies, evaluating the safety of drug therapy, administering vaccines, and counseling patients on services ranging from self-care to disease management," according to the American Pharmacists Association.

The Health Resources and Services Administration has identified some major trends in the field. It reports that more women are entering the field; they now make up half of all employed pharmacists. Women are expected to comprise 62 percent of pharmacists by 2030. Minorities are still underrepresented in the field. Only 18 percent of pharmacists were from minority groups in 2000, despite making up 25 percent of the U.S. population (as cited in the 2000 Census). Shortages of pharmacists are especially pronounced in "rural areas, low-income urban areas, and select federal institutions such as prisons."

Interview: John Hertig

Dr. John Hertig is a health-system pharmacist at Duke University Hospital in Durham, North Carolina. He discussed his career with the editors of *Hot Jobs*.

Q.   What made you want to enter this career?

A.   Throughout high school and into college, the world of health care always interested me. I enjoyed the idea of being able to provide medical care for those in need. While a high school student, I took interest in math and science; pharmacy was a great way to combine these academic interests. Once I started pharmacy school, I realized I wanted to practice in a fast-paced environment caring for patients needing urgent attention. Health-systems enable pharmacists to practice in a variety of settings, treating diverse patient populations. Importantly, I never wanted a career where I would be stuck at a desk all day. As a health-system pharmacist, every day is different and I enjoy the variety and the challenge.

Q.   What is one thing that young people may not know about a career as a health-system pharmacist?

A.   Health-system pharmacists aren't just in a retail pharmacy store, or hidden in the hospital basement. Although these pharmacists provide an important service, hospital-based pharmacists also round with physicians on patient-care floors, educate fellow health care professionals, adjust medication therapy in outpatient clinics, proactively identify medication-related problems, and counsel patients on their medicines. In addition, health-system pharmacists can specialize in a myriad of practice areas. Many hospitals have pharmacists who specialize in critical care, hematology/oncology, cardiology, infectious diseases, transplant, internal medication, and many more areas. These pharmacists are on the frontline of patient care and make a tangible positive impact every day.

Q. Can you briefly describe a typical day in your life on the job?

A. One of the best things about being a health-system pharmacist is that there are very few typical days. Health-system pharmacists fill a variety of roles including: specialty practice pharmacists on patient care floors, pharmacists in outpatient clinics, pharmacists in order review areas, and pharmacy in administrative functions. As an example, a typical specialty practice health-system pharmacist arrives and reviews his or her daily patient census. The pharmacist checks each patient's medication list for any drug-drug interactions, allergies, incomplete therapy, or inappropriate therapy. The pharmacist will then either round with the physician-based team or confer with physicians and nurses, offering recommendations on each patient. Once these "rounds" are complete, the pharmacist will spend the afternoon following up on issues that have arisen, engage in medication order review, research, and/or education and teaching. Each day presents new challenges and opportunities for continual learning.

Q. What are the most important qualities for pharmacists?

A. Pharmacy has long been regarded as one of the most trusted professions in the country. Pharmacists, including health-system pharmacists, take great pride in their profession. We are often the most accessible patient-care provider and are expected to treat all patients with respect and empathy. Our "Oath of a Pharmacist" speaks of humanity, service, knowledge, ethics, and responsibility. A person in this profession must be dedicated, compassionate, and willing to be a continual learner. New medications, protocols, and best practices are constantly released and a health-system pharmacist must keep updated on these new developments and maintain consistent professional competency.

Q. What are some of the pros and cons of your job?

A. The biggest pro of a health-system pharmacist is the positive impact you make on patient's lives every day. Hospitalized patients need urgent care, and health-system pharmacists play a vital role in managing medication therapy. Nearly every patient in the hospital needs medications; having a medication expert involved is essential to effective treatment and recovery. The other great positive about this career is that every day brings new opportunities and exciting experiences. I am always challenged in my job and feel great personal satisfaction, even after a long and taxing day.

The only potential con for health-system pharmacists can be the schedule. Many pharmacists need to work long hours to ensure patients receive optimum care. Some pharmacists work weekends, and others work evenings; some hospitals even need pharmacists overnight to ensure medications are properly dispensed. For many, however, this potential con represents a great opportunity. Pharmacists who enjoy flexible schedules find these nontraditional hours perfect for their lifestyle.

Q. What advice would you give to young people who are interested in becoming health-system pharmacists?

A. Do your research. Start looking at various schools and colleges of pharmacy. Talk with friends, relatives, or your local pharmacist about the pharmacy career path. Attempt to volunteer in a hospital and request to work in the pharmacy department. Volunteering will give you a snapshot of how a health-system pharmacy works and may give you the opportunity to shadow various health-system pharmacists. Finally, continue to work hard. Health care professions are academically rigorous and challenge your professional dedication. Yet, if you are like me, you may find your passion is health-system pharmacy and will wake up every morning loving what you do.

Interview: Brent Reed

Brent Reed, PharmD is a cardiology pharmacotherapy resident at the University of North Carolina Hospitals & Clinics. He discussed his career with the editors of *Hot Jobs*.

Q. What made you want to enter this career?

A. The feature that interested me most about pharmacy was that it was a career that would balance my interests in science and health care with my desire to work with people. I learned that pharmacists are considered one of the most trusted professionals, so the thought of patients confiding in me as their health advisor was also appealing. Pharmacists have become an integral part of the health care team and the opportunity to work with physicians, nurses, and other health care providers excited me. As I learned more about the complexity of the human body and the expertise that a pharmacy education provides, I realized how important pharmacists are in ensuring medications are both safe and effective.

Q. What is one thing that people may not know about a career as a pharmacist?

A. In addition to working in community pharmacies, pharmacists are also employed in variety of health care settings, including hospitals, clinics, community health centers, and long-term care facilities. Pharmacists also hold positions in the local, state, and federal governments, where they may serve as advisors, regulators, or in supervisory roles. Some pharmacists seek academic positions, where they provide education to student pharmacists, engage in practice-based or pharmaceutical research, or both. Others find career opportunities in the pharmaceutical industry.

Q. Can you briefly describe a typical day in your life on the job?

A. While the specific duties may differ based on practice setting, the primary responsibility of a pharmacist is to evaluate and manage medication therapy, ensuring it is both safe and effective in each individual patient. Community pharmacists verify prescriptions written by other health care providers and provide counseling on the appropriate use of medications. Hospital and health-system pharmacists often serve in consultation with physicians and other health care providers at the time medications are ordered. Regardless of practice setting, a pharmacist's work environment is often fast-paced and requires significant concentration to ensure each medication order or prescription is appropriate. Most pharmacists work between 40 and 50 hours per week, although this may also differ based on practice setting.

Q. What are the most important qualities for pharmacists?

A. Because one of the primary roles of a pharmacist is to provide medication-related care for patients, an important personal quality is empathy and a service-orientation. Additionally, pharmacists must make ethically-sound decisions, so trustworthiness and honesty are also important characteristics. As health care continues to become a team-based approach, pharmacists must share responsibility for health outcomes with physicians, nurses, and other health care providers.

Professionally, pharmacists must make a commitment to education, both in terms of the education and training required to become licensed as well as the lifelong learning required to remain an active practitioner. While on the job, pharmacists must effectively manage their time and pay close attention to detail. Finally, pharmacists must develop the communication skills necessary to counsel patients in terms they can understand while also engaging in discussions with physicians and other highly-trained health care professionals.

Q. What are some of the pros and cons of your job?

A. Pros: Pharmacy education and training provides specialized knowledge in the area of medication therapy, so I feel my contributions are valued by members of the health care team. My career also gives me an opportunity to interact with a variety of people, including physicians, nurses, patients, and the public. As health care and medication therapy continues to evolve, I feel there is always something new and exciting to learn and experience. The career also provides the flexibility necessary to have a balance between personal and professional responsibilities. Finally, the opportunity to make a difference in people's lives provides me with both personal and professional satisfaction.

Cons: The training required to become a practicing pharmacist can be long and demanding. Licensure requires a minimum of six years of education, and a growing number of student pharmacists have undergraduate degrees when they enroll in the four-year doctor of pharmacy program. Specific practice settings may also require additional credentials, such as one to two years of postgraduate residency or fellowship training. Pharmacists must also adapt and be receptive to change as both the profession of pharmacy and the health care industry continue to evolve. Pharmacist salaries increase only minimally with experience unless promoted to a management or administrative role. Finally, the pharmacist shortage appears to be abating, so job growth may slow significantly in the near future.

Q. What advice would you give to aspiring pharmacists?

A. Pharmacy education is based largely on science and math, so young people should find opportunities to improve their skills in these areas. Successful pharmacists must also be well-rounded, so young people interested in becoming a pharmacist should find opportunities that allow them to grow and develop personally and professionally. Examples include complementing academic pursuits with leadership and extracurricular activities. People interested in pharmacy should also seek opportunities to improve their communication skills, as more pharmacists engage in direct patient care and fewer are involved in handling medications. Finally, because the practice of pharmacy is so diverse, young people interested in pharmacy should shadow pharmacists in a variety of settings to identify areas that interests, them most.

PHYSICAL THERAPISTS

OVERVIEW

Physical therapists, also known as *physiotherapists,* are licensed professionals who provide health care services to individuals suffering from functional problems caused by arthritis, burns, amputations, stroke, back and neck injuries, traumatic brain injuries, sprains/strains and fractures, headaches, carpal tunnel syndrome, incontinence, multiple sclerosis, cerebral palsy, spina bifida, limitations caused by old age, and work- and sports-related injuries. They evaluate, design, and implement individualized programs to help reduce pain, improve mobility, and increase the quality of life for patients of all ages. Physical therapists use many different techniques for their work including exercise equipment, massage, and electrotherapy. A minimum of a post-baccalaureate degree in physical therapy is required to work in the field. Approximately 185,500 physical therapists are employed in the United States. Employment for physical therapists is expected to grow much faster than the average for all careers through 2018.

THE JOB

Many individuals suffer from functional limitations due to injury, disease, surgery, advanced age, or other medical conditions. Their limitations may include difficulty in walking, problems shifting weight, a limited range of motion in their arms or legs, a weak grip, or even decreased endurance. Physical therapists provide therapy services to help patients eliminate or reduce these problems. They also develop and implement therapy programs to help people retain their mobility and flexibility and generally have a healthy lifestyle.

When working with a new patient, physical therapists must first evaluate the individual. They conduct a physical assessment to gauge the patient's physical condition and limitations, as well as a short interview to learn more about the patient's lifestyle, work habits, degree of pain, degree of mobility, and therapy goals. Oftentimes, physical therapists consult with other health care professionals such as doctors, nurses, speech-language pathologists, audiologists, dentists, and social workers, as well as members of the patient's family, to complete the assessment. Once a diagnosis of the patient's movement dysfunction is made, physical therapists design a therapy plan to suit the patient's capabilities and schedule. Therapy plans, depending on the extent of the patient's disability or injury, can include a series of exercises, muscle manipulation and massage, traction, hot or cold therapy, ultrasound, and electrotherapy. Physical therapists use many different tools and techniques to achieve positive results such as hand weights, exercise balls and bands, risers, and cardiovascular equipment (treadmills, stationary bicycles, etc.).

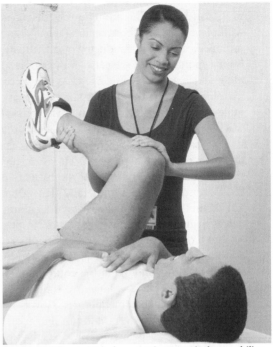

A physical therapist helps a patient regain leg mobility. The U.S. Department of Labor predicts that more than 56,000 new jobs will be available for physical therapists through 2018. (Getty Images/Thinkstock)

Many physical therapists specialize in a specific clinical area and may implement therapy plans that are customized to meet different needs and goals. Patients suffering from cardiopulmonary disease or those who have undergone recent cardiac or pulmonary surgery often have decreased endurance or lung function. For example, physical therapists use manual therapy to help remove excess secretions from the lungs, or they use chest mobilization exercises to increase lung capacity.

Physical therapists often work with elderly patients who have arthritis, osteoporosis, balance disorders, joint replacements, and Alzheimer's disease. Techniques used with geriatric patients include water aerobics, stretching exercises, and light weight lifting to improve their mobility. Physical therapists also teach geriatric patients better ways to conduct daily activities, such as the proper way to safely climb and descend stairs or how to use a walker or other aid.

Pediatric physical therapy is another specialty. When working with infants, children, and young adolescents, physical therapists create a plan to address not only areas of concern, but also the capabilities and attention spans of their young patients. Infants needing physical therapy may be those born with a congenital disorder such as spina bifida. Physical therapists may suggest leg braces or specific exercises and massages to keep limbs flexible and avoid contracting. Children with developmental delays also benefit from physical therapy. For example, balls and other squeezable toys may be incorporated into an exercise plan to increase mobility and strength.

Orthopedic physical therapy, the most common and identifiable specialty, treats patients suffering from injuries sustained at home, on the field, or at the workplace as well as those needing rehabilitation after orthopedic surgery. Most orthopedic therapy is conducted on an outpatient basis. For patients recovering from a sports injury to the arm, for example, physical therapists may use techniques such as therapeutic exercises, hot or cold packs, and even electrotherapy to expedite neuromuscular stimulation and retraining. They may use arm pulleys or resist-a-bands to increase strength. Continuous passive motion machines can be used to increase a patient's rotator cuff flexibility and strength.

Physical therapists are responsible for charting their patients' scheduled therapy sessions and progress. They consult with other health care professionals to keep them abreast of the patient's progress or to discuss or update them regarding changes in therapy plans. Depending on their employer, physical therapists may also complete and submit billing sheets for services rendered, maintain equipment, and order supplies and equipment.

The work of physical therapists is physically demanding. They spend a considerable amount of time each day standing, stooping, walking, bending, reaching, lifting, and operating equipment or using various tools.

A normal workweek for a full-time physical therapist is 40 hours, with time off on weekends or holidays. However, many physical therapists have some weekend and evening hours in order to accommodate patient loads. Approximately 27 percent of physical therapists work part-time. Some travel may be necessary, especially for those providing home health therapy.

Physical therapists may be required to wear a uniform, which often consists of hospital scrubs, pants, and smock, and comfortable, non-skid shoes.

REQUIREMENTS

HIGH SCHOOL

In high school, take science courses (especially anatomy, biology, chemistry, and physics), as well as classes in mathematics, statistics, social science, psychology, computer science, English, and speech. If you plan to work in an area with a large number of people who do not speak English as a first language, you should take a foreign language—especially Spanish.

POSTSECONDARY TRAINING

A minimum of a post-baccalaureate degree in physical therapy from an accredited physical therapy program is required to work in the field. The Commission on Accreditation of Physical Therapy Education (www.apta.org/CAPTE), which accredits entry-level academic programs in physical therapy, has accredited 212 education programs. Nine of these programs award master's degrees, and 203 award doctoral degrees. Typical courses in a doctorate program include Introduction to Physical Therapy, Gross Human Anatomy, Physiology,

Books to Read

Krumhansl, Bernice. *Opportunities in Physical Therapy Careers.* New York: McGraw-Hill, 2005.

Lais, Toni. *Career Diary of a Physical Therapist.* New York: Garth Gardner Company, 2008.

Pagliarulo, Michael A. *Introduction to Physical Therapy.* St. Louis: Mosby, 2006.

Functional Histology, Neuroanatomy, Joint Function and Movement, Biophysics, Clinical Applications, Psychosocial Theory and Practice, Musculoskeletal Dysfunction, Neuromuscular Dysfunction, Cardiopulmonary Dysfunction, Applied Pathophysiology, Case Management in Physical Therapy Practice, and Clinical Fieldwork.

Aspiring physical therapy students can use the PT Centralized Application Service (www.ptcas.org), which allows one to apply to multiple accredited physical therapy programs at one time.

CERTIFICATION AND LICENSING

Certification, while voluntary, is highly recommended. It is an excellent way to stand out from other job applicants and demonstrate your abilities to prospective employers. The American Board of Physical Therapy Specialities offers certification in the following specialties: cardiovascular and pulmonary, clinical electrophysiology, geriatrics, neurology, orthopaedics, pediatrics, sports physical therapy, and women's health. Contact the board for more information.

All states require physical therapists to be licensed. Licensing requirements vary by state but typically include graduation from an accredited physical therapy education program; passing the National Physical Therapy Examination, which is administered by the Federation of State Boards of Physical Therapy (www.fsbpt.org); and fulfilling state requirements (which may involve passing additional examinations).

OTHER REQUIREMENTS

Physical therapists must be in optimum physical condition in order to lift patients and assist them in turning, standing, or walking. A positive disposition is also helpful when working with patients who may be suffering from chronic pain or limited mobility. Physical therapists must often motivate their patients during therapy sessions, and this is best done with a smile and encouraging words. Other important traits include compassion, an interest in helping others, and good time-management skills.

EXPLORING

There are many ways to learn more about a career as a physical therapist. You can read books and magazines about the field (such as *Physical Therapy,* which is published by the American Physical Therapy Association, APTA), visit the websites of college physical therapy programs to learn about typical classes and possible career paths, and ask your teacher or school counselor to arrange an information interview with a physical therapist. Professional associations can also provide information about the field. The APTA, the leading physical therapy association in the United States, provides a wealth of information on education and careers at its website, www.apta.org. You should also try to land a part-time job in a setting where physical therapists are employed. This will give you a chance to interact with physical therapists and see if the career is a good fit for your interests and abilities.

EMPLOYERS

Approximately 185,500 physical therapists are employed in the United States. About 60 percent of physical therapists work in hospitals or in offices of health practitioners. Employment opportunities also exist at nursing homes, home health services providers, outpatient care centers, adult day-care programs, industrial settings, schools, and government agencies (such as the Department of Defense and Veterans Affairs and the Indian Health Service). Other physical therapists work as professors and researchers at colleges and universities. Some have their own businesses. In fact, the American Physical Therapy Association reports that nearly 22 percent of physical therapists are owners of, or partners in, a physical therapy practice.

GETTING A JOB

Many physical therapists obtain their first jobs as a result of contacts made through college internships, clinical experiences, or networking events. Others seek assistance in obtaining job leads from college career services offices, newspaper want ads, and employment websites. Additionally, the American Physical Therapy Association provides job listings at its website, www.apta.org/applications/careercenter.aspx. Those interested in positions with the federal government should visit the U.S. Office of Personnel Management's website, www.usajobs.opm.gov.

ADVANCEMENT

At large therapy providers, physical therapists may advance to managerial and supervisory positions. Others may start their own businesses and offer their services on a contract basis to hospitals, nursing facilities, and other therapy providers.

EARNINGS

Salaries for physical therapists vary by type of employer, geographic region, and the worker's experience level and skills. Median annual salaries for physical therapists were $74,480 in 2009, according to the U.S. Department of Labor (USDL). Salaries ranged from less than $52,170 to $105,900 or more. The USDL reports the following mean annual earnings for physical therapists by industry: home health care services, $83,500; nursing care facilities, $78,990; offices of physicians, $77,120; offices of other health practitioners, $75,760; and general medical and surgical hospitals, $75,030.

Physical therapists usually receive benefits such as health and life insurance, vacation days, sick leave, and a savings and pension plan. Self-employed workers must provide their own benefits.

FOR MORE INFORMATION

For detailed information on education and careers, contact
American Physical Therapy Association
1111 North Fairfax Street
Alexandria, VA 22314-1488
800-999-2782
www.apta.org

For information on accredited programs, contact
Commission on Accreditation in Physical Therapy Education
accreditation@apta.org
www.apta.org/CAPTE

EMPLOYMENT OUTLOOK

Employment for physical therapists is expected to grow by 30 percent through 2018, according to the U.S. Department of Labor—or much faster than the average for all careers. Factors that are fueling growth include an increasing elderly population, which has a strong need for physical therapy services; changes in insurance reimbursement, which will allow more people to have access to physical therapy services; the implementation of the Individuals with Disabilities Education Act, which ensures that disabled students will have better access to physical therapy and other rehabilitative services in schools; and advances in medicine and technology that are allowing people with severe trauma, serious illness, and birth defects to survive, which will create the need for more physical therapists to treat these patients.

Physical therapists who specialize in treating the elderly will have especially strong job prospects. Typical employers for these workers include acute care hospitals, skilled nursing facilities, and orthopedic settings. Opportunities will also be good in rural areas, where there is a shortage of trained physical therapists.

Interview: Jennie Gregory

Jennie Gregory is a seasoned physical therapist and a past member of the Arkansas State Board of Physical Therapy. She discussed her career with the editors of *Hot Jobs*.

Q. Where do you work?

A. I work in a hospital system where, as a physical therapist, I, with others on staff, provide therapy for inpatients and outpatients. We have, in the-not-too-distant past, had a SNF (skilled nursing facility or long-term care unit with rehab component) unit and an inpatient acute rehab unit, but do not staff or manage those any longer. The hospital system has more than one campus. The bulk of the services provided are for the acute inpatient population. Orthopedic surgery (trauma, fractures, spine and total joints), neurosurgery (craniotomy and aneurysm), neuro diagnosis, (stroke), and cardiovascular surgery (cardiac bypass surgery), valve replacements make up 65 percent of our patient population. The rest are the medically frail or those with skin or lymph system compromises.

Q.   How long have you worked in the field?

A.   I have been in this field, in this type of practice setting, for 35 years and have watched the transformation from 10- to 14-day length of stays to two- to three-day length of stays—even for the very involved surgery patients. Inpatient therapy goals have evolved from returning the patient to their prior level of function to preparing the patient for the next level of care whether that is home with home care and/or care giver, long-term care with continued rehab, or acute rehab for intensive therapy. Our outpatient services serve a more "acute population" than we did when I entered the profession. The orders/referrals that we receive from our referral sources are not specific, but rather are "evaluate and treat" or physical therapy consult." It is up to the therapist to evaluate the patient and determine the plan of care, including the intensity and frequency of treatment. The plan of care is altered based on the patient's response/ability to tolerate.

Q.   What made you want to enter this career?

A.   I chose the field of physical therapy for a variety of reasons. I felt "called" to health care as my "ministry" as a young teen. My initial plan was to go to medical school to be a pediatrician. Prior to beginning college I did some exploring and observing in other health care fields and was drawn to physical therapy. The one-on-one time that could be and would be spent on an ongoing basis with the patients is engaging. Being a part of restoring men, women, and children to a prior level of function or teaching them how to use assistive devices to improve their level of independence is challenging and rewarding. (The hours are much better than those of a physician, too!) As I applied to college, I looked for universities and colleges with physical therapy programs as by that time I had decided that was my career of choice.

Q.   What is one thing that young people may not know about a career in physical therapy?

A.   Physical therapy in most states is now a direct access practice. Although many insurance companies and third-party payers still require a physician/LIP (Licensed Independent Practitioner) referral, the practice does not. The level of education is now that of a clinical doctorate so the differential diagnosis and patient problem identification skills are at a much higher level at the time of graduation than they were in the past. Years of practice and experience gave the practicing therapist those skills, but now the new grad, newly licensed therapist has those skills. There are parts of physical therapy that can be mundane and repetitious, but there are far more aspects of therapy that allow for creativity, individualization, and thinking outside the box.

Q.   What high school classes and activities should students participate in to prepare for the field?

A.   In high school (and in college) students looking to enter the field of physical therapy need to have a good background in sciences, both physical and life sciences. They also need a good basic math background with geometry and algebra. An interest in anatomy and physiology and the ability to see body parts dissected without becoming squeamish is extremely important as well. Any activity or organization that will enable you to interact with a variety of different age groups and types of people is helpful in preparing you for this profession and for the interview process to be accepted into the program. If being in one-on-one situations is not comfortable, therapy is not for you. If completing mandatory paperwork with deadlines is not something that you can deal with, a career in therapy is not for you.

Q. What advice would you offer physical therapy majors as they graduate and look for jobs? What's the best way to land a job today?

A. All therapy students do "internship rotations" prior to the completion of their programs. During this time, the student should take advantage of the opportunity to experience what "fits" for them. Size-up the therapy staff and become aware of your strengths. Request opportunities with the management to go through the interview process, even if there is not an opening at that facility or if that is not the setting that you would like to work in at graduation. The experience makes you more at ease when you go for your "real" interviews. Be prepared to answer questions that tell the interviewer something about your personal beliefs or views and not always directly job related. Be prepared to explain what you bring to the table. Do not start your part of the interview with questions about salary, benefits, and what the job will do for you. Do not jump at your first job offer unless you are 100 percent sure that is where you want to work.

Interview: Kip Schick

Kip Schick works a physical therapist for the University of Wisconsin Hospital and Clinics in Madison, Wisconsin. He is also the president of the Wisconsin Physical Therapy Association. Kip discussed his career with the editors of *Hot Jobs*.

Q. How long have you worked in the field?

A. I have been a physical therapist for more than 16 years, and I have been an administrator for the past 12 years.

Q. What made you want to enter this career?

A. My interest was centered in serving and helping others as well as working in a science field and the medical profession.

Q. What is one thing that young people may not know about a career in physical therapy?

A. As with other careers, unless someone has a firsthand experience, it is difficult to understand what various professionals due as part of their practice. Physical therapy is incredibly diverse, serving a wide range of people and conditions (i.e., orthopedics; sports; neurology; pediatrics; geriatrics; women's health; and many others) while being offered in numerous practice settings (i.e., acute/hospital care; inpatient rehabilitation; outpatient clinics; private practice; school-based care; colleges/universities; sports teams; dance organizations; home health; skilled nursing facilities; nursing homes; and many others).

Q. What are the most important personal and professional qualities for physical therapists?

A. Physical therapy requires individuals to interact well with others through effective communication, teamwork, and problem solving. Physical therapists also need to commit to life-long learning while providing compassionate care that is patient centered.

Q. What are some of the pros and cons of your job?

A. I enjoy having the ability to interact with people and to challenge myself on a continual basis, which requires me to be adaptive, flexible, and thoughtful when working with people to develop an effective treatment plan. I wouldn't describe the job as having cons, although challenges certainly exist, including increased scrutiny for providers to demonstrate highly effective treatment at a low cost as well as having sufficient time to document the services provided.

Q. What advice would you give to aspiring physical therapists?

A. If you are interested in the field, be sure to talk to others who practice in the field to get their feedback on the profession. Volunteer with a local company (private practice, school, or health facility) or at an event that involves some type of medical coverage such as a local 5K race or marathon. The physical therapy curriculum is very demanding and virtually all entry degrees in physical therapy are at the doctorate level. Physical therapy curriculum places an emphasis on math, science, and communication (written and oral).

Q. What are the best ways to find a job?

A. In order to get a job, physical therapy students must graduate from physical therapy school and pass the national licensure examination. After that, I encourage new graduates to work in setting that will give them an opportunity to learn from others. Currently the job market is favorable and the outlook for the profession is favorable in terms of demand.

Q. Can you tell us about the Wisconsin Physical Therapy Association (WPTA)?

A. The WPTA is the statewide association that supports physical therapists and physical therapist assistants. It is a component chapter of our national association, the American Physical Therapy Association. Essentially the association at the state and national level serves to support the advancement and protect the interests of the physical therapy profession, including consumers, payers, and practitioners. The association also fosters advancement in physical therapy practice, research, and education.

Q. How important is association membership to career success?

A. Membership is not required in the association, but membership brings many advantages, including the ability to receive professional journals to stay current with research as well as several ways to access information and fellow members to stay current with research and other issues that impact contemporary practice. Membership also provides the association with additional resources, which are needed to remain an active voice in the legislative and policy arenas. This is especially important with the on-going debate specific to health care reform.

PHYSICIANS

OVERVIEW

Physicians, also known as *doctors,* are licensed health professionals who assess, diagnose, and treat patients of all ages and with many different conditions. Their methods of treatment may include prescribing medications and diagnostic tests, offering counseling on nutrition and exercise, and conducting surgery and other medical procedures. Many physicians specialize by focusing on a particular system or part of the body. A medical degree is necessary to enter the field. Approximately 661,400 physicians are employed in the United States. Employment opportunities for physicians should be very good through 2018.

THE JOB

Physicians play an important role in our society. We rely on their knowledge of medical technology and treatment methods to help us when we are sick, or in order to stay healthy. There are two types of physicians: the designation, M.D., for Doctor of Medicine, and D.O., for Doctor of Osteopathic Medicine. M.D.s, also known as *allopathic physicians,* use surgery and drugs to treat patients, while D.O.s, also known as *osteopaths,* practice holistic patient care in addition to prescribing medicine and surgery. They pay special attention to the body's musculoskeletal system when examining patients and stress preventive medicine.

Physicians diagnosis illnesses, prescribe medications, and/or administer treatments. Sometimes they perform diagnostic tests to help confirm a diagnosis or refer patients to a *medical specialist* (such as an *oncologist* if they suspect

FAST FACTS

High School Subjects
Biology
Health

Personal Skills
Communication
Helping
Scientific
Technical

Minimum Education Level
Medical degree

Salary Range
$51,000 to $173,000 to $700,000+

Employment Outlook
Faster than the average

O*NET-SOC
29-1061.00, 29-1062.00,
29-1063.00, 29-1064.00,
29-1065.00, 29-1066.00,
29-1067.00, 29-1069.01,
29-1069.02, 29-1069.03,
29-1069.04, 29-1069.05,
29-1069.06, 29-1069.07,
29-1069.08, 29-1069.09,
29-1069.10, 29-1069.11,
29-1069.12, 29-1069.99

GOE
14.02.01

DOT
070

NOC
3112

that a patient has cancer) or laboratory for additional testing. Physicians may see patients suffering from injuries or pain, and they perform procedures ranging from suturing lacerations, to setting broken bones, to prescribing medications to help alleviate pain and discomfort. Physicians also counsel patients on health and may suggest dietary or lifestyle changes to improve patients' condition.

Some physicians are *primary care doctors,* providing a wide range of general services. They often have a group of long-term patients that they see on a regular basis. Primary care doctors see patients for a variety of reasons including wellness care, routine physicals and immunizations, and the treatment of minor injuries, infections, or diseases. If the patient has more specific health needs, primary care physicians will then refer him or her to a specialist. Some examples of primary care doctors are those practicing *family and general medicine, internal medicine,* and *pediatrics. Family and general medicine practitioners* are typically the first physician practitioners an individual sees when ill or injured. They diagnose and treat a wide variety of illnesses or injuries—from broken bones, to the flu, to respiratory infections. *General internists* treat problems that affect the internal organ systems, such as the liver, stomach, kidneys, and digestive tract. *General pediatricians* provide health care services to infants, children, teens, and young adults.

Physician specialists are trained to focus on a particular system or part of the body. Some specialties, especially those involving surgery or other procedures, require additional training during residency or fellowship. Specialists work with primary care doctors in treating patients for a particular medical condition, or for complete care throughout life. Examples of medical specialties include *neurology, obstetrics and gynecology, anesthesiology,* and *orthopedic surgery.*

The following paragraphs detail some of the largest medical specialties:

Anesthesiologists are specially trained in anesthesia and peri-operative medicine. They treat patients before, during, and after surgery or any other medical procedure that requires anesthesia. Before a surgery begins, anesthesiologists assess the patient and consult with the surgical team to create an anesthesiology plan customized for the patient's needs. They take into account airway management and provisions for pain management. During surgery, they administer anesthesia and monitor the patient's vital life functions—heart rate, blood pressure, body temperature, and breathing. After surgery, they make sure the patient is stabilized and monitor him or her for any adverse reactions to the anesthesia.

Dermatologists treat conditions and diseases of the skin, scalp, hair, and nails. They treat patients suffering from conditions ranging from acne to cancerous lesions.

Emergency medicine physicians, also known as *emergency room physicians,* are specially trained to care for patients with illnesses or injuries that require immediate medical attention. Emergency medicine covers the field of general medicine, but it also involves practically all fields of medicine, surgery, and surgical sub-specialties. Emergency medicine physicians diagnose, treat, and stabilize patients with conditions ranging from lacerations to heart attacks. They may also treat patients suffering from injuries caused by sports or trauma (such as a car accident or a gunshot wound). Some emergency physicians also train staff members regarding cardiopulmonary resuscitation, advanced cardiac life support, and advanced trauma life support. Some participate in mock disaster drills with other health care professionals in order to be ready when a real emergency occurs.

In the 1990s, a movement to introduce medical professionals who focused solely on the care of hospital inpatients began. These physicians are known as *hospitalists*. Since that time, there has been much debate about whether their existence is a good thing. But one thing is certain: their numbers are growing, from approximately 800 in 1990 to 30,000 today, partly due to the increasing number of people admitted to hospitals nationwide and partly due to the movement to reform health care. Hospitalists are doctors who work only in hospitals. They take over for primary care physicians or internists who have to juggle their inpatient and outpatient workloads. In addition to patient care, hospitalists handle administrative tasks such as ordering tests and medications and ensuring that their orders are carried out correctly, filling out paperwork that details patient care, and overseeing patient discharge. Approximately "82.3 percent of practicing hospitalists are trained in general internal medicine, 6.5 percent in general pediatrics, 4 percent in an internal medicine subspecialty, 3.7 percent in family practice, 3.1 percent in internal medicine pediatrics, and 0.4 percent in a pediatrics subspecialty," according to the Society of Hospital Medicine.

Obstetricians and gynecologists (OB/GYNs) are responsible for the general health of women. They also provide care related to pregnancy and the reproductive system. OB/GYNs give patients annual physicals and important tests such as Pap smears or breast exams. They try to catch early occurrences of cancer in the breast, cervix, or reproductive system. OB/GYNs also specialize in prenatal care, delivery, and postnatal care.

Psychiatrists are trained in the study and treatment of mental disorders. Their patient assessment includes a mental status examination and compilation of case history. Diagnostic tests may be prescribed, including neuroimaging and other neurophysiological techniques. Psychiatrists can prescribe treatments such as medication, psychotherapy, or transcranial magnetic stimulation. Depending on the severity of the patient's condition, treatment can be conducted during hospitalization or on an outpatient basis.

Radiologists are specially trained to take and interpret medical images. Through the use of x-rays, radioactive substances, sound waves, or the body's natural magnetism, radiologists can determine the presence and severity of injuries and diseases. Some radiologists sub-specialize in a particular area of the body or system, such as head and neck radiology or breast imaging. Others sub-specialize in interventional radiology, which allows them to treat patients with minimally invasive interventional techniques. Angioplasty, stent placement, and biopsy procedures are some examples of interventional radiology techniques.

Surgeons specialize in the treatment of injury or disease through surgical procedures. Physicians perform general surgery or may specialize in surgery on a specific area of the body or system. For example, *orthopedic surgeons* perform procedures related to the musculoskeletal system, *neurosurgeons* specialize in surgical procedures on the brain and nervous system, and *cardiothoracic surgeons* specialize in conducting surgeries on the chest, heart, and lungs. Other surgical specialists include *otolaryngologists* (treatment and surgery for conditions or injuries to the ear, nose, and throat) and *plastic or reconstructive surgeons.*

Physicians, regardless of their specialty, have additional duties including charting patients' progress and treatments; consulting with other physicians, health care workers, and patients and their families; and participating in staff meetings. Depending on the size and scope of their medical practice, some physicians may be responsible for other office management duties including billing, staff education, and administrative tasks. Some physicians, especially those employed by university or teaching hospitals, may supervise, train, and mentor medical students, interns, and residents. Some physicians also teach at medical schools or conduct scientific research and publish their findings in medical journals or other scholarly publications. Physicians sometimes provide expert testimony in legal proceedings.

Physicians work in hospitals, private offices, or clinics. Certain specialties, such as family medicine, pediatrics, or obstetrics/gynecology, lend themselves to private practice, while others—such as radiology, emergency medicine, and urology—are practiced in physician groups, hospitals, or other health care settings.

Physicians work in clean and sterile conditions. Their uniform consists of either hospital scrubs and gown, or other professional attire. They are often aided by a staff of other health care professionals such as nurses, physician assistants, nurse aides, therapists, technicians, and medical secretaries. Their days are often stressful; physicians can expect to work with multiple patients with varying degrees of illness.

Many physicians work long and irregular hours. More than 40 percent of all doctors working in the United States log 50 or more hours a week, including evening, weekend, and holiday hours. Depending on their specialty, physicians are "on call" day and night and deal with many patient complaints or emergencies outside the office.

REQUIREMENTS

HIGH SCHOOL

You will need to study for many years before you can become a physician. In high school, take a college-preparatory track that includes as many science classes as possible (especially chemistry, biology, and anatomy and physiology), as well as courses in mathematics, computer science, psychology, English, speech, foreign languages (especially Latin), and social studies.

POSTSECONDARY TRAINING

A medical degree is necessary to enter the field. Preparation for this career is very demanding. Medical students must complete eight years of training after high school, plus three to eight years of internship and residency. Applying to and succeeding in medical school can be challenging. Aspiring medical students must also take and pass the very demanding Medical College Admission Test (www.aamc.org/students/applying/mcat), a national examination that is administered by the Association of American Medical Colleges (AAMC). To assist students in this process, the AAMC has developed a useful publication, *The Road to Becoming a Doctor,* which can be accessed by visiting www.aamc.org/students/considering.

Approximately 65 percent of medical school applicants major in biology or another physical science at the undergraduate or graduate levels. Others major in pre-med.

More medical schools are reaching out to students with nonscience backgrounds, including those in the humanities, according to *Newsweek.* For example, 40 percent of students recently accepted to the University of Pennsylvania's medical school had nonscience backgrounds. By accepting students from nonscience backgrounds, medical schools are trying to create more well-rounded students "who can be molded into caring and analytical doctors."

There are 129 medical schools accredited by the Liaison Committee on Medical Education, which accredits M.D. medical education programs. The American Osteopathic Association (AOA) accredits colleges that award a D.O. degree. The AOA has accredited 25 schools in 31 locations.

According to the AAMC, a typical medical school curriculum is as follows: Year 1—biochemistry, cell biology, medical genetics, gross anatomy, structure and function of the organ systems, neuroscience, and immunology; Year 2—infectious diseases, pharmacology, pathology, clinical diagnoses and therapeutics, and health law; Years 3 and 4—generalist core (family and community medicine, obstetrics and gynecology, surgery, etc.), neurology, psychiatry, subspecialty segment (anesthesia, dermatology, orthopedics, urology, radiology, ophthalmology, otolaryngology), continuity-of-care segment (sub internships, emergency room and intensive-care experiences), and electives.

As they approach their fourth year of school, medical students choose a specialty area in which they want to practice and begin applying to graduate medical education programs, which are known as residencies. Students obtain residencies through the National Resident Matching Program. Residencies can last anywhere from three to seven years depending on the specialty.

Students who plan to conduct biomedical research often attend joint M.D./Ph.D. programs. In these programs, which typically last seven or eight years, students learn the research skills that will help them as scientists and the clinical skills that will allow them to practice medicine. Visit www.aamc.org/students/considering/exploring_medical/research/mdphd to learn more about M.D./Ph.D. dual degree training.

Medical school tuition is high. The AAMC reports that "annual tuition and fees at state medical schools in 2008-2009 averaged $23,581 for state residents and $43,587 for non-residents. At private schools, tuition and fees averaged $41,225 for residents and $42,519 for non-resident students." Housing and living expenses were not included in these figures. A number of private and government financial aid programs are available to help students pay for medical school. Visit the websites of the associations in the For More Information section for details.

CERTIFICATION AND LICENSING

Physicians can earn voluntary board certification in a variety of medical specialties. They must participate in medical residencies and pass an examination by a member board of the American Osteopathic Association or the American Board of Medical Specialties.

Once they complete their medical training, physicians must take an examination in order to be licensed to practice medicine. Licensing is required in all 50 states and U.S. territories. The board of medical examiners in each state administers the examinations.

OTHER REQUIREMENTS

Physicians must be able to think quickly and clearly and must stay calm—especially when dealing with patient emergencies. Good bedside manners are a must—meaning physicians should have empathy toward their patients' conditions, be good listeners, and be able to have a kind and sincere disposition when counseling patients and their families.

EXPLORING

There are many ways to learn more about a career as a physician. You can read books about the field. Here is one suggestion: *White Coat Wisdom*, by Stephen J. Busalacchi (Apollo's Voice, 2008). You can also visit the websites of medical schools to learn about typical classes and medical specialties, and you can ask your teacher or school counselor to arrange an information interview with a physician or talk to your doctor about his or her career. Professional associations also provide information about the field. The American Medical Association provides a wealth of information at its website, www.ama-assn.org. The Association of American Medical Colleges (AAMC) also offers two useful websites: Considering a Medical Career (www.aamc.org/students/considering) and AspiringDocs.org (www.aspiringdocs.org), which aims to increase diversity in medicine. The AAMC also offers an annual career fair for students who are interested in learning more about careers in medicine. Visit the AAMC website for more information. You should also try to land a part-time job in a doctor's office. This will give you a chance to interact with physicians and see if the career is a good fit for your interests and abilities.

EMPLOYERS

Approximately 661,400 physicians are employed in the United States. About 53 percent of physicians and surgeons work in offices of physicians. Nineteen percent are employed by hospitals. Other physicians are employed by government agencies, schools, correctional facilities, and outpatient care centers. Approximately 12 percent are self-employed.

According to the American Medical Association, the following medical areas employed the most physicians: internal medicine, 20.1 percent; family medicine/general practice, 12.4 percent; pediatrics, 9.6 percent; obstetrics and gynecology, 5.6 percent; anesthesiology, 5.5 percent; psychiatry, 5.2 percent; general surgery, 5.0 percent; and emergency medicine, 4.1 percent.

GETTING A JOB

Many physicians obtain their first jobs as a result of contacts made during their residencies. Others seek assistance in obtaining job leads from medical school career services offices, newspaper want ads, and employment websites. Some professional associations, such as the American Academy of Family Physicians, provide job listings at their websites. See For More Information for a list of organizations. Job listings can also be found at the *Journal of the American Medical Association*'s website, www.jamacareer-center.com. Some new graduates start their own solo private practices, enter into a partnership with other physicians, or enter into a group practice. Those interested in positions with the federal government should visit the U.S. Office of Personnel Management's website, www.usajobs.opm.gov.

ADVANCEMENT

Physicians advance by assuming managerial duties, becoming well-known for their medical skills, by becoming experts in their medical specialty, or by opening their own practices. Some physicians become medical administrators or college professors.

EARNINGS

Salaries for physicians vary by type of employer, geographic region, and the employee's experience level, specialty, and skills. The U.S. Department of Labor (USDL) reports the following mean annual earnings for physicians by specialty in 2009: anesthesiology, $271,264; family and general practice, $167,245; internal medicine, $181,081; obstetrics/gynecology, $279,635; pediatrics, $126,955; psychiatry, $149,866; and general surgery, $219,770. Mean annual salaries for physicians and surgeons, not otherwise classified were $173,860 in 2009. Some physicians earned less than $51,750. Top specialists can earn much higher salaries. For example, very experienced plastic surgeons can earn more than $700,000.

While work in these careers is lucrative, earnings are offset by high medical malpractice insurance and the higher-than-average number of hours worked. For example, OB/GYNs worked an average of 2,637 hours a year, according to the USDL—much higher than the average of 2,008 annual hours for all workers.

Employers offer a variety of benefits, including the following: medical, dental, and life insurance; paid holidays, vacations, and sick and personal days; 401(k) plans; profit-sharing plans; retirement and pension plans; and educational assistance programs. Physicians who own their own practices or who are in a partnership with other doctors must provide their own benefits.

EMPLOYMENT OUTLOOK

Employment opportunities for physicians should be very good through 2018. In fact, the U.S. Department of Labor predicts that 144,100 new jobs will become available for physicians from 2008 to 2018.

The rapidly growing U.S. population, the predicted doubling of the number of people over age 65 between 2000 and 2030, rising expectations about the quality and ready availability of health care services, an aging physician workforce, the increasing availability of health insurance as a result of health insurance reform, and a trend toward reduced hours for physicians has created a potential physician shortage in coming years, according to the Association of American Medical Colleges (AAMC).

To address this shortage, the AAMC recommends that enrollment at U.S. medical schools be increased by 30 percent (or 5,000 students annually) by 2015. The Association says that this goal can be accomplished by increasing enrollment at existing schools and by founding new allopathic medical schools.

Physicians who are willing to work in rural and low-income areas will have the best job prospects. Opportunities will also be good for physicians who specialize in caring for the elderly because this segment of the population is growing rapidly and its members require more medical care than people in other demographics.

FOR MORE INFORMATION

For information on accredited post-M.D. medical training programs in the United States, visit the council's website.
**Accreditation Council
for Graduate Medical Education**
515 North State Street, Suite 2000
Chicago, IL 60654-4865
www.acgme.org

For information on family medicine, contact
**American Academy
of Family Physicians**
PO Box 11210
Shawnee Mission, KS 66207-1210
www.aafp.org

To read the *Osteopathic Medical College Information Book,* and for information on careers and financial aid, visit the AACOM website.
**American Association of Colleges
of Osteopathic Medicine (AACOM)**
5550 Friendship Boulevard, Suite 310
Chevy Chase, MD 20815-7231
www.aacom.org

For information on board certification, contact

American Board of Medical Specialties
222 North LaSalle Street, Suite 1500
Chicago, IL 60601-1117
www.abms.org

For comprehensive information on medical education and careers, contact
American Medical Association
515 North State Street
Chicago, IL 60654-4854
www.ama-assn.org

For information on osteopathic medicine, contact
American Osteopathic Association
142 East Ontario Street
Chicago, IL 60611-2864
www.osteopathic.org

For information on accredited medical schools in the U.S. and Canada, contact
**Association of
American Medical Colleges**
2450 N Street, NW
Washington, DC 20037-1126
www.aamc.org

For information about the career of hospitalist, contact
Society of Hospital Medicine
1500 Spring Garden, Suite 501
Philadelphia, PA 19130-4070
www.hospitalmedicine.org

Interview: Victor DeJesus

Dr. Victor DeJesus is a board-certified physician in internal medicine who currently works in private practice. He discussed his career with the editors of *Hot Jobs*.

Q. What made you want to enter this career?

A.   My father's death due to an abdominal wound affected me greatly and was my motivation in becoming a doctor. At a young age, I envisioned myself someday becoming a doctor with the skills and knowledge to prevent such an untimely death and spare other families the bitter pain of losing a loved one.

Q.   What is one thing that young people may not know about a career as a physician?

A.   It's not a walk in the park. A doctor's job can never be nine to five. Our responsibility to each patient continues even after the office visit. We get called any time of the day and as a solo practitioner, even an out-of-town vacation doesn't spare me from patient demands and frantic calls from my office staff.

Q.   What are the most important qualities for physicians?

A.   I believe that perseverance and a good memory are the two most important qualities that a medical student should possess to finish medical school. Once in private practice, a doctor who shows sincere compassion and attentiveness to the patients' needs will surely be rewarded with a good patient following and a financially stable practice.

Q.   What do you like most about your job?

A.   The actual patient care experience is my biggest fulfillment. Seeing my patients' quality of life improve is the best feeling I can ever get.

Q.   What advice would you give to young people who are interested in becoming physicians?

A.   The practice of medicine is a lifetime commitment with more challenges than ever: 1) lower insurance reimbursements with more cuts in the near future; 2) unpredictable work schedules and long working hours; 3) malpractice lawsuits, which can potentially wipe out all life savings; 4) a steep learning curve for the business part of the practice; and 5) a gloomy outlook on the horizon with the federal government's new health care reform. However, an aspiring doctor who can accept these challenges as part of the job and sees fulfillment in making people's lives better should pursue this career.

Q.   What is the employment outlook for physicians?

A.   Medical doctors need not worry about job security. With President Obama's plan of adding another 30 million Americans to the ranks of the insured, there is a plenty of work for every doctor in every field of medicine. In fact, the American Medical Association confirms a large physician shortage in the field of primary care (pediatrics, family medicine, and internal medicine) and projects the use of more physician extenders, such as nurse practitioners and physician assistants, to improve patient flow and prevent a crisis.

PUBLIC RELATIONS SPECIALISTS

OVERVIEW

Public relations (PR) specialists, also known as *communications specialists, media specialists,* and *press secretaries* and *public affairs specialists* (in government), communicate with the public on behalf of well-known individuals, companies, nonprofit organizations, and government agencies. They draft internal and external communications and work to ensure such messages are delivered in a manner that is pleasing to their client. A minimum of a bachelor's degree in public relations or a related field is required to work as a PR specialist. Approximately 275,200 public relations specialists are employed in the United States. Employment is projected to grow much faster than the average for all careers through 2018.

THE JOB

If you have excellent communication skills (both oral and writ-

FAST FACTS

High School Subjects
Business
English
Journalism

Personal Skills
Communication
Judgment and decision making
Leadership

Minimum Education Level
Bachelor's degree

Salary Range
$30,000 to $51,000 to
$125,000+

Employment Outlook
Much faster than the average

O*NET-SOC
11-2031.00, 27-3031.00

GOE
01.03.01

DOT
165

NOC
5124

ten), grace under pressure, and the ability to help companies and other organizations tell the world about their achievements and good deeds, improve their negative reputations, and create positive buzz about their products and services, you might have a future in public relations.

Public relations specialists help organizations build and promote their products and services by seeking out the support of the public and organizations that influence the public, such as media outlets including TV, radio, print, and the Internet. Newer Internet tools—blogs, podcasts, social network sites, and wikis, to name a few—have added to the resources that PR specialists use to reach the public. By helping to establish credibility, these professionals play a valuable strategic role in building a business, government interest, or client base.

The field of public relations is often confused with advertising. However, there is one key difference: advertisers pay for media coverage, so they can develop and control the exact message they are trying to convey to the public. Conversely, public relations relies on unsolicited media coverage or third-party endorsements. This offers much less control over how a message will be conveyed to the public, making the job of public relations specialists that much harder.

For PR specialists, no day is the same. They work with multiple clients who have differing PR needs and requests. Whether they are employed directly by a business or hired under a contract by a firm, PR specialists must quickly assess what their client does in business and the issues it faces. This will drive PR decisions. They need to consider what concerns the company's stakeholders. They discover this by attending industry conferences and conducting research on the views of opinion leaders such as reporters that follow their client's business.

PR specialists must be confident and maintain their composure under pressure. For example, a business may hire a PR specialist to diffuse negative publicity endured because of a company mistake. Reporters "digging for dirt" will pepper the PR specialist with a steady stream of questions in an attempt to catch him or her off guard. Conversely, a business may actually be looking for additional publicity, and it is the job of the PR specialist to engage reporters and get them interested enough to cover a story about a company when there's no controversy. This takes creativity and a keen business sense.

Public relations specialists must have good communication and problem-solving skills and must be flexible when facing new challenges. Responding to issues on the fly requires grace under pressure. Public relations professionals must communicate with a broad range of audiences, from customers, to employees, to shareholders, to government officials.

Employees are a particularly important audience for public relations specialists. Businesses hire them to craft internal communications to ensure that a company's message is clear to its staff and that staff members understand their respective roles in achieving that vision. Because morale and productivity are often linked, and employees are the public face of a company, clients hire PR specialists to ensure that their staff members are positive ambassadors who believe in the products and services offered by the organization—as well as its overall goals.

The health care and high-technology industries are increasingly hiring PR specialists. Specialists who work in the health sciences may work for a pharmaceutical company that is launching a new drug. Specialists work with pharmaceutical scientists to complete applications to obtain Food and Drug Administration approval, network with physicians to build acceptance of the drug, educate the public about the potential positive impacts of the medication, and inspire stockholder confidence in the company's vision for the new product. PR specialists hired to work in technology may be employed to represent a tiny startup and build it into a powerhouse such as YouTube or Google. They might also be hired by a large company to help reduce bad publicity received by the company's owner or as a result of the company's business practices.

PR specialists are employed directly by companies or nonprofit organizations. Others work for PR firms that provide services on a temporary contract basis. These specialists work with a variety of clients.

Regardless of their employer, PR specialists often work a standard 35- to 40-hour week. Overtime is common during crunch times, however, and schedules can be irregular. Since deadlines for speeches or other communication needs can come quickly, PR specialists must often "drop everything" to deliver on time.

Success for a PR specialist is readily apparent, manifesting itself in the form of satisfied clients and repeat business for the individual or firm. There are also opportunities to travel and even to apply for transfer to other cities or countries.

So what's the catch? Work in public relations can be demanding and often stressful. For the same reason you can see successful PR strategies, you can easily spot a lack of results. PR specialists are the first to be blamed when a PR plan fails to deliver business or positive press.

REQUIREMENTS

HIGH SCHOOL

High school classes that will help prepare you for a career in public relations include English (especially creative writing), speech, psychology, journalism, and computer science. Since the United States is becoming more ethnically diverse and U.S. businesses are competing at a global level, it is a good idea to take at least one foreign language in high school so that you can communicate with people in the United States who do not speak English as a first language or people in foreign countries.

POSTSECONDARY TRAINING

PR specialists typically enter the field with a bachelor's degree in public relations, journalism, marketing, or communications. Some companies prefer applicants to have experience in print or electronic journalism. Others seek applicants with specialized knowledge and/or experience in their particular industry—such as finance, health care, science, engineering, information technology, or sales. In addition to course work, students can participate in one or more public relations internships. Some programs may offer minors or concentrations in business, government, and nonprofit public relations. A master's degree or higher may be required for managerial positions. PR specialists who want to teach at the college level will also need a graduate degree.

CERTIFICATION AND LICENSING

Voluntary certification is offered by the Public Relations Society of America and the International Association of Business Communicators. Contact these organizations for more information. There is no licensing required for PR specialists.

OTHER REQUIREMENTS

Some of the most important traits for successful PR specialists include excellent communication skills, confidence, creativity, the ability to solve problems, persistence, the ability to think on one's feet, good judgment, the ability to motivate others, and an understanding of human psychology.

EXPLORING

Do you think you would be a good PR specialist? If so, there are many ways to learn more about a career in the field. You can read books and periodicals (such as *Communication World* and *Student Connection*, which are published by the International Association of Business Communicators) about the field, visit the websites of college public relations programs to learn about typical classes and possible career paths, and ask your teacher or school counselor to arrange an information interview with a PR specialist. You can check out The Museum of Public Relations online at www.prmuseum.com to read about public relations pioneers such as Edward L. Bernays, Arthur W. Page, and Chet Burger.

Professional associations can also provide information. The Public Relations Society of America provides an overview of PR careers via its online publication, *Public Relations Professional Career Guide*, which can be accessed at www.prsa.org/Jobcenter/CareerGuidePRSAFoundation/Career%20Guide.pdf.

Finally, try to participate in activities that help you develop your communication and promotional skills. You might find a part-time or summer job at a newspaper, radio or television station, or Internet news site. Or you could work in a retail job that involves a lot of customer interaction, or volunteer your services to a political campaign or a grassroots organization in your community. You should also try to land a part-time job at a public relations firm or the PR department of a company, nonprofit organization, or government agency. This will give you a chance to interact with PR specialists and see if the career is a good fit for your interests and abilities.

EMPLOYERS

Approximately 275,200 public relations specialists are employed in the United States. Specialists work for PR firms that contract professionals out to organizations, or they may be employed directly by an individual, corporation, nonprofit, or government agency. According to the U.S. Department of Labor, PR specialists primarily work in "service-providing industries, such as advertising and related services; health care and social assistance; educational services; and government; others work for communications firms, financial institutions, and government agencies."

GETTING A JOB

Many PR specialists obtain their first jobs as a result of contacts made through college internships or networking events. Others seek assistance in obtaining job leads from college career services offices, newspaper want ads, and employment websites. Additionally, professional associations, such as the Public Relations Society of America and the Council of Public Relations Firms, provide job listings at their websites. See For More Information for a list of organizations. Those interested in positions with the federal government should visit the U.S. Office of Personnel Management's website, www.usajobs.opm.gov.

ADVANCEMENT

Public relations specialists advance by receiving pay raises or by moving up the ladder from junior account executive, to account executive, to senior account executive, to account manager, and to vice president. Some PR specialists open their own firms.

EARNINGS

Salaries for public relations specialists vary by type of employer, geographic region, and the worker's experience , education, and skill level. Median annual salaries for PR specialists were $51,960 in 2009, according to the U.S. Department of Labor (USDL). Salaries ranged from less than $30,520 to $96,630 or more. The USDL reports the following mean annual earnings for PR specialists by industry: oil and gas extraction, $86,640; advertising, public relations, and related services, $69,630; business, professional, labor, political, and similar organizations, $62,040; local government, $54,720; and colleges, universities, and professional schools, $52,540. Salaries for public relations managers ranged from less than $47,800 to $125,220 or more.

Public relations specialists usually receive benefits such as health and life insurance, vacation days, sick leave, and a savings and pension plan. Self-employed workers must provide their own benefits.

EMPLOYMENT OUTLOOK

The U.S. Department of Labor predicts that employment for public relations specialists will grow much faster than the average for all careers through 2018. In 2009, spending on public relations in the U.S. grew by nearly 3 percent from 2008 to 2009—to $3.7 billion, according to Veronis Suhler Stevenson (VSS), a private-equity firm. VSS predicts that spending on public relations will exceed $8 billion by 2013.

Many factors are fueling job growth in the field. Scandals and government bailouts in the financial services industry have created a need for PR specialists to "spin" bad news into good and help companies regain the respect of the public. Public relations campaigns are also less expensive than advertising campaigns. PR workers are now being hired, according to *The Economist,* "to pitch story ideas to media outlets and try to get their clients mentioned in newspapers . . . and dream up and orchestrate live events, web launches, and the like." The growth of Internet and social media has also created new opportunities for PR specialists. PR specialists manage their company's presence on social networking sites such as Twitter and Facebook. Their skills recently came in handy when two employees of pizza giant Domino's uploaded video of themselves sticking pizza ingredients up their noses. PR specialists quickly posted a video of a company executive apologizing for the incident and stressed the cleanliness of the company's pizza-making operations.

Opportunities will be best for those with knowledge of international business, expertise in social media, certification, experience in the field, and fluency in one or more foreign languages.

FOR MORE INFORMATION

For industry information, contact
**Automotive Public
Relations Council**
1301 West Long Lake, Suite 225
Troy, MI 48098-6371
248-952-6401
www.autopr.org

For information on PR careers, contact
Council of Public Relations Firms
317 Madison Avenue, Suite 2320
New York, NY 10017-5205
877-773-4767
www.prfirms.org

For certification information, contact
**International Association
of Business Communicators**
601 Montgomery Street, Suite 1900
San Francisco, CA 94111-2623

415-544-4700
www.iabc.com

To learn about opportunities in
school public relations, contact
**National School Public
Relations Association**
15948 Derwood Road
Rockville, MD 20855-2123
301-519-0496
info@nspra.org
www.nspra.org

Visit the society's website for information about earnings, publications, certification, and careers, as well as a
blog about public relations.
Public Relations Society of America
33 Maiden Lane, 11th Floor
New York, NY 10038-5150
212-460-1400
www.prsa.org

Interview: Deborah Radman

Deborah Radman has worked in the field of public relations since 1984. She is the past president of the New York Chapter of the Public Relations Society of America (PRSA), a PRSA Fellow, and past chair of The Counselors Academy. Deborah discussed her career with the editors of *Hot Jobs*.

Q.   Where do you work? What made you want to enter this career?

A.   I am currently consulting with three to four mid-size public relations agencies and directly with some clients of my own. I became involved in this career initially because of a love of writing and interest in journalism.

Q.   What is one thing that young people may not know about a career in public relations?

A.   They should remain mindful at all times that their role in public relations is not just tactical execution. Rather, their role is to help their clients or employers communicate a relevant message to key influencers.

Q.   What are the most important qualities for people in your career?

A.   Curiosity, determination, and ability to demonstrate good thinking through strong writing.

Q.   What are some of the pros and cons of your job?

A.   This profession is not 9-5. That can be either a pro or a con depending on who you are and how you like to work. Another pro is that PR is finally on the front foot and being given credit for the uniquely useful and essential contributions it makes at all levels of companies and organizations. The con side of this one is that many in the worlds of advertising and media, as well as in the C-suite, simply don't get earned media and its impact on reputation. It's a battle that has been fought for decades and will no doubt continue. Be prepared to join the skirmish.

Q. What advice would you give to young people who are interested in becoming public relations specialists?

A. Be inspired by opportunity and the idea of taking a risk, rather than just getting paid.

Q. What is the employment outlook for public relations specialists? How is the field changing?

A. The job market has opened up quite a bit from this time last year. The field has changed significantly in terms of how we distribute information and how we reach and engage influencers. But what hasn't changed is this: the key role of the PR professional is to help management or clients understand and interpret the world around them and respond effectively in that constantly changing environment.

Interview: Gerard F. Corbett

Gerard F. Corbett is the founder and CEO of Redphlag LLC in San Bruno, California. He is also on the board of directors of the Public Relations Society of America. Gerard discussed his career with the editors of *Hot Jobs*.

Q. Can you tell us about Redphlag LLC? What made you want to enter this career?

A. Redphlag LLC is a California corporation founded in 2008 that focuses on public relations and marketing consulting and career coaching services. Previously, I managed public relations (PR) and corporate marketing for Hitachi in the Americas as vice president and general manager. I have spent four decades in the field and had a strong desire to be in the communications field since high school.

Q. What is one thing that young people may not know about a career as a public relations specialist?

A. A career in public relations is not only about working with people. A career in PR is about advocating for people, organizations, causes, points of view, and societal benefit.

Q. What are some of the pros and cons of your job?

A. Pros of the job include freedom to excel, ability to learn, and opportunity to perform. There are no cons if PR folks are patient, professional, and prepared.

Q. What advice would you give to young people who are interested in becoming public relations specialists?

A. Learn to write well, be well read, develop patience, and have an open mind and truthful heart.

Q. What is the employment outlook for public relations specialists? How is the field changing?

A. The field is wide open and starting to recover following the toughest job environment in many years. With the growth and evolution in social media, public relations people have the opportunity to be the primary gatekeepers and actuators of the complete communications function. The field is not changing. What is changing is the proliferation of technology, tools, and channels of communications.

Interview: Judith Phair

Judith Phair is the President of PhairAdvantage Communications in Laurel, Maryland (just outside of Washington, D.C.) In 2010, she received the Public Relations Society of America's Gold Anvil Award, its highest individual award. Judith discussed her career with the editors of *Hot Jobs*.

Q. How long have you worked in the field? What made you want to enter this career?

A. My career in public relations spans more than 35 years. I began my career in public relations by accident—I started out as a newspaper reporter and moved from Chicago to Cincinnati early in my career because of my husband's job. I got a better offer from the University of Cincinnati in a public relations (PR) position than from one of the then two-city dailies, and that was it. I loved my new line of work, and that love affair has continued. Our profession exists because it serves the public—communication is critical to democracy and to a well-functioning society. We facilitate that communication for the mutual benefit of our clients and their publics. It's an exciting, challenging, and ever-changing business. You never know what their day is going to be like—we expect the unexpected.

Q. What is one thing that young people may not know about a career in public relations?

A. Recent TV shows and movies have tended to focus more on the "glamour" of public relations—putting on and attending posh special events—or on negative perceptions of the PR person, such as "spinning" to manipulate public opinion, presenting false images of people and products, and the like. The great majority of public relations professionals bring talent and integrity to their work every day. They work hard and frequently have very long hours, especially in this 24/7 news world. We are there when the crisis hits, immediately strategizing solutions, organizing response teams, preparing spokespeople, communicating with stakeholders—and we stay with the crisis long after the TV cameras have left, continuing to do our jobs. At the special event, we are working, not socializing—and generally making sure that countless details and unexpected problems are handled quickly and correctly. Our work is not glamorous, but it is rewarding and certainly not boring.

On another note, many young people do not realize how critically important good writing is to their careers. It is a "must" in just about every public relations job.

Q. What are the most important qualities for PR workers?

A. Personal: integrity; curiosity; energy; strong worth ethic; sense of fair play; respect for others, as well as self-respect; caring about the needs and concerns of others

Professional: strong interpersonal skills; excellent oral and written communications skills; strategic thinking/approach to the job; professional demeanor and attitude; business knowledge; understanding and appreciation of cultural and ethnic diversity; deadline-oriented; works well under pressure

Q. What are some of the pros and cons of your job?

A. I worked for many wonderful employers for many years before opening my own consulting business—and, in fact, I recently took a four-year hiatus from full-time consulting to work full-time for another organization because of the opportunities it offered me. In fact, that organization is now a major client, and I am enjoying one of the perks of returning to consulting life: no daily commute. Other pluses are, of course, being your own boss and being able to define exactly how you operate and what kind of work you will focus on, dealing with a variety of projects that are stimulating and challenging, managing your own time to accommodate client needs, volunteer activities, and family (even, though, on the negative side, that can mean late hours and lots of weekend work), and gaining enormous satisfaction from your work.

Challenges include work-family balance (exactly because of the round-the-clock nature of handling the needs of multiple clients with both anticipated and unexpected demands), financial management (with no "steady" paycheck), and, at least for me, dealing with some days of solo work (I'm a pretty social person). Fortunately, my volunteer activities—including [those with the] Public Relations Society of America—ensure a lot of daily connection with colleagues.

Q. What advice would you give to aspiring public relations specialists?

A. Embrace leadership opportunities, especially through such organizations as Public Relations Student Society of America; become global—learn another language, study and travel abroad, read about what is going on around the world; develop or enhance your technological expertise; network and cultivate relationships; keep on learning—through formal and informal classes, conferences, webinars, etc.; and be flexible—be willing to do something outside of your job definition.

Q. What is the employment outlook for public relations specialists? How is the field changing?

A. The economy may be down, but there are still jobs in public relations, especially at the entry level. Among areas that are hiring are government, nonprofits, and health care. Young professionals have an edge in terms of critical communications needs today—they are comfortable and facile with technology and social media. In fact, a friend with a major agency told me recently that they are always on the lookout for talent in digital media; it's a growth market for them because of the needs of their clients. Among changes in the field: expansion of social media, coupled with continuing importance of traditional media to reach some key stakeholders; less trust in traditional opinion leaders; more in our peers ("people like me"); the need to engage with audiences in a customized way through multiple voices and channels; internationalization; and greater need for business and legal knowledge.

REGISTERED NURSES

OVERVIEW

Registered nurses work to promote health, prevent disease, and help patients who are sick or injured. They also serve as health educators for patients, families, and communities. Registered nurses train for the field by earning a bachelor's degree, an associate degree, or a diploma in nursing from an approved nursing program. Registered nurses who decide to become advanced practice nurses (clinical nurse specialists, nurse anesthetists, nurse-midwives, and nurse practitioners) must earn master's degrees and industry certifications. Registered nurses (RNs) are the largest health care population, comprising approximately 2.6 million jobs. Employment opportunities for RNs are expected to be excellent through 2018.

THE JOB

Most RNs provide direct patient care. They observe, assess, and record patient symptoms, reactions, and progress. Nurses collaborate with physicians and other medical professionals on patient care, treatments, and examinations, and they administer medications.

RNs work closely with physicians to care for patients. It is their job to implement the doctor's orders regarding the treatment of a patient. In addition to interacting with patients, RNs also have a lot of contact with patients' families, so they must have good "bedside manner" and put people at ease.

Specific work responsibilities vary from one RN to the next. An RN's duties and title are often determined by his or her work setting, such as *emergency room nurses,* who work in hospital emergency rooms, or *radiology nurses,* who administer x-rays and other body scans to patients or care for those undergoing radiation treatments for cancer. These nurses generally work in hospitals, clinics, or outpatient care facilities. RNs can also work outside of health care facilities, in settings such as schools, workplaces, and summer camps.

FAST FACTS

High School Subjects
Biology
Chemistry
Health

Personal Skills
Active listening
Communication
Critical thinking
Helping

Minimum Education Level
Some postsecondary training

Salary Range
$43,000 to $63,000 to $93,000+

Employment Outlook
Much faster than the average

O*NET-SOC
29-1111.00

GOE
14.02.01

DOT
075

NOC
3152

Other nurses are defined by the types of patients served. *Hematology nurses,* for example, help patients with blood disorders. *Oncology nurses* specialize in treating patients with cancer. These nurses are employed virtually anywhere, including physicians' offices, outpatient treatment facilities, home health care agencies, and hospitals. Those that specialize in a disease or condition may also specialize in the age of the patients served. Some examples include *neonatal nurses* (newborns), *pediatric nurses* (children and adolescents), and *geriatric nurses* (the elderly).

A nurse studies a patient's chart. Employment for registered nurses is expected to grow by 22 percent through 2018. (Comstock)

Finally, other RNs specialize in working with one or more organs or systems, such as *respiratory nurses,* who care for those with respiratory illnesses such as cystic fibrosis or asthma. RNs specializing in treatment of a particular organ or body system usually are employed in hospital specialty or critical care units, specialty clinics, and outpatient care facilities.

RNs can be one or a combination of these nursing types, such as a *geriatric dialysis nurse,* who specializes in care for elderly patients with kidney failure.

Registered nurses who pursue advanced degrees and certification are called *advanced practice nurses (APNs).* There are four advanced practice nursing specialties: *clinical nurse specialists, nurse anesthetists, nurse-midwives,* and *nurse practitioners.* For detailed information on these specialties, see the article, Advanced Practice Nurses, in this book.

Instead of working in teams under the direction of a physician, APNs work relatively independently. Clinical nurse specialists provide specialized expertise in a specific area of nursing, such as rehabilitation, mental health, or geriatrics. Nurse anesthetists administer anesthesia and provide pain management services before and after surgical, therapeutic, diagnostic, and obstetric procedures. Nurse-midwives provide primary care to women, including gynecological exams, prenatal and neonatal care, and direct assistance in labor and delivery. Finally, nurse practitioners serve as primary and specialty care providers, providing a blend of nursing and health care services to patients and families. Specialties include pediatrics, family practice, and women's health, among others.

Books to Read

Catalano, Joseph T. *Nursing Now: Today's Issues, Tomorrow's Trends.* 5th ed. Philadelphia: F. A. Davis Company, 2008.

Novotny, Jeanne M., Doris T. Lippman, Nicole K. Sanders, and Joyce J. Fitzpatrick. *101 Careers in Nursing.* New York: Springer Publishing Company, 2006.

Peterson, Veronica. *Just the Facts: A Pocket Guide to Nursing.* 4th ed. St. Louis: Mosby, 2008.

Potter, Patricia A., and Anne Griffin Perry. *Fundamentals of Nursing.* 6th ed. St. Louis: Mosby, 2008.

Vallano, Annette. *Your Career In Nursing: Manage Your Future in the Changing World of Healthcare.* 5th ed. New York: Kaplan Publishing, 2008.

In addition to caring for patients with existing conditions and illnesses, nurses also perform a valuable service by providing education and preventive care to healthy populations. A good example of this type of nurse includes an *occupational health nurse,* who seeks to prevent job-related injuries and illnesses and supports employers in implementing health and safety standards.

Some RNs work in applied nursing jobs, or positions that require the medical knowledge of a nurse without the traditional hands-on work with patients. The following paragraphs detail some popular applied nursing specialties:

Nurse educators evaluate existing or create new professional development plans for student nurses and RNs. They teach a variety of nursing classes to students.

Forensics nurses provide legal testimony in investigations of accidents or crimes.

Legal nurse consultants are registered nurses with considerable nursing experience and knowledge of the legal system. They use these skills to assist lawyers in health-care-related cases. According to the American Association of Legal Nurse Consultants (www.aalnc.org), legal nurse consultants offer support to the law profession in the following practice areas: personal injury, product liability, medical malpractice, workers' compensation, toxic torts, risk management, medical licensure investigation, criminal law, elder law, and fraud and abuse compliance.

Nursing informatics specialists organize a database of patients' medical information in an accessible format. They may customize and test the database according to the needs of different medical departments or specialties. Nursing informatics specialists also train nurses on computer charting, which consists of adding information to or retrieving it from the database. They may also write and install new programs or software applications to help nursing staffs work more efficiently.

As the types of nursing varieties are numerous, so are the settings in which nurses work. In addition to hospitals, doctor's offices, and medical clinics, nurses work in patients' homes, schools, large corporations, community centers, and other locations. Hospitals or other 24-hour facilities must be staffed around the clock, so some nurses work holidays, weekends, and overnight shifts.

Nurses follow strict guidelines in handling hazardous medical waste or dangerous instruments such as needles. They are also exposed to patients with contagious diseases, so they must wear protective gear such as masks and gloves. Hand washing is constant and methodical in nursing to prevent the transmission of communicable diseases.

While their jobs may be stressful, most nurses find caring for others enjoyable and rewarding.

REQUIREMENTS

HIGH SCHOOL

Take health, mathematics, biology, anatomy and physiology, chemistry, physics, English, speech, and computer science classes in high school to prepare for a career in nursing.

POSTSECONDARY TRAINING

Prospective RNs have the option of pursuing one of three training paths: associate's degree, diploma, and bachelor's degree. Associate's degree programs in nursing last two years and are offered by community colleges. Diploma programs in nursing typically last three years and are offered by hospitals and independent schools. Bachelor of science in nursing programs are offered by colleges and universities. They typically take four—and sometimes five—years to complete. Graduates of all three paths are known as graduate nurses and must take a licensing exam in their state to obtain the RN designation. Visit Discover Nursing (www.discovernursing.com) for a database of nursing programs.

Students who are interested in becoming nurse managers should earn at least a bachelor's degree. Those interested in becoming nursing educators, advanced practice nurses, or advancing as an RN should earn at least a master's degree in nursing, plus industry certifications.

CERTIFICATION AND LICENSING

Certification or credentialing, while voluntary, is highly recommended. It is an excellent way to stand out from other job applicants and demonstrate your abilities to prospective employers. Certification is offered by the American Nursing Credentialing Center, the National League for Nursing, and many other nursing organizations.

Nurses must be licensed to practice nursing in all states and the District of Columbia. Licensure requirements vary by state but typically include graduating from an approved nursing school and passing the National Council Licensure Examination, which is administered by the National Council of State Boards of Nursing.

OTHER REQUIREMENTS

To be a successful registered nurse, you should be detail oriented, have excellent communication skills, be sympathetic and caring, be calm under pressure, have leadership skills, and be willing to continue to learn throughout your career. You will need to be emotionally strong, since you will encounter many heartbreaking cases and emergency situations. You will also need to be physically fit, since you will spend many hours on your feet and often bend and stoop, and lift patients, as needed.

EXPLORING

Read books about nursing, talk with your counselor or teacher about setting up a presentation by a nurse, take a tour of a hospital or other health care setting, or volunteer at one of these facilities. Nursing websites, including those of professional associations, can also be a good source of information. Here are a few suggestions: Cybernurse.com (www.cybernurse.com), Discover Nursing (www.discovernursing.com), Nurse.com (www.nurse.com), and Futures in Nursing (http://futuresinnursing.org). You should also join Future Nurses organizations or student health clubs at your school.

EMPLOYERS

Approximately 2.6 million registered nurses are employed in the United States. The U.S. Department of Labor reports that 60 percent of registered nurses work at hospitals, 8 percent in offices of physicians, 5 percent in home health care services, 5 percent in nursing care facilities, and 3 percent in employment services. Other RNs are employed by colleges and universities, prisons, corporations, government agencies, and social assistance agencies. Some RNs with advanced education work as college nursing professors.

GETTING A JOB

Many registered nurses obtain their first jobs as a result of contacts made through college internships, clinical rotations, or networking events. Others seek assistance in obtaining job leads from college career services offices, newspaper want ads, and employment websites. Additionally, professional associations, such as the American Nurses Association, provide job listings at their websites. See For More Information for a list of organizations. Those interested in positions with the federal government should visit the U.S. Office of Personnel Management's website, www.usajobs.opm.gov.

ADVANCEMENT

There are many advancement opportunities for registered nurses. Those who start their careers as staff nurses can become nurse managers or head nurses. Those already in management positions can advance from assistant unit manager or head nurse to more senior-level administrative roles such as assistant director, director, vice president, or chief of nursing. Registered nurses can earn a master's degree and industry certifications and become advanced practice nurses. Some nurses become college professors. Others work in research or serve as consultants for insurance companies, pharmaceutical manufacturers, and law firms.

EARNINGS

Salaries for registered nurses vary by type of employer, geographic region, and the worker's experience level and skills. Median annual salaries for registered nurses were $63,750 in 2009, according to the U.S. Department of Labor (USDL). Salaries ranged from less than $43,970 to $93,700 or more. The USDL reports the following mean annual earnings for registered nurses by industry: federal government, $77,830; general medical and surgical hospitals, $67,740; offices of physicians, $67,290; outpatient care centers, $65,690; home health care services, $63,300; and nursing care facilities, $59,320.

Employers offer a variety of benefits, including the following: medical, dental, and life insurance; paid holidays, vacations, and sick days; personal days; 401(k) plans; profit-sharing plans; retirement and pension plans; and educational assistance programs. Self-employed workers must provide their own benefits.

Emerging Career: Dementia Care Nurse

Approximately 4.5 million people in the United States have been diagnosed with Alzheimer's disease (one of many types of dementia)—more than twice the number in 1980. This number is expected to grow to 11 to 16 million by 2050. As a result, nurses who care for dementia patients will be in strong demand in the coming decades. There is no specialized certification or training available for this career; nurses learn these skills on the job. *Dementia care nurses* need a strong love of others, patience to deal with patients who are sometimes confused or even violent, and familiarity with the special care that is necessary for those with dementia.

EMPLOYMENT OUTLOOK

The career outlook for nurses is excellent. The US Department of Labor (USDL) predicts that more than 737,000 new and replacement nurses will be needed by 2018 to care for the growing—and aging—U.S. population. The next several years will be an excellent time to pursue a career in nursing. Employment for nurses will be best in offices of physicians. This sector will experience growth of 48 percent through 2018, according to the USDL. Employment for nurses in home health care services will grow by 33 percent; by 25 percent in nursing care facilities; by 24 percent in employment services; and by 17 percent in hospitals, public and private.

Many nursing specialties are experiencing strong growth. One of the fastest-growing areas is the care of geriatric populations. As baby boomers continue to reach their mid-60s and beyond, there will be increasing demand for nurses with specialized training in geriatric care. According to *Who Will Care for Each of Us?: America's Coming Health Care Crisis*, the ratio of potential caregivers to those who need care (including the growing elderly population) will decrease by 40 percent between 2010 and 2030, creating a strong

FOR MORE INFORMATION

The following organizations provide a wealth of resources and information related to registered nursing. For a list of advanced practice nursing associations, see the For More Information section of the Advanced Practice Nurses article in this book.

For information on opportunities for men in nursing, contact

**American Assembly
for Men in Nursing**
PO Box 130220
Birmingham, AL 35213-0220
www.aamn.org

For information on careers in assisted living facilities, contact

**American Assisted
Living Nurses Association**
PO Box 10469
Napa, CA 94581-2469
www.alnursing.org

For information on accredited nursing programs, contact

**American Association
of Colleges of Nursing**
One Dupont Circle, NW, Suite 530
Washington, DC 20036-1135
www.aacn.nche.edu

The ANA is the largest nursing organization in the United States. Visit its website for a wealth of information about education, careers, and credentialing.

American Nurses Association (ANA)
8515 Georgia Avenue, Suite 400
Silver Spring, MD 20910-3492
www.nursingworld.org

For certification information, contact

**American Nurses
Credentialing Center**
c/o American Nurses Association
8515 Georgia Avenue, Suite 400
Silver Spring, MD 20910-3492
800-284-2378
www.nursecredentialing.org

For industry news, visit the society's website.

**American Society
of Registered Nurses**
1001 Bridgeway, Suite 233
Sausalito, CA 94965-2104
www.asrn.org

For information on licensing, contact

**National Council of
State Boards of Nursing**
111 East Wacker Drive, Suite 2900
Chicago, IL 60601-4277
www.ncsbn.org

For general information about nursing, contact

National League for Nursing
61 Broadway, 33rd Floor
New York, NY 10006-2701
www.nln.org

The N-OADN serves as an advocate for registered nurses who have earned an associate degree. Visit its website for more information.

**National Organization for Associate
Degree Nursing (N-OADN)**
7794 Grow Drive
Pensacola, FL 32514-7072
www.noadn.org

For information on membership, contact

**National Student
Nurses' Association**
45 Main Street, Suite 606
Brooklyn, NY 11201-1099
nsna@nsna.org
www.nsna.org

For resources for aspiring and current nurses with disabilities, visit

ExceptionalNurse.com
www.exceptionalnurse.com

need for health care professionals, including nurses. In addition, the USDL reports that clinical nurse specialists, nurse practitioners, nurse-midwives, and nurse anesthetists will be in strong demand. Opportunities should also be good for nurses who "provide specialized long-term rehabilitation for stroke and head injury patients."

Despite the rosy outlook, the American Association of Colleges of Nursing (AACN) reports that enrollment in entry-level baccalaureate nursing programs grew by only 2.2 percent from 2007 to 2008. This growth is not enough to fill all available openings. The Health Resources and Services Administration states that "to meet the projected growth in demand for RN services, the U.S. must graduate approximately 90 percent more nurses from U.S. nursing programs."

Many students are interested in studying nursing, but they are finding it hard to land a coveted spot in nursing school. The AACN notes that 49,948 qualified applicants to baccalaureate and graduate nursing programs were turned away in 2008 due to "insufficient number of faculty, clinical sites, classroom space, clinical preceptors, and budget constraints."

What is causing the faculty shortages? Earnings and age are two of the most significant factors. According to the *New York Times,* nursing educators earn 40 to 50 percent less than nurses employed in clinical settings, which keeps qualified nurses who might be interested in pursuing a career in academe on the sidelines due to financial considerations. Additionally, many nurses are becoming educators late in their careers—the average age of nursing educators is 57—and many educators are retiring without being replaced.

To address these shortages, professional nursing organizations are working to secure federal funding for faculty development programs, creating scholarship programs for doctoral education (the typical educational requirement for top positions in nursing education), and attempting to develop a more direct route to the Ph.D. in order to encourage students to pursue nursing education at a younger age.

Interview: Thara   Gagni

Thara Gagni is a registered nurse in the Medical Intensive Care Unit at Northwestern Memorial Hospital in Chicago, Illinois. She discussed her career with the editors of *Hot Jobs.*

Q.   What made you want to enter this career?

A.   I entered this career because I always knew that I wanted to be in the medical field. It was not until my freshmen year of college that I narrowed my choice to nursing. My reasons were really quite simple: I enjoyed providing bedside care; I appreciated being able to build personal relationships with my patients and their families; as a nurse I appreciated the focus on taking care of and being the advocate of the patient (whereas I felt doctors took care of the disease); and there was plenty of directions a career in nursing could take.

Q. What is one thing that young people may not know about a career in nursing?

A. There are so many directions a career in nursing can take you. Some people enjoy bedside nursing, but you can go into politics, law, even business with a career in nursing. Our profession is needed literally EVERYWHERE in the world, so whether you're looking for jobs or volunteer opportunities, all you have to do is seek out where and what you want to be with your degree in nursing. The world is truly your oyster.

Q. What are the most important qualities for people in your career?

A. The most personal qualities for people in nursing, in my opinion, are understanding and compassion. If you take time to put yourself in your patient's shoes, or that of his or her family, you show more compassion. Compassion in nursing will always be an important quality, because when you show it and work with it, you provide the best care for your patients.

Professional qualities that are important in nursing are accountability, advocacy, cultural awareness, and flexibility. Nurses need to be aware they will be held accountable for their practice and the care they provide their patients. We deal with peoples' lives, and so being an advocate for our patients, their health and safety, is always a priority. We deal with many cultures and people of different backgrounds; it is important for nurses to be aware that our care may affect them culturally and vice versa. Being sensitive to a patient's culture and background is always important when trying to holistically care for their needs. In nursing, there is constant research, which means new practices, regulations, and evidence-based practice are always emerging. As nurses, we need to be flexible in this evolving profession.

Q. What do you like most and least about your career?

A. I am gratified after making connections with people despite what their admitting diagnosis may have been. I learn so much from their life experiences. And just when you think you've just had it sometimes in this profession, there will always be one family/patient that expresses their sincerest gratitude and appreciation for you and the work you have done. Now THAT makes anything and everything you go through worth it.

What I like the least? Being told that "you are just the nurse." And yes, it happens and it is said more often than you would like to admit.

Q. What advice would you give to aspiring nurses?

A. GO FOR IT! The opportunities are truly endless, and there is always room for improvement and advancement in this field. It is a gratifying profession and all that you do will always be of a great service to the rest of the community...and if you want, to the rest of the world.

Q. What is the employment outlook for registered nurses?

A. Due to the recent decline of our economy, job opportunities are not as easy to come by. But in all honesty, I truly believe that there will never come a time when nurses are not needed. They will always be a crucial part of the health care system; it is just a matter of initially finding your first experiences and from there discovering your true niche in the nursing profession.

Renewable Energy and Green Industry Workers

OVERVIEW

Public concerns about pollution from fossil fuels (oil, coal, etc.), rising prices for conventional energy sources, and our overdependence on foreign energy supplies have created strong interest in energy resources that are environmentally friendly and offer unlimited supplies. These renewable energy resources include wind, solar, hydropower, ocean, geothermal, and bioenergy. There is also increasing public interest in energy efficiency, sustainability practices in business, green construction, and the creation of advanced energy technologies, which is creating new career opportunities in these areas. *Renewable energy and green industry workers* are the people who work in these fields. They help us to live healthier lives while ensuring that we have enough sustainable energy to heat, cool, and light our homes; power our cars, computers, and other electronics; and generally have a less negative effect on our environment. In the United States, green industries currently provide 8.5 million jobs, according to the American Solar Energy Society (ASES). The ASES predicts that the renewable energy industry could grow to offer an additional 4.5 million jobs by 2030. Educational

FAST FACTS

High School Subjects
Biology
Business
Chemistry
Mathematics
Physics

Personal Skills
Mechanical
Scientific
Technical

Minimum Education Level
High school diploma (support positions)
Bachelor's degree (technical and professional positions)

Salary Range
$19,000 to $50,000 to $151,000+

Employment Outlook
Faster than the average

O*NET-SOC
11-2011.01, 13-2051.00, 11-3051.03, 11-3051.04, 11-3051.02, 11-3051.06, 11-3051.00, 11-3051.05, 11-3051.01, 11-9012.00, 11-9199.10, 13-1199.01, 13-1199.05, 17-2199.03, 17-2141.01, 17-2199.10, 17-2199.11, 19-2041.01, 19-3011.01, 19-3051.00, 41-3099.01, 47-1011.03, 49-9021.01, 51-8012.00

GOE
02.07.04, 02.08.04

DOT
007, 637, 809

NOC
7441

requirements vary for workers in the field. Some train for the field by completing apprenticeships or receiving on-the-job training. Others earn college degrees or certificates. Employment in the renewable energy industry is expected to be strong during the next decade.

THE JOB

The renewable energy industry can be broken up into the following sub-industries: wind, solar, hydropower, ocean, geothermal, and bioenergy. (Nuclear energy is considered an alternative energy source by some, but environmentalists fiercely disagree on whether its use is good or bad for the environment.) Renewable energy made up approximately 8 percent of energy consumption in the United States in 2009, according to the U.S. Department of Energy. In addition to opportunities in renewable energy, there are opportunities in energy efficiency, sustainable business practices, green construction, advanced vehicle technologies, and fuel cell technology. The following paragraphs detail these fields.

WIND

Wind energy (or wind power) is created by the conversion of wind into electricity. The energy of the wind is captured by wind turbines (or wind farms—a group of turbines). The wind turns the turbine blades, which then turn a shaft that is connected to a generator that makes the electricity. Wind industry professionals are employed in a variety of areas, including turbine component manufacturing, construction and installation of wind turbines, wind turbine operations and maintenance, marketing, legal services, customer support, transportation and logistical support, and office support. Career paths include *windsmiths* (sometimes called *mechanical* or *electrical technicians*), *construction workers and managers, electricians, civil engineers, crane operators, site managers, manufacturing workers, accountants, business development managers, electrical and mechanical engineers,* and *meteorologists.*

SOLAR

The sun has provided humans with light and warmth for hundreds of thousands of years; today, we are beginning to utilize the sun to create renewable energy. Referred to as solar energy, it can be harnessed wherever and whenever the sun shines on Earth. We capture solar energy via several methods. Sunlight is captured using solar thermal collectors and converted to solar thermal energy. This form of energy is used to heat water for residential use, including bathing and swimming pools. Thermal heat is also used to heat residential and large business spaces. Thermal heat is often referred to as passive, since it relies on location, design, or particular building materials to take advantage of the sun's heat or light. Solar energy is also captured and converted into another form, considered active—electricity. Solar-collecting power plants use the heat from the sun to heat and turn fluids into steam. This steam creates combustion, similar to that created by fossil fuels, to power generators. Photovoltaic (PV) or solar cells are another way of harnessing solar energy. PV cells, made from silicon alloys, are grouped into panels—the larger the group, the more electricity that is generated. PV cells work similarly to household batteries, generating direct current for small load equipment or alternating current for larger commercial applications.

While solar energy is free and a clean source of energy, it does have its drawbacks. The amount of sunlight changes depending on the time of day and season. Also, a large surface collecting area is needed to harness enough power to be useful.

There are many career options in the solar power industry, including *photovoltaic installers* (also known as *solar panel installers), solar designers and engineers, electrical engineers, chemical engineers, mechanical engineers, architects, solar installation managers, sales representatives, estimators, site assessors, mechanics, electricians, electrical equipment assemblers,* and *construction equipment operators.*

HYDROPOWER

The ancient Greeks took advantage of the power of water more than 2,000 years ago, relying on paddle wheels turned by flowing water to grind grain. Today, we use water to power machinery and create electricity. Hydropower is one of the cleanest sources of renewable energy; in fact, it creates 70 percent of all electricity produced from a renewable source, according to the National Energy Education Development Project. There are several ways to harness hydropower. Impoundment, the most common, is a large hydropower system that uses a dam to store water, creating a reservoir. When water is released from the reservoir, it flows through and spins a turbine. This spinning action activates a generator, thus producing electricity. The diversion system, also known as a "run of river" facility, channels a river through a specially made canal or penstock. Water is diverted through a turbine without use of a reservoir. Pumped storage facilities can control the amount of water flow. When the demand for electricity is low, water is pumped from a lower reservoir to an upper reservoir. Water is released back to the lower reservoir when demand for electricity increases.

While hydropower is a free and clean source of power, available on demand, it does have some disadvantages. Reservoirs and dams are expensive to build and maintain. They, at times, have a negative impact on the environment—mineral levels in the water are altered, and animals and plants can lose their natural habitats. Also, proper water levels are difficult to maintain during times of extreme drought.

Career options in the field include *electrical and mechanical engineers and technicians, civil engineers, architects, biologists* (to conduct environmental impact studies), *fish farmers* (to develop ways for fish to migrate past hydropower infrastructure), and *trail planners* and *land managers* (to create recreational paths and areas near reservoirs or dams).

OCEAN

Ocean energy consists of four main areas: wind, wave, current, and thermal. Wind energy utilizes turbines that are anchored offshore. Wave power involves the use of several different types of technologies that power electricity-generating turbines. In current power, turbines are placed horizontally in the water where strong currents exist (such as the Gulf Stream). Finally, thermal power uses the differences in temperature between the cold depths and the warm surface for power generation.

The ocean energy industry offers many opportunities for workers with multidisciplinary backgrounds. *Marine scientists* and *electronics, materials, acoustics,* and *fluid power engineers* should be in especially strong demand. *Maintenance* and *installation workers* will also be needed to maintain and build systems.

The Electric Power Research Institute has identified Alaska, Washington, Oregon, Maine, Massachusetts, Hawaii, and California as potentially viable wave power sites, although other states may also be considered with further study.

GEOTHERMAL

Geothermal energy taps the heat that is located deep inside the Earth. According to the U.S. Department of Energy (USDE), "geothermal resources include the heat retained in shallow ground, hot water and rock found a few miles beneath the Earth's surface, and extremely high-temperature molten rock called magma located deep in the Earth." It reports that the U.S. leads the world in existing geothermal capacity, and the field continues to enjoy strong growth. There are many job opportunities in geothermal energy. The USDE divides career paths into four areas: Physical and Earth Sciences (*chemists, geologists, hydrologists,* and *physicists);* Field Work and Operations (*carpenters, construction workers, designers, drilling equipment operators, electrical engineers, electricians, excavators, machinists, mechanical engineers, mechanics, pipefitters, plumbers, structural engineers, surveyors,* and *welders);* Sales and Finance (*accountants, attorneys, computer technicians, developers, entrepreneurs, financiers, investors,* and *suppliers);* and Policy and Permitting (*environmental consultants, land leasing specialists,* and *land surveyors).*

BIOENERGY

Bioenergy, or biomass, production involves the conversion of trees, crops (especially corn), wood chips, farm and municipal waste, algae, grass clippings, and straw into advanced biofuels. Bioenergy made up 50 percent of all renewable energy in the United States in 2009, according to the Energy Information Administration. According to the U.S. Department of Energy, there are career opportunities in four main areas: Feedstocks (*agricultural engineers, biochemists, chemical applications specialists, chemical engineers, chemical production workers, equipment production workers, farmers, genetic engineers and scientists, harvesting equipment mechanics, mechanical engineers,* and *tree farm workers);* Conversion (*chemical engineers, clean room technicians, industrial engineers, mechanical engineers, microbiologists,* and *plant operators);* End Use (*chemists, codes and standards developers, construction workers, consultants, regulation compliance workers,* and *station workers);* and Transport of Foodstocks and Biofuels (*barge operators, railcar operators, pipeline operators, truck drivers,* and *truck filling station workers).*

ENERGY EFFICIENCY

Our nation's focus on developing alternative energy resources and saving money by improving energy efficiency has created demand for energy efficiency workers. *Energy conservation technicians,* sometimes known as *energy auditors,* help businesses and consumers identify areas in which they can reduce energy usage. For example, they check heating and air-conditioning systems to make sure that they are not wasting energy and check for the presence of insulation, which can reduce heating and cooling costs. *Energy efficiency engineers* design and supervise the construction of equipment and systems that improve energy efficiency. Other opportunities are available for *roofers, insulation installers,* and *carpenters.*

ADVANCED VEHICLE TECHNOLOGIES

Efforts to attain energy security and reduce the effects of fossil fuels on the environment have prompted the auto manufacturing industry to develop new ecologically friendly technologies and products. These include biofuels, electric and hybrid vehicles, sustainable business practices, and manufacturing processes that create less pollution. According to the U.S. Department of Energy, there are career opportunities in three main areas: Technology Development (*chemical, electrical,* and *mechanical engineers; laboratory technicians;* and *materials scientists*); Technology Manufacturers (*industrial engineers, factory workers,* and *machinists*); and Technology Users (*automotive technicians; bus, truck,* and *fleet drivers;* and *fueling infrastructure installers*).

FUEL CELL TECHNOLOGY

Fuel cells provide cleaner, more renewable energy than conventional power generation sources. They are like batteries, but they do not run out of energy as long as they are provided with hydrogen. According to the USDE, fuel cells "can be used in a wide range of applications—from portable electronics, to stationary electricity generation, to passenger vehicles." Career options in the field include *chemical engineers, chemists, electrical engineers, factory workers, fueling infrastructure installers, hydrogen production technicians, industrial engineers, laboratory technicians, machinists, materials scientists, mechanical engineers, power plant operators,* and *vehicle technicians.*

GREEN CONSTRUCTION

The U.S. Environmental Protection Agency defines *green construction* as "the practice of creating structures and using processes that are environmentally responsible and resource-efficient throughout a building's lifecycle from siting to design, construction, operation, maintenance, renovation and deconstruction." Green construction is also known as *green building* or *sustainable* or *high-performance building. Construction workers* from all the trades work in this industry, but they have special training and experience in green construction techniques. They use sustainable building materials during construction or renovation, ensure that products used in indoor environments are ecologically friendly and have fewer toxic emissions than traditional building materials, and plant native trees, plants, and shrubs that require less water and fertilizers—which reduces water usage and protects the local soil and water supply from pollution.

SUSTAINABLE BUSINESS PRACTICES

Sustainable business practices aim to build profitability and economic stability while being mindful of the environment and promoting local communities. By using materials and/or operations that are less harmful to the environment, not only do the local community and physical environment benefit, but the company employing sustainable business practices can benefit too:

for example, by saving expenses from not having to handle potentially harmful raw materials and/or byproducts, or by possibly creating a superior product. Sustainable business practices embrace such concepts as biomimicry (studying nature and then imitating or adapting it to solve human problems), recycling, a "triple-bottom line" mindset (measuring success not only by the traditional "bottom line" benchmark of economic profit, but by also evaluating social justice and environmental "profit"), and whole-system thinking. *Sustainable business consultants* help businesses, government agencies, and other organizations develop sustainable business practices.

REQUIREMENTS

HIGH SCHOOL

If you plan to work in technical or professional positions, take a college-preparatory curriculum that includes classes in mathematics, science, English, speech, business, government, social studies, and computer science. Take shop, math, and physics classes if you know that you want to work in the construction aspect of the field. All aspiring renewable energy industry workers should take as many environmental classes as possible to learn more about environmental issues. If you want to work abroad, you should consider taking a foreign language.

POSTSECONDARY TRAINING

Educational requirements vary greatly by career. Technical workers, for example, typically require an associate or bachelor's degree. Construction trades workers usually prepare for the field by combining an apprenticeship with on-the-job training. Those who work in research and development typically have bachelor's or master's degrees in engineering or science. Some policy experts have master's degrees and Ph.D.s.

Courses in renewable-energy-related topics are offered by two- and four-year colleges throughout the United States, and a growing number of institutions offer certificates and degrees in the field. For a list of programs, visit www1.eere.energy.gov/education/educational_professional.html   or http://irecusa.org/irec-programs/workforce-development/education-information/university-courses. A list of wind energy educational programs can be accessed at www.windpoweringamerica.gov.

Typical classes vary by specialty, but a student in a general renewable energy education program will take the following courses: Physics; Mathematics; Introduction to Renewable Energy; Introduction to Energy Management; Renewable Energy Applications; Photovoltaic Theory and System Design; Photovoltaic Installation; Electrical Systems; Introduction to Wind Energy; Introduction to Solar Energy; Introduction to Hydropower; Introduction to Geothermal Energy; and Introduction to Bioenergy.

In addition to the creation of new renewable energy degrees in environmental science departments, colleges are also creating interdisciplinary majors that combine classes from a variety of departments, such as chemistry, biology, engineering, and environmental science. Montana State University, for example, recently launched a Sustainable Food and Bioenergy Systems interdisciplinary degree. According to the program's website (http://sfbs. montana.edu), the degree "promotes sustainable production, distribution and consumption of food and bioenergy by growing a new generation of leaders through collaborative learning and hands-on experience." College business and engineering departments are also adding environmentally-oriented courses to their curricula. A 2008 study by the National Wildlife Federation found that almost 30 percent of business departments and 22 percent of engineering departments offer environment-related courses.

Environmental sustainability has also become a popular focus of industry and on college campuses. The Association for the Advancement of Sustainability in Higher Education (www.aashe.org) reports that approximately 70 colleges now have sustainability-related academic programs. Sustainable-business programs attract socially and environmentally conscious students with an interest in business and a desire to help others acquire an understanding of the natural world's role in our lives. There are a wide variety of sustainability-related degrees available. Some are linked with business or traditional liberal arts majors such as economics. Others are more closely aligned with environmental science departments.

CERTIFICATION AND LICENSING

Certification is highly recommended. It is an excellent way to stand out from other job applicants and demonstrate your abilities to prospective employers. Certification is offered by state and national associations including the Association of Energy Engineers, the North American Board of Certified Energy Practitioners, the National Institute for Certification in Engineering Technologies, and the National Society of Professional Engineers. Certifications are typically voluntary, but photovoltaic technicians must be certified to work on most projects, especially those that are funded by the government. Other careers that may require licensing or certification include contractors, engineers, electricians, architects, and truck drivers.

OTHER REQUIREMENTS

Skill requirements vary by type of position, but all workers in the field should be highly organized, able to work well with others, be good at solving problems, have excellent communication skills, and be willing to continue to learn throughout their careers. An interest in protecting the environment is also important. Field workers must be in excellent physical condition; those who service wind towers or work in other above-ground areas must not be afraid of heights.

EXPLORING

There are many ways to learn more about a career as a renewable energy or green-industry worker. You can read books about the field such as *Careers in Renewable Energy,* by Gregory McNamee (PixyJack Press, 2008); *75 Green Businesses You Can Start to Make Money and Make a Difference,* by Glenn Croston (Entrepreneur Media Inc., 2008); *Green Jobs: Working for People and the Environment* (Worldwatch Report 177), by Michael Renner, Sean

Sweeney, and Jill Kubit (The Worldwatch Institute, 2008); *Green Jobs: A Guide to Eco-Friendly Employment,* by A. Bronwyn Llewellyn (Adams Media, 2008); and *Green Building & Remodeling For Dummies,* by Eric Corey Freed (For Dummies, 2007). Periodicals such as *Green Careers Journal* (http://environmentalcareer.com/green-careers-journal) will provide you with an excellent introduction to the field. You can also visit the websites of college programs to learn about typical classes and possible career paths, and you can ask your teacher or school counselor to arrange an information interview with a renewable energy professional.

There are also many competitions for students in grades K-12 that can help you get hands-on experience and allow you to interact with teachers and fellow students who are interested in the field. These include ExploraVision (www.exploravision.org), National Junior Solar Sprint/Hydrogen Fuel Cell Car Competitions (www.nrel.gov/education/jss_hfc.html), and the Igniting Creative Energy Challenge (www.ignitingcreativeenergy.org). Visit www1.eere.energy.gov/education/k12_competitions.html and www.nrel.gov/education/k12_students.html for a list of more competitions.

Professional associations can also provide information about the field. See the organizations listed in the For More Information section for contact information.

EMPLOYERS

Renewable energy workers are employed by manufacturing companies; research and development firms; utility companies; government agencies (such as the National Renewable Energy Laboratory); nonprofit groups and agencies; colleges and universities; trade associations; engineering firms; and architectural firms.

Approximately 85,000 people are employed in the wind power industry. States with the largest wind power generating capacity (in descending order) are Texas, Iowa, California, Washington, and Oregon.

About 60,000 people are employed in the solar energy industry.

Approximately 25,000 people work in the geothermal industry, according to the Geothermal Energy Association.

The U.S. Green Building Council reports that the green construction market currently supports more than 2.4 million jobs.

GETTING A JOB

Many renewable energy workers obtain their first jobs as a result of contacts made through college internships or networking events. Others seek assistance in obtaining job leads from college career services offices, newspaper want ads, and career fairs. Additionally, professional associations, such as the National Society of Professional Engineers, the U.S. Green Building Council, and the American Solar Energy Society, provide job listings at their websites. See For More Information for a list of organizations. Employment websites are also a good source of jobs. Some popular sites include RenewableEnergyWorld.com (www.renewableenergyworld.com/rea/careers); Green Jobs (www.greenjobs.

com), EnergyVortex.com (www.energyvortex.com/careercenter), Careers in Wind (www.careersinwind.com), Ethanol-Jobs.com (www.ethanol-jobs.com), and Environmental Career.com (http://environmental-jobs.com). Those interested in positions with the federal government should visit the U.S. Office of Personnel Management's website, www.usajobs.opm.gov.

ADVANCEMENT

Advancement opportunities vary by specialty, but most workers can advance by receiving higher earnings, being asked to take on managerial duties, returning to school to improve their credentials and advance to different careers or job levels, and moving to larger companies or organizations. Some workers become college professors or start their own consulting firms. Others write books about renewable energy and green-industry practices.

EARNINGS

Earnings for renewable energy and green-industry workers vary by type of employer, geographic region, and the worker's education, experience, and skill level. Salaries for green-industry workers are similar or slightly lower than those earned by their counterparts in traditional industries. But industry experts report that this is offset by the fact that green-industry careers provide workers with better and more frequent opportunities to advance and expand their skill sets—as well as work in employment sectors that will experience long-term growth. Here are some typical salary ranges for workers in the field (courtesy of the U.S. Department of Labor, with salary data from 2009): architects, $42,320 to $122,640; biological scientists, $36,750 to $100,580; carpenters, $24,600 to $70,750; chemical engineers, $56,090 to $132,980; civil engineers, $49,620 to $118,320; conservation scientists, $35,570 to $87,890; construction managers, $49,320 to $151,630; electrical engineers, $53,510 to $126,810; electricians, $28,690 to $80,260; engineering technicians, $30,910 to $86,510; environmental engineers, $47,660 to $115,750; hydrologists, $46,290 to $110,110; lawyers, $55,270 to $113,240; materials engineers, $52,670 to $125,660; mechanical engineers, $49,730 to $117,550; secretaries, $19,190 to $45,170; and surveyors, $30,130 to $89,120.

In 2010, the Association of Energy Engineers conducted a survey of its members. It found that they earned an average salary of $96,001. Nearly 10 percent of respondents earned less than $60,000, and nearly 10 percent earned more than $130,000.

Employers offer a variety of benefits, including the following: medical, dental, and life insurance; paid holidays, vacations, and sick and personal days; 401(k) plans; profit-sharing plans; retirement and pension plans; and educational assistance programs. Self-employed workers must provide their own benefits.

EMPLOYMENT OUTLOOK

Overall employment in the renewable energy industry and related fields is expected to be very good through 2018. Faced with rising fuel prices and increasing pollution of our air, water, and soil, the U.S. government is strongly focusing on developing renewable energy resources. Summaries for specific sub-industries are provided in the following paragraphs.

Employment in the wind industry is booming. According to a report from the American Wind Energy Association (AWEA), wind energy has been the fastest-growing energy technology in the world since 2006. The U.S. wind industry employs more than 85,000 people. The AWEA estimates that the U.S. wind energy industry will grow by 300 to 400 percent in the next decade—which will create excellent opportunities for windsmiths, technicians, engineers, and electricians.

Opportunities are expected to be excellent in the solar power industry. The U.S. ranks fourth in the world (after Germany,. Italy, and Japan) for new solar electric installations, and the industry will continue to expand during the next decade.

Employment should also be good in the hydropower industry. A Navigant Consulting, Inc. study commissioned by the National Hydropower Association estimates that anywhere from 480,000 to 1.4 million jobs will be created by 2025 if "existing federal and state incentives for renewable energy development, such as tax incentives and state Renewable Energy Standards programs, remain in place." Although jobs are available throughout the United States, opportunities are expected to be best in the Western states.

The geothermal industry is undergoing rapid expansion, In fact, the number of domestic geothermal projects grew by 26 percent from 2009 to 2010, according to the U.S. Department of Energy. The Geothermal Energy Association reports that "six million Americans use geothermal energy in their homes...three million receive electricity from geothermal power plants...and another three million use geothermal heat pumps to heat and cool their homes." As a result, more workers will be needed to locate new geothermal resources and build and monitor infrastructure.

The National Energy Foundation predicts that the use of biomass to produce energy will grow by 33 percent through 2013. The Energy Independence and Security Act of 2007 calls for renewable fuels to make up a larger portion of motor fuels by 2022, and current biofuel output is only 25 percent of what is mandated by law by 2022.

The market research firm Frost & Sullivan estimates that ocean energy output will increase from "almost nothing to more than 3,000 megawatts, equivalent to four coal power plants by 2020."

In addition to renewable energy careers, opportunities in the general environmental industry are also good. Energy efficiency, and environmental engineering are especially strong fields at the moment. Other good options include those with clean technology companies (which "create products and services that improve performance, productivity, or efficiency while reducing costs, inputs, or pollution," according to WetFeet.com) and those in green building (a $12 billion industry that is expected to support more than 7.9 million jobs from 2009 to 2013, according to the U.S. Green Building Council).

One major trend in the environmental/renewable industries is the emergence of green-collar jobs, which require more than a high-school diploma but less than a four-year degree. Experts predict that the number of green-collar jobs will grow by anywhere from 100,000 in the next few years (according to the School of Public and International Affairs at North Carolina State University) to three million jobs in the next decade (according to The Apollo Alliance, an environmental coalition).

Finally, a report by the American Solar Energy Society predicts that tackling climate change will be a great job creator in coming years. According to *Estimating the Jobs Impact of Tackling Climate Change,* "aggressive deployment of renewable energy and energy efficiency may net up to 4.5 million new U.S. jobs by 2030." Job opportunities will be available throughout the United States to people from all educational backgrounds. Some of the careers that will enjoy strong growth include plumbers, electricians, carpenters, machinists, administrative assistants, cashiers, management analysts, civil engineers, and sheet metal workers.

FOR MORE INFORMATION

GENERAL RESOURCES
For information on energy efficiency, contact
**American Council for
an Energy-Efficient Economy**
529 14th Street, NW, Suite 600
Washington, DC 20045-1000
202-507-4000
www.aceee.org

For more information on green-collar jobs and education, contact the following organizations
Apollo Alliance
330 Townsend Street, Suite 205
San Francisco, CA 94107-1662
415-371-1700
http://apolloalliance.org

Green for All
1611 Telegraph Avenue, Suite 600
Oakland, CA 94612-2149
510-663-6500
www.greenforall.org

For information on careers and certification, contact
Association of Energy Engineers
4025 Pleasantdale Road, Suite 420
Atlanta, GA 30340-4260
770-447-5083
www.aeecenter.org

For information on renewable energy and careers in the field, visit
**Energy Efficiency
and Renewable Energy**
U.S. Department of Energy
Mail Stop EE-1
Washington, DC 20585
877-337-3463
www.eere.energy.gov

For industry statistics, contact
Energy Information Administration
1000 Independence Avenue, SW
Washington, DC 20585-0001
www.eia.doe.gov/fuelrenewable.html

For information about renewable energy and a database of postsecondary training programs, contact
**Interstate Renewable
Energy Council**
PO Box 1156
Latham, NY 12110-1156
518-458-6059
info@irecusa.org
www.irecusa.org

For industry information, contact
**Midwest Renewable
Energy Association**
7558 Deer Road
Custer, WI 54423-9734
info@the-mrea.org
www.the-mrea.org

For information on renewable energy, internships, and careers, contact

**National Renewable
Energy Laboratory**
1617 Cole Boulevard
Golden, CO 80401-3305
303-275-3000
www.nrel.gov

For information on licensure, contact

**National Society
of Professional Engineers**
1420 King Street
Alexandria, VA 22314-2794
703-684-2800
www.nspe.org

For information on green construction, contact

U.S. Green Building Council
2101 L Street, NW, Suite 500
Washington, DC 20037-1599
www.usgbc.org

WIND
For information on wind energy and postsecondary training programs, contact

American Wind Energy Association
1501 M Street, NW, Suite 1000
Washington, DC 20005-1769
202-383-2500
windmail@awea.org
www.awea.org

SOLAR
For information about solar energy, contact the following organizations

American Solar Energy Society
2400 Central Avenue, Suite A
Boulder, CO 80301-2862
303-443-3130
ases@ases.org
www.ases.org

Solar Electric Power Association
1220 19th Street, NW, Suite 401
Washington, DC 20036-2405
202-857-0898
www.solarelectricpower.org

Solar Energy Industries Association
575 7th Street, NW, Suite 400
Washington DC 20004-1612
202-682-0556
info@seia.org
www.seia.org

HYDROPOWER
For information about hydropower, contact

National Hydropower Association
25 Massachusetts Avenue, NW,
Suite 450
Washington, DC 20001-7405
202-682-1700
help@hydro.org
www.hydro.org

OCEAN ENERGY
For information on ocean energy, visit the coalition's website.

Ocean Renewable Energy Coalition
www.oceanrenewable.com

GEOTHERMAL
Contact the following organizations for more information about geothermal energy.

Geothermal Education Office
664 Hilary Drive
Tiburon, CA 94920-1446
415-435-4574
geo@marin.org
www.geothermal.marin.org

Geothermal Energy Association
209 Pennsylvania Avenue, SE
Washington, DC 20003-1107
202-454-5261
research@geo-energy.org
www.geo-energy.org

BIOENERGY
For information on bioenergy, contact

Renewable Fuels Association
425 Third Street, SW, Suite 1150
Washington, DC 20024-3231
202-289-3835
www.ethanolrfa.org

SOFTWARE ENGINEERS

OVERVIEW

Software engineers design, develop, and test software that is used for businesses' operating systems, network management, or database management. Many times software engineers may adapt a software program to fit the specific needs of a client or its business. They also develop a wide variety of software that is used by consumers, including computer games, operating systems, business applications, network control systems, and middleware. A minimum of a bachelor's degree in computer information systems, computer science, mathematics, or software engineering is required to work in the field; some employers prefer applicants to have a master's degree. Approximately 909,600 software engineers work in the United States. Employment for these workers is expected to grow much faster than the average for all careers through 2018.

FAST FACTS

High School Subjects
  Computer science
  Mathematics

Personal Skills
  Communication
  Complex problem solving
  Critical thinking
  Technical

Minimum Education Level
  Bachelor's degree

Salary Range
  $54,000 to $90,000 to
  $139,000+

Employment Outlook
  Much faster than the average

O*NET-SOC
  15-1031.00, 15-1032.00

GOE
  02.07.01

DOT
  030

NOC
  2173

THE JOB

What would life be like without software? There would be no computers as we know them today. No Internet. No modern cars!—software is used in their electronic systems. No video games, cell phones, or countless other electronic gadgets that we have come to take for granted in our fast-paced, highly technological lives. Without software, it would be much harder to design and lay-out books like this one and create animated movies and television shows. In short, our lives have become easier—and more fun—as a result of software, and most people wouldn't want to return to the days when it did not exist.

Many businesses rely on software to store and manage data, sell products, track inventory, and perform a variety of other tasks. Software engineers create many of these applications. Using theories and principles of computer science and mathematics, they design, develop, and test software for many different companies, businesses, and individual consumers. Their projects range from business applications, to operating systems, to computer games.

When working on a new project, software engineers identify the potential user. Are they designing accounting software to be used by an international company? Software for a handheld GPS unit? A video game? A cell phone? An app for an iPhone? Or a new feature for a website? They often travel to the company headquarters or client's office to consult on the design and maintenance of the software system.

Software engineers often consult with hardware engineers regarding certain aspects of the project. They work together to evaluate the interface between hardware and software and to determine if the company's main computer hardware has the performance capacity to handle the new software. Software engineers also analyze the time needed to develop the software and the final cost of the project.

Software engineers create flowcharts, diagrams, and other documentation during the design process to help them get a handle on the project. Then they create algorithms, which act as instructions, telling the computer what actions to execute. These algorithms are converted into special coding or programming by *computer programmers*. However, some software engineers also play a role in the actual programming. Popular program languages include C, C++, Java, and Python.

There are two types of software engineers: *applications software engineers* and *systems software engineers*. Applications software engineers create customized applications as determined by the client's needs. After deployment, these applications or special utility programs are often tested and debugged until the applications run smoothly. Software engineers may use existing diagnostic computer programs or design a unique program to detect potential flaws in the system. Applications engineers may also create or develop databases.

Systems software engineers work with a company's existing computer system. They expand, construct, or maintain the system based to the company's needs. For example, they may coordinate computer software for different departments—such as customer service, inventory, or billing. They may develop a file transfer or a network protocol such as TCP/IP or IPX/SPX. Systems engineers also create computer networks that allow departments to access shared information or create easier departmental communication. Depending on the size and location of the company and any satellite offices, they may use WAN (wide area network) or LAN (local area network) connectivity and network management software. Engineers are also responsible for ensuring system and data security using passwords, firewalls, and other security measures.

Some software engineers create and maintain technical documentation for a project. Others coordinate the installation of a software system, often supervising the work of programmers, analysts, and technicians.

Full-time software engineers work about 40 hours a week. However, overtime is necessary, and often unavoidable, especially when an important deadline is looming. Approximately 15 percent of software engineers work more than 50 hours a week. Most software engineers work in comfortable offices. They spend a considerable amount of time in front of a computer but also attend meetings and travel to meet with clients. When assigned a new project, software engineers often meet with the client to identify the client's needs and goals. Once the project is underway, engineers can often telecommute from their homes via the Internet, accessing the computers of clients remotely via special software programs.

Overall duties will vary depending on the size of the company or organization and the nature of its business. For example, a large insurance company may employ many software engineers to manage a large-scale project, with one of two engineers assigned to perform a small role within the project. However, a smaller company, such as an independent clothing store, may employ one computer professional on staff. That one person may be responsible for duties ranging from all software programming needs to training coworkers on how to use new software and navigate the company's computer network.

REQUIREMENTS

High School

Take as many mathematics and computer science classes as possible in high school. Those that help you develop your problem-solving and critical-thinking skills will be most useful. Other important classes include English and speech.

Postsecondary Training

A minimum of a bachelor's degree is required to work in the field; some employers require applicants to have a master's degree. Applications software engineers usually have degrees in computer science, software engineering, or mathematics. Systems software engineers usually have majored in computer science or computer information systems. It also helps to have industry-specific knowledge. For example, a software engineer who works in the health information management industry should have an understanding of the health care field and the way in which computers are used to store, manage, and analyze patient information.

The Accreditation Board for Engineering and Technology accredits software engineering programs. Visit its website, www.abet.org, for a searchable database of accredited programs.

Software engineering technology is constantly changing and evolving. Software engineers must keep abreast of these innovations through continuing education classes, seminars, and conferences.

Certification and Licensing

Product vendors and software firms offer voluntary certification to software engineers. Certification is also offered by professional computing associations such as the Institute for Certification of Computing Professionals (www.iccp.org) and the IEEE Computer Society. Contact these organizations for more information. Certification, while voluntary, is highly recommended. It is an excellent way to stand out from other job applicants and demonstrate your abilities to prospective employers.

OTHER REQUIREMENTS

To be a successful software engineer, you will need excellent analytical and technical skills. You must be able to solve problems and "think outside the box" to come up with solutions for difficult design challenges. Other important traits include strong communication skills, the ability to multitask, attention to detail, the ability to work well under pressure, and a willingness to continue to learn throughout your career.

Pros and Cons

Kathy Land, a principal software and systems engineer at The MITRE Corp, describes what she likes least and most about her job:

"I am now at the later stages of my career and really cannot think of any con that stands out. The cons that really got to me early in my career were issues associated with bad management. Having project managers in charge of Information Technology (IT) projects who were not qualified IT managers; they were not software engineers. Fortunately, the field of software engineering is maturing and the depth and breadth of qualified individuals in our profession is growing.

As far as pros, there are a few that stand out. 1) As with any technical field, your capability is a great equalizer. If you are talented and you work hard, you will have a great career. The field of software engineering is a level one; 2) there is always something new to learn, work never gets stale; and 3) if you are talented, you do not have to tolerate a bad employer."

EXPLORING

Does a career as a software engineer sound exciting? If so, there are many ways to explore the career while still in school. You can read books and magazines (such as *Computerworld*) to learn more about the computer industry. Visit the websites of college computer science departments to learn about typical classes and possible career paths. Ask your teacher or school counselor to arrange an information interview with a software engineer.

To help young people explore opportunities in computer science, the Association for Computing Machinery and other organizations have created a useful website, Computing Degrees and Careers (http://computingcareers.acm.org), that provides a wealth of information about important skills, educational requirements, and career paths; interviews with computer science students and recent graduates; and answers to frequently asked questions about the field, such as Didn't the opportunities in the field disappear when the dot-com bubble collapsed in 2000? and Aren't computing jobs solitary and boring? Here are a few other useful sites for those interested in learning more about software engineering careers: Why Choose Computer Science & Engineering? (www.cs.washington.edu/WhyCSE), Junior Engineering Technical Society (www.jets.org/explore/what/software.html), and Sloan Career Cornerstone Center (http://careercornerstone.org).

EMPLOYERS

Approximately 909,600 software engineers are employed in the United States. Approximately 57 percent specialize in applications software, while 43 percent focus on systems software. About 32 percent of software engineers work for computer systems design and related services firms. Other major employers include government agencies, the computer security industry, software publishers, the computer manufacturing industry, financial institutions, insurance companies, telecommunications companies, and virtually any industry (medical, industrial, aerospace, scientific, etc.) that produces products or services that require software engineering.

GETTING A JOB

Many software engineers obtain their first jobs as a result of contacts made through college internships or networking events. Others seek assistance in obtaining job leads from college career services offices and newspaper want ads. Additionally, professional associations, such as the IEEE Computer Society, provide job listings and career articles at their websites. See For More Information for a list of organizations. Many computer professionals also seek out job opportunities at job-search websites such as Dice (www.dice.com), Robert Half Technology (www.roberthalftechnology.com), ComputerJobs.com (www.computerjobs.com), and Crunchboard (www.crunchboard.com). Those interested in positions with the federal government should visit the U.S. Office of Personnel Management's website, www.usajobs.opm.gov.

ADVANCEMENT

In addition to receiving pay increases or working on larger projects, software engineers with advanced training and experience can be promoted to the position of project manager, manager of information systems, or chief information officer. The U.S. Department of Labor reports that others "can find lucrative opportunities as systems designers or independent consultants, particularly in specialized fields such as business-to-business transactions or security and data assurance." Others become college professors.

EARNINGS

Salaries for software engineers vary by type of employer, geographic region, and the worker's education, experience, and skill level. New graduates with a bachelor's degree in computer science received average starting salary offers of $61,407 in July 2009, according to the National Association of Colleges and Employers.

Median annual salaries for software engineers-applications were $87,480 in 2009, according to the U.S. Department of Labor. Salaries ranged from less than $54,840 to $132,080 or more. Software engineers-systems software earned median annual salaries of $93,470. Ten percent earned less than $59,600, and 10 percent earned $139,930 or more.

According to *Computerworld*'s 2010 Salary Survey, software engineers earned an average base salary of $88,697 and an additional $4,250 in bonuses.

Employers offer a variety of benefits, including the following: medical, dental, and life insurance; paid holidays, vacations, and sick and personal days; 401(k) plans; profit-sharing plans; retirement and pension plans; and educational assistance programs. Self-employed workers must provide their own benefits.

EMPLOYMENT OUTLOOK

Opportunities should be excellent for software engineers. Employment in software publishing is expected to increase by 32 percent from 2008 to 2018, according to the U.S. Department of Labor (USDL)—or nearly three times as fast as the average for all industries. The USDL projects that the career of

FOR MORE INFORMATION

For information on education and careers, visit the association's websites.

**Association for
Computing Machinery**
2 Penn Plaza, Suite 701
New York, NY 10121-0701
800-342-6626
http://computingcareers.acm.org
www.acm.org

For membership information, contact
Association for Women in Computing
41 Sutter Street, Suite 1006
San Francisco, CA 94104-4905
info@awc-hq.org
www.awc-hq.org

For industry news, contact
**Association of Information
Technology Professionals**
401 North Michigan Avenue,
Suite 2400
Chicago, IL 60611-4267
www.aitp.org

For information on careers and certification, contact
IEEE Computer Society
2001 L Street, NW, Suite 700
Washington, DC 20036-4910
202-371-0101
help@computer.org
www.computer.org

For information about software engineers, "extreme" software engineers, and student competitions, contact
**Junior Engineering
Technical Society**
1420 King Street, Suite 405
Alexandria, VA 22314-2750
703-548-5387
info@jets.org
www.jets.org

For information on high school competitions and women in the computer industry, contact
**National Center for Women
and Information Technology**
University of Colorado
Campus Box 322 UCB
Boulder, CO 80309-0322
www.ncwit.org

For news about software engineering, visit the SIIA website.
**Software and Information
Industry Association (SIIA)**
1090 Vermont Avenue, NW, Sixth Floor
Washington, DC 20005-4095
202-289-7442
www.siia.net

software engineer is among the occupations that is expected to grow the fastest and add the most new jobs through 2018. Additionally, the career of software engineer was chosen by CareerCast.com as the second-best job in 2010 based on five criteria (income, work environment, stress level, employment outlook, and physical demands of the job).

Employment will grow as a result of the increasing use of computer networking, expanding Internet technologies, growing emphasis on computer security, and increasing demand for new mobile applications and software systems (including those that are used by businesses).

Advanced manufacturing, which requires the merger of manufacturing and information technology, is one of the key industries fueling demand for these workers. Other industries that will need software engineers include information security, Internet consulting, and telecommunications. Software engineers with "strong programming, systems analysis, interpersonal, and business skills" and at least a bachelor's degree will have the best employment opportunities, according to the USDL.

Interview: Kathy Land

Kathy Land is a principal software and systems engineer at The MITRE Corp. She has worked in the field for more than 20 years, and is the author or co-author of four books on software engineering. Kathy discussed her career with the editors of *Hot Jobs*.

Q. **What made you want to enter this career?**

A. I do not know if I really 'chose' to enter the field initially, but rather sort of fell into it. My degree was not in computer science. In fact, the University of Georgia did not initially offer a degree in computer science until 1984, the year I graduated. My first job was working in the Department of Genetics at the University, and I helped the professors develop their grant proposals. It was challenging because this was prior to the advances we now see in what is available in the most basic word processing programs. We were using some type of IBM mainframe system to layout the fruit fly (a.k.a., drosophilia melanogaster) genetic mappings. While the Ph.D.s were breaking genetic codes, I was able to decipher how the system worked and was able to translate their most complex diagrams. I was also able to keep the IBM system up and operational. I helped them, in a very real way, get their research accomplished.

When I went to school, programming courses were offered, but they were not attractive. All I could see at the time were the bleary-eyed folks carrying stacks of strange rectangular cards coming from the engineering building. I discovered, during this first job, that computers and programming were much more than what I saw on campus, and I was hooked.

I was lucky enough to parlay this first job into a second as a computer systems programmer working at the Pacific Missile Test Center in the Standard Missile Laboratory. The languages don't really matter now, because they are all extinct, what does really matter is that I was fortunate to work during a time when technology was rapidly changing, much more so than it does today. I was around when Sperry's were the

rage, when the first Mac's came out in the Department of Defense laboratories (what an impact!), and have seen how the increases in processing
power and storage capabilities daily affected our abilities to compute.

Q.   What is one thing that young people may not know about a career in software engineering?

A.   Individuals have to constantly learn and adapt. Although the pace of
change associated with our field has slowed down somewhat over the
past five to 10 years, the field is still pretty dynamic. Folks cannot just
think that they are going to get a degree and that this will be followed
with success without years of additional hard work. The degree is the
starting point. If you do not love solving complex problems, do not enter
this field. The challenges will be there with every new project.

Employers are looking for more than an individual who can program;
they are looking for folks who understand the software life cycle and
who can adapt to changing requirements. Each specific application
domain requires a slightly different software engineering expertise. Here
is what I mean, if you go into the Department of Defense as opposed to
commercial game development or if you are developing software for
banking as opposed to software to support safety critical infrastructure
associated with say, a nuclear power facility. While the core knowledge
requirements are common, a slightly differing set of software engineering skills are required to support each of these specific domains to deliver successfully.

Did You Know?

Only 21 college software engineering programs are accredited by the
Accreditation Board for Engineering Technology. Visit www.abet.org for a
list of programs.

Q.   What advice would you give to aspiring software engineers? What is the best way to land a job?

A.   Start early working to gain as much experience as possible. Working as a
waiter may get you more cash in tips, but interning during the summer
helping the network guy maintain the local college IT infrastructure will
do more to help you in your career (and on your résumé) down the road.
Think long term when looking for summer employment.

For new graduates, attend job fairs, etc. However, a reality check, just
because you graduated with a tremendous GPA does not mean that you
are guaranteed an offer, or will even be placed at the top of some
recruiter's list. You are still behind all those who may be temporally
unemployed with significantly more experience (and with active security
clearances). Today's job market is particularly tough on those looking to
break into the field. My advice is to take any entry-level position. It is
easier to get a job once you have a job.

Q.   What are the most important skills for software engineers?

A.   Software engineers should understand and uphold the Software Engineering
Code of Ethics (www.acm.org/about/se-code) and should have a solid work-

ing knowledge of the areas described in the Software Engineering Body of Knowledge. Software engineers are responsible for designing, implementing, and modifying software. The biggest issue that I see is that although many software engineers are not involved in the direct development of code, many of these same individuals who are categorized as software engineers have NEVER written a line of code. This is a problem, particularly if these folks are managing development efforts. As they say, 'you have to have ridden a horse to understand how high one can jump.'

Q. What has been one (or more) of the most rewarding experiences in your career and why?

A. When I think back on my career, almost every project I have been on comes to mind. It is not only the work, but the teams that have made this such a great career. Every project has had its own type of reward and has left its own unique positive stamp on my career. I think that testimony could be offered up as a pretty strong argument to those who might be considering software engineering as a career field.

There have been some pretty 'cool' things that I have been able to do. My work has taken me inside the Department of Justice, the FBI, and a Black Hawk helicopter. While working to support the America's Army gaming platform I live-fired every type of weapon in game at the time. I have developed software that runs the applications gamut in size and scope. The most rewarding thing about my career is that I am looking forward to the next 20 years.

SPECIAL EDUCATION TEACHERS

OVERVIEW

Special education teachers design and modify curriculum and teaching methods to work with children and adolescents who have special needs—from the hearing or visually impaired, to students with physical or mental/emotional disabilities, to students with specific learning disabilities. Some also work with intellectually gifted students, those who have suffered physical or mental abuse, and those who do not speak English proficiently. Special education teachers work in schools (pre-K through high school) either within general education classes or in separate classrooms. They also work in hospitals and make home visits. All special education teachers must be licensed. Some states require teachers to have a bachelor's degree in special education as part of their licensing requirements; others require a master's degree. Approximately 473,000 special education teachers work in the United States. Employment opportunities should be excellent through 2018.

FAST FACTS

High School Subjects
English
Speech

Personal Skills
Communication
Helping
Leadership

Minimum Education Level
Bachelor's degree

Salary Range
$34,000 to $51,000 to $83,000+

Employment Outlook
Faster than the average

O*NET-SOC
25-2041.00, 25-2042.00, 25-2043.00

GOE
12.03.03

DOT
094

NOC
4141, 4142

THE JOB

A typical day for a special education teacher varies depending on the age and disability of the students they serve and on the work setting. Disabilities that may require students to participate in special education include autism, combined deafness and blindness, emotional disturbance, hearing impairments, mental retardation, multiple disabilities, orthopedic impairments, specific learning disabilities, speech or language impairments, traumatic brain injury, visual impairments, and other health problems. The most common work settings include preschools and elementary, middle, and secondary schools. A few special education teachers work with infants and toddlers.

Educators who work with young children focus on using play to teach, much like general elementary teachers. However, these special educators have to consider the emotional or physical constraints of their students when developing their lessons. For example, they may have to use modified toys to help a student who is visually impaired. *Middle* and *high school special education educators* teach older students with special needs. As curriculum and testing become more advanced, these teachers must modify teaching and assessment tools to ensure that students have an equal opportunity to learn and advance. For example, they may discover that one student may learn better through oral lessons rather than reading a textbook. In this instance, they prepare special audio recordings or CDs for the student to listen to at home. A student with a physical disability might need to learn with the assistance of computer touch-screen technology. Another student may have challenges with time constraints when taking tests, so the special educator will administer tests untimed in order to provide him or her with extra time to complete the test.

In addition to varieties in ages and disabilities, special education teachers' careers vary by employment setting. Some work in general classrooms alongside teachers (this approach is called "mainstreaming"). These classes, also called "inclusive" or "self-contained" classes, mix general education students with students with special needs. The special educator will take the classroom teacher's lesson plans or unit goals and modify them to better suit the special-needs student. Some may create lesson plans from scratch. Other special education teachers work in resource rooms with students coming in and out all day based on specific schedules. This method, called the "pull-out classroom," allows the teacher to work one-on-one with the student, but it has disadvantages in that it can make the student feel singled out or isolated from his or her peers. Some schools mix the two methods.

All students, regardless of their needs, have what is called an Individualized Education Plan (IEP). The IEP establishes personalized goals for the student based on his or her disability and learning style. The ultimate goal of the IEP is to prepare the student for advancement to the next educational level and/or employment. It is usually the job of the special education teacher to develop and record progress on the student's IEP. This is used to communicate progress and goals to parents and all teachers within the school who work with the student. The IEP is also used for state reporting. Preparing and maintaining students' IEPs can be challenging—especially because the teacher must also grade student performance, take attendance, meet with other teachers to discuss student performance and education goals, and correspond and/or meet with parents regarding their children's progress.

All special education teachers, whether they work in classrooms or in special resource rooms, need to be able to collaborate with others. Students with special needs achieve more when they have the full cooperation of teachers, special education teachers and assistants, parents, community agencies, and school administrators, who all work together to assist the student. Each member of the team brings unique insight and expertise that can be used to help the child remain challenged and focused and continue to learn.

Some special education teachers specialize in preparing students for life after graduation by assisting with job training and placement or life skills development (such as balancing a checkbook, developing good grooming habits, or learning how to use public transportation). They work with community agencies to line up jobs, training programs, or other resources for a student once he or she transitions out of the school.

Special education teachers may also conduct home visits or visit hospitalized children with disabilities.

A career as a special education teacher can be physically and emotionally draining. Educators may become frustrated by uncooperative students or get overwhelmed working with a student who has an increasing number of setbacks. The amount of paperwork required for the job can also be frustrating. However, most special educators agree that helping students succeed in life and in school is incredibly rewarding and outweighs the frustrations. They also cite their ability to build strong relationships with students as another perk of the job.

REQUIREMENTS

High School

In high school, take courses in health, mathematics, English, speech, computer science, and psychology. Participate in any activities in which you can help or teach others.

Postsecondary Training

All special education teachers must be licensed. Some states require teachers to have a bachelor's degree in special education as part of the licensing requirements; others require a master's degree. Some states offer alternative qualification programs for people with bachelor's degrees but no experience in education. Special education training programs are offered at the undergraduate, master's, and doctoral degree levels. Visit www.personnelcenter.org/get.cfm for a searchable database of programs.

Certification and Licensing

The American Academy of Special Education Professionals offers voluntary board certification to special education teachers who have at least a master's degree and pass an examination. Contact the academy for more information.

All 50 states and the District of Columbia require special education teachers to be licensed. The National Center for Special Education Personnel and Related Service Providers offers information on licensing requirements for each state at its website, www.personnelcenter.org/licensure.cfm.

Other Requirements

Successful special education teachers are empathetic, emotionally stable, open-minded, creative, organized, patient, and good motivators. They also have strong communication skills. In addition to working closely with students, they interact frequently with parents, other teachers, social workers, psychologists, therapists, and school administrators. Approximately 64 percent of special education teachers belong to a union or are covered by a union contract.

EXPLORING

There are many ways to learn more about a career as a special education teacher. You can read books and periodicals about the field, visit the websites of college special education programs to learn about typical classes and possible career paths, and talk to a special education teacher at your school about the rewards and challenges of his or her career. Perhaps you can observe a special education class while it is in session. You should also consider volunteering to work with people with special needs at a day camp, community agency, residential facility, or other employer. Professional associations can also provide information about the field.

EMPLOYERS

Approximately 473,000 special education teachers are employed in the United States. Most work in private and public schools. A few work at residential facilities, social assistance agencies, home settings, correctional facilities, and hospitals. Others pursue careers as teachers in higher education.

GETTING A JOB

Many special education teachers obtain their first jobs as a result of contacts made through college internships, career fairs, or networking events. Others seek assistance in obtaining job leads from college career services offices, newspaper want ads, and employment websites. Additionally, professional associations such as the National Association of Special Education Teachers (www.naset.org), American Academy of Special Education Professionals (http://aasep.org), and Council for Exceptional Children (www.specialedcareers.org) provide job listings at their websites. The National Center for Special Education Personnel and Related Service Providers offers information on state teacher employment clearinghouses, job banks, and recruitment initiatives at its website, www.personnelcenter.org/tate_clearinghouses.cfm. Other job-search sites and teacher placement services include TopSchoolJobs (www.topschooljobs.org), USteach (www.usteach.com), and Project Connect (http://careers.education.wisc.edu/projectconnect/MainMenu.cfm).

ADVANCEMENT

Experienced special education teachers advance by receiving salary increases and by becoming supervisors or school administrators. Others pursue graduate degrees and teach special education classes at colleges and universities.

EARNINGS

Salaries for special education teachers vary by type of employer, geographic region, and the worker's experience, education, and skill level. The U.S. Department of Labor reports that special education teachers earned the following mean annual salaries by employer in 2009: preschool, kindergarten, and elementary school, $50,950; middle school, $51,970; and secondary school, $52,900. Salaries for all special education teachers ranged from less than $34,010 to $83,590 or more.

Special education teachers usually receive benefits such as health and life insurance, vacation days, sick leave, and a savings and pension plan. Self-employed teachers must provide their own benefits.

Did You Know?

The employment outlook for special education teachers varies by grade level. The U.S. Department of Labor reports that employment for those at the preschool, kindergarten, and elementary school levels will grow much faster than the average for all careers. Faster-than-average employment growth is expected for middle-school special education teachers. Employment for teachers at the high-school level is expected to grow about as fast as the average for all careers.

EMPLOYMENT OUTLOOK

The U.S. Department of Labor predicts that employment for special education teachers will grow faster than the average for all occupations through 2018. Opportunities will vary by geographic region; for example, positions in rural areas and inner cities will be more readily available than those in suburban or affluent urban areas. Employment will also be strong in the South and West due to increases in the student populations in these areas. Finally, employment prospects will vary by specialty. Teachers who work with children with multiple disabilities and severe disabilities (such as autism), as well as those who work with young children and those with bilingual skills, will be in strong demand.

Nearly seven million students between the ages of six and 21 are enrolled in special education programs, according to the National Association of Special Education Teachers. This number is expected to rise as the U.S. population continues to grow and more children become eligible for special education programs under the Individuals with Disabilities Education Improvement Act. Unfortunately, there is a shortage of qualified special education teachers to meet these increases.

Several factors are causing this shortage. Certification requirements have become more demanding, which is making it harder for people to become qualified to enter the field. Another key factor causing the shortage is the fact that special education teachers leave the field after one year at a higher rate than general educators due to the demanding nature of the career, lack of support from school administration, and isolation from other educators.

States and school districts are seeking to attract special education candidates by creating recruitment, retention, and mentoring programs; offering financial aid; and creating alternative routes to certification for those who have bachelor's degrees in subjects other than education.

FOR MORE INFORMATION

For information on careers and board certification, contact

American Academy of Special Education Professionals
700 12th Street, NW, Suite 700
Washington, DC 20005-4052
800-754-4421, ext. 106
info@aasep.org
http://aasep.org

The council works to improve the educational achievement of individuals with disabilities and/or gifts and talents. Visit its website to read teachers' blogs and other publications.

Council for Exceptional Children
1110 North Glebe Road, Suite 300
Arlington, VA 22201-5704
888-232-7733
www.cec.sped.org

For special education resources, contact
Council of Administrators of Special Education
101 Katelyn Circle, Suite E
Warner Robins, GA 31088-6484
478-333-6892
www.casecec.org

Visit the association's website for resources for special education teachers, information on board certification, and answers to FAQs about special education teachers.

National Association of Special Education Teachers
1250 Connecticut Avenue, NW, Suite 200
Washington, DC 20036-2643
contactus@naset.org
www.naset.org

Visit the center's website for a database of postsecondary training programs and information on careers and licensing.

National Center for Special Education Personnel and Related Service Providers
National Association of State Directors of Special Education
1800 Diagonal Road, Suite 320
Alexandria, VA 22314-2862
866-BECOME1
www.personnelcenter.org

For information on government-sponsored special education programs, contact
U.S. Department of Education
Office of Special Education and Rehabilitative Services
400 Maryland Avenue, SW
Washington, DC 20202-7100
www.ed.gov/about/offices/list/osers/index.html

Interview: Audra Chadwell

Audra Chadwell is an intervention specialist working with students in grades 2-4 for Three Rivers Local School District in Cincinnati, Ohio. She discussed her career with the editors of *Hot Jobs*.

Q. What made you want to enter this career?

A. I work with students who have moderate to intense disabilities, such as cognitively delayed and emotionally disturbed children. As a young student, I always struggled with reading comprehension, and when I was held back in second grade I felt like a failure. From the day that I got the report card that told me I would be retained, I have always wanted to be a teacher. I wanted to help students learn how to read, so that they did not have to go through what I went through. The decision to become a special education teacher came about 10 years later when my little cousin was born and was identified as autistic. When I would be around him he would always attach to me and listen to what needed to be done. The things that he did fascinated me so when I was deciding which path to pursue in college I chose special education.

Q. What is one thing that young people may not know about a career in special education?

A. Every day is a new day in the classroom and students are not always predictable. No two days are alike and you cannot expect students to perform like they did during a previous day. The issues that arise in the classroom come and go and you never know when to expect a child to get upset or when they are going to act out.

Q. What are the most important qualities for people in your career?

A. To be a special education teacher you need to personally want to be there every day to make a difference in your students' lives. You also need to have patience and love for each and every student in your class because everyone is different. One professional quality that is important in being a special education teacher is learning about each and every student's disabilities and what you can do to help improve his or her education. Every student with disabilities learns in a different way, so knowing how each child learns helps you to prepare better lessons. You also always need to be learning about new techniques in the classroom, new instructional strategies, and ways to deal with students with behavioral problems.

Q. What do you like most and least about your job?

A. The thing I like most about my job is coming into school every day and seeing my students. I also like knowing that every day I am making a difference in their life even though there may be days that it does not feel like it. The thing I least like about my job is that there are no two days alike. I cannot go in everyday thinking that the routine from yesterday was successful so let's do it again. Everything I do has to be fun, unique, and inviting to keep them interested in learning. Down the road, I can try that routine again and it may work, but everything is best understood when the lessons are not taught in the same manner.

Q. Any advice for young people who are interested in the field?

A. You will make a difference in so many lives. There may be days that are challenging but you need to stay strong and get through them. If you show weakness your students will sense that and take advantage of it. Every day is a new day and you need to go into everyday knowing that it is a new day. Also, live in the moment. Do not hold students accountable for something that occurred yesterday if you did not address it that day.

Q. What is the employment outlook for your field?

A. The employment outlook in special education is typically very good if you have a pre K-12 certificate and you can work with any disabilities. There are always plenty of openings; however, you need to be open to various grade levels and disabilities.

TEACHERS—KINDERGARTEN, ELEMENTARY, AND MIDDLE SCHOOL

OVERVIEW

Kindergarten, elementary, and middle-school teachers instruct young and adolescent children on subjects such as reading, writing, math, spelling, history, and science. These teachers are critically important to young children's development. The way children view themselves and the world is shaped by what they learn and experience during their early years. This image has a strong influence during their later years, whether in high school, in college, at work, or even in their personal lives. Teachers prepare for the field by earning at least a bachelor's degree from a teacher education program. There are nearly 2.4 million kindergarten, elementary, and middle-school teachers employed in the United States. Employment is expected to grow faster than the average for all careers through 2018.

FAST FACTS

High School Subjects
English
Speech

Personal Skills
Communication
Helping
Leadership

Minimum Education Level
Bachelor's degree

Salary Range
$31,000 to $50,000 to $79,000+

Employment Outlook
Faster than the average

O*NET-SOC
25-2012.00, 25-2021.00, 25-2022.00

GOE
12.03.03

DOT
092

NOC
4142

THE JOB

Think about a favorite teacher from your past. What set him or her apart? Was it his or her passion for the subject? Did he or she inspire you to love mathematics or science? Did the teacher use creative means to teach lessons? Or did he or she just make you laugh and help you through some of your early challenges? Chances are it was a combination of all these factors that made this teacher stand out.

Kindergarten, elementary, and middle-school teachers are responsible for laying the educational foundation for young children and adolescents. Early childhood education in basic skills such as reading, writing, and counting sets children up for success in later classes in literature, composition, and algebra. It is the job of these early educators to make their lessons interesting and engaging to emphasize early on the importance and even the enjoyment that can be found in education.

What these teachers instruct varies greatly depending on the age of the student.

Kindergarten teachers work with young children, roughly between the ages of four and six. Because the students are so young, these teachers build upon skills learned in preschool and often use play to impart their lessons. For example, they may use blocks to start children thinking about counting and basic math operations. They may use sing-along songs to teach about rhyming and spelling. They may use role playing to teach about kindness, sharing, and other social skills. At this age, students are taught letter and number recognition, phonics, and basic nature concepts.

An elementary school teacher supervises students as they work on an art project. (Katy McDonnell, Thinkstock)

Elementary-school teachers teach all subjects, working with children roughly ages six to 10. They use textbooks, chalkboards, activity workbooks, computers, and other tools to teach early skills such as basic math, spelling, and writing. They also introduce history and cover other science subjects besides what can be found in nature. It is during this time that children learn math skills such as adding and subtracting numbers, memorizing timetables, and doing basic division.

Middle-school teachers typically focus on one subject and work with students roughly ages 10 to 14. They use textbooks, workbooks, chalk or whiteboards, videos, computer programs, and more in their lessons. These teachers begin approaching more advanced levels of math, such as long division, and introduce variables to lay the foundations for algebra and even precalculus. Students will start to write short papers on reading assignments to develop writing skills as well as be tested regarding their reading comprehension and analysis skills. In general, middle-school teachers assign a larger quantity, as well as more complex, homework as children advance in grade level to prepare them for high school and beyond.

Regardless of the age of their students, much of teachers' time is spent outside the classroom, preparing lessons, creating assignments and tests, and grading homework and tests. They also meet with pupils before and after class and make time to meet with parents or other education professionals to discuss students' progress.

Teachers sometimes attend workshops to learn about new methods or technologies or teaching strategies that they can apply in their own classrooms. Many are also involved in other school-based activities, such as participating in field trips, coaching a sports team, supervising a club, or leading the school band.

Teachers work with students of many different cultures. Some students may speak English only as a second language. Teachers learn about different ethnic backgrounds so that they can be more helpful to these students. Those who are bilingual—especially speaking Spanish as a second language—will be more marketable.

Most teachers enjoy seeing children learn and develop. However, sometimes teaching a whole class of young children or adolescents—some of whom may misbehave, act out, struggle, or have emotional outbursts—can be stressful.

Summer vacation is a definite perk to the job. Teachers may travel, enjoy free time, or pursue professional development during their vacations. Some teachers may work, whether choosing to teach summer school or working for a school that has a year-round schedule. These schools break up vacations more evenly throughout the school year.

Some states offer tenure to public school teachers who have put in their time and proved their excellence with the district. These teachers cannot be fired without just cause and due process. Tenure does not guarantee a job, but it does provide some security with a school district.

REQUIREMENTS

HIGH SCHOOL

Take a college-preparatory curricula in high school that includes classes in mathematics, science, English, speech, government, social studies, computer science, and psychology.

POSTSECONDARY TRAINING

Teachers prepare for the field by earning at least a bachelor's degree from a teacher education program. They may earn a degree in education, childhood education, or a particular major, such as biology or mathematics. The National Council for Accreditation of Teacher Education (www.ncate.org) and the Teacher Education Accreditation Council (www.teac.org) accredit teacher education programs.

CERTIFICATION AND LICENSING

Voluntary national certification is offered by the National Board for Professional Teaching Standards (www.nbpts.org). The Council for

Professional Recognition (www.cdacouncil.org) also provides certification. Obtaining certification is highly recommended. It is an excellent way to stand out from other job applicants and demonstrate your abilities to prospective employers. Certified teachers also typically earn higher salaries and are reimbursed for continuing education and certification fees.

All public school teachers must be licensed by the state in which they plan to teach. Licensing requirements typically include attending an approved teacher education program and having a bachelor's degree. Some states require teachers to obtain a master's degree within a specified amount of time after they begin teaching. Contact your state department of education for more information on licensing requirements.

Many states are now offering alternative routes to licensing for people who do not have a degree in education but want to become teachers.

OTHER REQUIREMENTS

To be a successful teacher, you need to have a strong desire to help young people learn. You should have patience, enthusiasm, good organizational skills, and the ability to motivate and inspire young people to learn. Other key traits include strong communication skills, leadership ability, dependability, creativity, and a willingness to work outside of traditional school hours to prepare lesson plans, grade papers and tests, and otherwise prepare for the next school day.

Most teachers belong to unions—mainly the American Federation of Teachers and the National Education Association. Unions represent the professional interests of teachers, negotiating with school districts regarding work hours, salaries, and other employment issues.

EXPLORING

There are many ways to learn more about a career as a teacher. You can talk to teachers at your school about their careers, read books and magazines about the field, and visit the websites of college teacher preparation programs to learn about typical classes. Professional associations can also provide information about the field. The American Federation of Teachers provides a useful publication called *Becoming a Teacher* at its website, www.aft.org/pdfs/tools4teachers/becomingateacher0608.pdf. You should also work as a teacher at a summer camp, community center, or other organization that offers classes.

EMPLOYERS

There are nearly 2.4 million kindergarten, elementary, and middle-school teachers employed in the United States. Opportunities are available throughout the United States at public and private schools.

GETTING A JOB

Many teachers obtain their first jobs as a result of contacts made through student teaching positions, career fairs, or networking events. Others seek assistance in obtaining job leads from college career services offices, newspaper want ads, and employment websites. Job-search sites and teacher placement services include Project Connect (http://careers.education.wisc.edu/projectconnect/MainMenu.cfm), USteach (www.usteach.com), and TopSchoolJobs (www.topschooljobs.org).

ADVANCEMENT

To advance as a teacher, you will need to become certified and pursue a graduate degree. With these qualifications, you will be eligible to receive higher pay than those who are not certified or do not have advanced degrees. Teachers also advance by transitioning into administrative or supervisory positions or by becoming instructional coordinators, school librarians, reading specialists, or guidance counselors. Some become *senior* or *mentor teachers,* who provide guidance to younger educators while still retaining most of their teaching duties. Some teachers earn master's degrees or Ph.D.s and become college educators.

EARNINGS

Salaries for teachers vary by type of employer, geographic region, and the individual's experience, education, and skill level. Median annual salaries for kindergarten teachers were $47,830 in 2009, according to the U.S. Department of Labor. Salaries ranged from less than $31,320 to $75,210 or more. Elementary school teachers earned median annual salaries of $50,510. Ten percent earned less than $33,830, and 10 percent earned $78,720 or more. Middle school teachers earned salaries that ranged from less than $34,360 to $79,200, with a median salary of $50,770. Some teachers earn extra pay for coaching sports, for supervising clubs and other extracurricular activities, or by receiving advanced degrees and/or certification.

Employers offer a variety of benefits, including the following: medical, dental, and life insurance; paid holidays, vacations, and sick and personal days; 401(k) plans; profit-sharing plans; retirement and pension plans; educational assistance programs; and free subsidized housing (some private school teachers).

EMPLOYMENT OUTLOOK

Employment for kindergarten, elementary, and middle school teachers is expected to grow faster than the average for all careers through 2018, according to the U.S. Department of Labor. Approximately 372,400 new positions are predicted to be available by 2018 as a result of a large number of expected retirements, as well as the fact that some teachers leave the profession after a few years due to job burnout or other factors. Middle school teachers with expertise in areas where there is a shortage of qualified educators—such as mathematics, science, special education, and bilingual education—will have the best job prospects. There is currently an oversupply of teachers in health education, physical education, and social studies.

FOR MORE INFORMATION

Contact the following organizations for information about education, careers, and union membership.

American Federation of Teachers
555 New Jersey Avenue, NW
Washington, DC 20001-2029
202-879-4400
www.aft.org

National Education Association
1201 16th Street, NW
Washington, DC 20036-3290
202-833-4000
www.nea.org

For information on training programs, contact
American Montessori Society
281 Park Avenue South
New York, NY 10010-6102
212-358-1250

ams@amshq.org
www.amshq.org

The NAEYC is "dedicated to improving the well-being of all young children, with particular focus on the quality of educational and developmental services for all children from birth through age eight." Visit its website for more information.

National Association for the Education of Young Children (NAEYC)
1313 L Street, NW, Suite 500
Washington, DC 20005-4110
800-424-2460
www.naeyc.org

For information for men who are interested in becoming teachers, visit
MenTeach
www.menteach.org

Strong opportunities will be available for all teachers who are willing to work in less-desirable urban or rural school districts. Teachers who are bilingual, certified, and willing to relocate for positions will have the best job prospects.

Opportunities will be strongest in geographic regions that are experiencing fast population growth. The largest enrollment growth is expected in states in the South and West. Enrollment is expected to remain about the same in the Midwest and decline in the Northeast.

Interview: Betsy Stewart

Betsy Stewart is a first-grade teacher at a private Roman Catholic school. She discussed her career with the editors of *Hot Jobs*.

Q. What made you want to enter this career?

A. I always knew I wanted to be a teacher. In some cases you will be called to your profession, and I certainly knew this at a young age. In my classroom I have a sign that I made when I was in first grade that says "When I grow up I want to be a teacher. I want to teach first grade because I like kids and I like to grade papers." I also had a classroom in my basement where all the neighborhood children came over to play school. I was always the teacher.

Q.   What is one thing that young people may not know about a career as a teacher?

A.   It is truly a rewarding and wonderful profession but your heart has to be in it 100 percent. You can't go in with anything less than your best every day. (If you are sick, stay home! You are of no use to your students and faculty.) Even if you had a rough morning or a disagreement with your significant other you need to leave that all at the door when you enter your class-room—which is hard. You have all these little faces looking up at you, depending on you to entertain and fill their heads with knowledge that day. Also, you might not know that as a teacher you wear many hats. You are also a nurse, counselor, advocate, cheerleader, referee, and disciplinarian.

Q.   What are the most important personal and professional qualities for elementary school teachers?

A.   Personally I think good teachers have patience and compassion, yet they have to know when to get tough. There is a very fine line that a teacher walks in order to get things done and have students rise to the occasion without having them crack under pressure.

Professionally you have to respect all the other teachers, parents, and anyone you come into contact with in the school environment. There will be people that challenge the way you run your classroom but you need to believe in yourself (again not always easy) and remain cool even in these sticky situations.

Q.   What do you like most and least about your job?

A.   I love that the day goes by so quickly! We are busy every moment and there is never any time to get bored. There is always something to do. The thing I like least is the conflict that sometimes comes with having to tell parents that there is an issue with their child's behavior or academics. This is always difficult but it is best to let the parents know that together you are on the same team working for their child's success.

Q.   What advice would you give to young people who are interested in becoming teachers?

A.   Spend some time in a classroom volunteering or tutor after school. Make sure that you like working with kids. I do not romanticize the profession and I think that everyone needs to know that there will be days in the classroom where the students are tired or awaiting the next day off or struggling with cabin fever, yet you still need to keep them motivated even when they are fighting you the whole way. Babysitting is also a great way to see how your rapport is with kids.

Q.   What is the employment outlook for your field?

A.   Many teachers have received their pink slips lately, and I find this very sad. However, there is a perpetual demand for good teachers and there will always be students and full classrooms—so if you are up for the chal-lenge, go for it, you'll find a job if you are persistent.

INDEX

A

A.C. Nielsen Center for Marketing Research, 115

AACSB International-Association to Advance Collegiate Schools of Business, 3, 6

Academy of Board Certified Environmental Professionals, 30

Academy of Managed Care Pharmacy, 137, 139

accountants and auditors, 1-9

Accreditation Board for Engineering and Technology, 29, 194, 199

Accreditation Commission for Midwifery Education, 12

Accreditation Council for Accountancy and Taxation, 3, 6

Accreditation Council for Graduate Medical Education, 160

Accreditation Council for Pharmacy Education, 137, 139

advanced practice nurses, 10-17, 172

advanced vehicle technologies workers, 184

Advertising Educational Foundation, 114

Allied Cleveland Tradeswomen, 25

allopathic physicians, 153

American Academy of Environmental Engineers, 29, 31

American Academy of Family Physicians, 159, 160

American Academy of Nurse Practitioners, 12, 13, 14, 16

American Academy of Special Education Professionals, 203, 204, 206

American Advertising Federation, 114

American Alliance of Paralegals, 126, 129

American Assembly for Men in Nursing, 15, 177

American Assisted Living Nurses Association, 177

American Association for Agricultural Education, 40

American Association for Marriage and Family Therapy, 81

American Association for Paralegal Education, 126, 129

American Association for Public Opinion Research, 114

American Association of Advertising Agencies, 113, 114

American Association of Colleges of Nursing, 12, 15, 177, 178

American Association of Colleges of Osteopathic Medicine, 160

American Association of Colleges of Pharmacy, 136, 137, 139

American Association of Critical Care Nurses Certification Corporation, 12

American Association of Legal Nurse Consultants, 173

American Association of Nurse Anesthetists, 11, 12, 15

American Association of Pharmaceutical Scientists, 121, 122

American Association of University Professors, 40

American Association of University Women, 40

American Bar Association, 126, 129

American Board of Clinical Pharmacology, 120

American Board of Genetic Counseling, 81

American Board of Medical Specialties, 158, 160

American Board of Physical Therapy Specialities, 147

American College Health Association, 80

American College of Nurse Practitioners, 16

American College of Nurse-Midwives, 15

American College, The, 94

American Council for an Energy-Efficient Economy, 190

American Council for Construction Education, 22, 62, 65

American Counseling Association, 79, 81

American Dental Association, 89, 90

American Dental Education Association, 90

American Dental Hygienists' Association, 88, 89, 90

American Federation of Teachers, 40, 211, 213

American Institute of Certified Public Accountants, 3, 4, 5, 6, 104

American Institute of Constructors, 63, 65

American Management Association, 103, 104

American Marketing Association, 112, 113, 114

American Medical Association, 158, 160

American Mental Health Counselors Association, 81

American Midwifery Certification Board, 12, 15

American Montessori Society, 213

American Nurses Association, 13, 175, 177

American Nursing Credentialing Center, 12, 13, 15, 174, 177

American Osteopathic Association, 157, 158, 160

American Pharmacists Association, 136, 138, 139, 140

American Physical Therapy Association, 147, 148, 149

American Rehabilitation and Counseling Association, 81

American School Counselor Association, 81

American Society for Engineering Education, 31

American Society for Microbiology, 123

American Society for Pharmacology and Experimental Therapeutics, 120, 121, 122

American Society of Civil Engineers, 29, 30, 31

American Society of Consultant Pharmacists, 139

American Society of Health-System Pharmacists, 135, 138, 139

American Society of Highway Engineers, 31

American Society of Human Genetics, 81

American Society of PeriAnesthesia Nurses, 13, 16

American Society of Professional Estimators, 71, 72, 73

American Society of Registered Nurses, 177

American Solar Energy Society, 180, 187, 190, 191

American Water Resources Association, 31

American Water Works Association, 31

American Wind Energy Association, 189, 191

anesthesiologists, 154

Apollo Alliance, 190

applications software engineers, 193

applied epidemiologists, 118

ASCEville.org, 30

AspiringDocs.org, 158

Associated General Contractors of America, 22, 65

Association for Computing Machinery, 44, 46, 52, 57, 58, 194, 197

Association for Library and Information Science Education, 40

Association for Professionals in Infection Control and Epidemiology, 120

Association for the Advancement of Cost Engineering, 71, 73

Association for the Advancement of Sustainability in Higher Education, 186

Association for Women in Computing, 46, 58, 197

Association of American Colleges and Universities, 38

Association of American Medical Colleges, 121, 157, 158, 160

Association of Certified Fraud Examiners, 3

Association of Energy Engineers, 186, 188, 190

Association of Environmental Engineering and Science Professors, 40

Association of Information Technology Professionals, 46, 58, 197

Association of Internal Management Consultants, 103, 104

Association of Legal Administrators, 129

Association of Management Consulting Firms, 104

Association of Professors of
    Dermatology, 40
Association of Support Professionals,
    48, 51, 52
Association of University Professors
    of Neurology, 40
Association of University Professors
    of Ophthalmology, 40
Automotive Public Relations
    Council, 167

B
BAI, 6
Becoming a Teacher, 211
behavioral disorder counselors, 76
Bennett, Lindsi, 84-85
Besser, Mianne, 129-132
bioenergy workers, 183
biologists, 182
biomedical scientists, 118
Biotechnology Industry
    Organization, 123
Biotechnology Institute, 123
Board of Pharmacy Specialties, 136,
    139
Bowman, Lindsey, 83-84
Branch, Kristin, 115-116
Branham, Michael, 98-99
Business Professionals of America,
    103

C
Calling Dr. Nurse, 12
cardiothoracic surgeons, 156
career counselors, 76
*Career in Construction Management:
    Build America's Future as You
    Build Your Own, A,* 63
CareerCast.com, 58, 198
Careers in Wind, 188
Careers Outside the Box-Survey
    Research: A Fun, Exciting,
    Rewarding Career, 113
carpenters, 18-25
Centers for Disease Control and
    Prevention, 123
Certification Board of Infection
    Control and Epidemiology,
    120, 123
CFP Board, 94
Chadwell, Audra, 206-207
civil engineers, 26-34
clinical nurse specialists, 10, 172
Coastal Ocean Ports & Rivers
    Institute, 29
Coates, Aaron, 99
College and University Professional
    Association for Human
    Resources, 38, 39
college and university professors
    2 (accounting), 35-40
college counselors, 76
College of Financial Planning, 96
college professors, 2, 35-40
Commission for Certification in
    Geriatric Pharmacy, 137
Commission on Accreditation of
    Physical Therapy Education,
    146, 149
Commission on Dental
    Accreditation, 88

Commission on Rehabilitation
    Counselor Certification, 81
communications specialists, 162
compliance auditors, 2
CompTIA TechCareer Compass, 44,
    50, 56
CompTIA, 43, 49, 50, 56
computer network administrators,
    41-46
computer network, systems, and
    database administrators, 41-46
computer programmers, 54, 193
Computer Science Teachers
    Association, 40
computer security specialists, 42
computer support specialists, 47-52
computer systems analysts, 53-59
ComputerJobs.com, 45, 51, 57, 196
Computing Degrees and Careers, 44,
    50, 56, 194
Computing Technology Industry
    Association, 44, 50, 56
Consider Pharmacy as a Career, 137
Considering a Medical Career, 158
construction engineers, 28
Construction Management
    Association of America,
    63, 64, 65
construction managers, 60-68
construction superintendents, 60
construction workers, 184
consulting pharmacists, 135
Corbett, Gerard, 168-169
cost accountants, 2
cost estimators, 69-74
Council for Accreditation of
    Counseling and Related
    Educational Programs, 81
Council for Exceptional Children,
    204, 206
Council for Professional
    Recognition, 210, 211
Council of Accreditation of Nurse
    Anesthesia Educational
    Programs, 12
Council of Administrators of Special
    Education, 206
Council of American Survey Research
    Organizations, 113, 114
Council of Graduate Schools, 37, 38
Council of Public Relations Firms,
    165, 167
Council of State and Territorial
    Epidemiologists, 123
Council on Certification of Nurse
    Anesthetists, 13
Council on Rehabilitation
    Education, 81
counselors, 75-85
Crunchboard, 45, 51, 57, 196
Cybernurse.com, 13, 175
cytologic scientists, 117

D
DAMA International, 43, 46
data communication analysts, 42
database administrators, 41-46
DeJesus, Victor, 161
dementia care nurses, 176
dental hygienists, 86-91
dermatologists, 154

Dice.com, 45, 51, 57, 196
Discover Nursing, 12, 13, 175
doctors, 153

E
Educational Foundation for Women
    in Accounting, The, 6
Electric Power Research Institute,
    183
elementary school counselors, 75
elementary teachers, 208-214
emergency medicine physicians, 154
emergency room nurses, 171
emergency room physicians, 154
Employment & Training
    Administration, 22
employment counselors, 76
energy auditors, 183
energy conservation technicians,
    183
Energy Efficiency and Renewable
    Energy, 190
energy efficiency engineers, 184
energy efficiency workers, 183-184
Energy Information Administration,
    183, 190
EnergyVortex.com, 188
Environmental & Water Resources
    Institute, 29
environmental accountants, 2
environmental auditors, 2
Environmental Career.com, 188
environmental engineers, 27
Epidemic Intelligence Service, 123
epidemiologists, 117
Ethanol-Jobs.com, 188
ExceptionalNurse.com, 15, 177
external auditors, 2

F
family medicine practitioners, 154
Federal Trade Commission, 127
Federation of American Societies for
    Experimental Biology, 123
Federation of State Boards of
    Physical Therapy, 147
Fi360, 94
financial advisors, 92
financial consultants, 1
financial planners, 92-99
Financial Planning Association,
    95, 96
fish farmers, 182
Flaherty, Christine, 67-68
forensic accountants, 2
forensics nurses, 173
fuel cell technologies workers, 184
Future Educators Association, 38
Future City Competition, 33
Futures in Nursing, 175

G
Gagni, Thara, 178-179
general accountants, 2
general contractors, 60
general internists, 154
general medicine practitioners, 154
general pediatricians, 154
genetic counselors, 77
Geo-Institute, 29
geotechnical engineers, 27

Geothermal Education Office, 191
Geothermal Energy Association, 189, 191
geothermal energy workers, 183
geriatric dialysis nurses, 172
geriatric nurses, 172
Gerontological Advanced Practice Nurses Association, 15
Gipson, Allyson, 66-67
Goldberg, Josette, 108-109
government accountants, 2
government auditors, 2
graphic designers, 54
Green for All, 190
Green Jobs, 187
green construction workers, 184
Gregory, Jennie, 149-151
gynecologists, 155

H
Habitat for Humanity, 20
Hard Hatted Women, 21, 25
HDI, 43, 49, 51, 52
head estimators, 70
Health Resources and Services Administration, 140, 178
health-system pharmacists, 140
help desk technicians, 47
hematology nurses, 172
Hertig, John, 140-142
high school counselors, 75
high school special education educators, 202
Home Builders Institute, 19, 22
hospitalists, 155
Howe, Fraser, 32-33
Hwasta, Rocky, 23-25
hydraulic engineers, 28
hydropower industry workers, 182

I
IEEE Computer Society, 43, 44, 46, 56, 194, 196, 197
immigration law paralegals, 125
Independent Pharmacy Career Guide, 137, 139
Indian Health Service, 137, 148
industrial accountants, 2
infectious disease specialists, 118
Infectious Diseases Society of America, 121, 123
information technology auditors, 2
Institute for Certification of Computing Professionals, 43, 49, 52, 56, 194
Institute of Internal Auditors, 3, 6
Institute of Management Accountants, 3, 6
Institute of Management Consultants USA, Inc., 102, 104
Institute of Professional Environmental Practice, 30
Institute of Transportation Engineers, 30, 31
internal auditors, 2
Internal Revenue Service, 127
International Association of Business Communicators, 164, 165, 167
Interstate Renewable Energy Council, 190
Investment Management Consultants Association, 94

ISACA, 3, 6

J
Job Corps, 22
Joint Commission on National Dental Examinations, 88
Journalism Education Association, 40
Junior Achievement, 103
Junior Engineering Technical Society, 30, 31, 194, 197

K
Kerr, Nora, 58-59
Khan, Maya Chahine, 7-8
kindergarten teachers, 208-214

L
land managers, 182
Land, Kathy, 195, 198-200
lead estimators, 70
League of Professional System Administrators, 46
legal assistants, 124
legal nurse consultants, 173
Lehman, Maria, 33-34
Liaison Committee on Medical Education, 157

M
management analysts, 100-109
management consultants, 100
managerial accountants, 2
Mapping Your Career in Managed Care Pharmacy, 137, 139
marketing research analysts, 110-116
Marketing Research Association, 112, 114
marriage and family counselors, 76
MathCounts, 33
McClanahan, Carolyn, 97-98
media specialists, 162
medical microbiologists, 117
medical scientists, 117-123
medical specialists, 153
mental health counselors, 76, 80
MenTeach, 213
middle-school special education educators, 202
middle-school teachers, 208-214
Midwest Renewable Energy Association, 190
Midwives Alliance of North America, 15
Monuments of the Millennium, 28

N
NALS...the association for legal professionals, 126, 127, 129
National Association for College Admission Counseling, 82
National Association for the Education of Young Children, 213
National Association of Boards of Pharmacy, 137, 139
National Association of Chain Drug Stores, 137, 139
National Association of Clinical Nurse Specialists, 12, 14, 15
National Association of Colleges and Employers, 5, 64

National Association of Geoscience Teachers, 40
National Association of Home Builders, 22
National Association of Legal Assistants, 126, 127, 128, 129
National Association of Nurse Practitioners in Women's Health, 16
National Association of Pediatric Nurse Practitioners, 16
National Association of Personal Financial Advisors, 95, 96
National Association of Special Education Teachers, 204, 205, 206
National Association of Women in Construction, 21
National Board for Certified Counselors, 75
National Board for Professional Teaching Standards, 210
National Center for Biotechnology Information, 123
National Center for Construction Education and Research, 65
National Center for Special Education Personnel and Related Service Providers, 203, 204, 206
National Center for Women and Information Technology, 46, 52, 58, 197
National Clearinghouse of Rehabilitation Training Materials, 82
National Community Pharmacists Association, 137, 139
National Council for Accreditation of Teacher Education, 210
National Council Licensure Examination, 174
National Council of Examiners for Engineering and Surveying, 30
National Council of State Boards of Nursing, 13, 174, 177
National Earth Science Teachers Association, 40
National Education Association, 211, 213
National Energy Foundation, 189
National Engineers Week, 33
National Federation of Paralegal Associations, 126, 127, 129
National Hydropower Association, 189, 191
National Institute for Certification in Engineering Technologies, 186
National League for Nursing, 15, 174, 177
National Marine Educators Association, 40
National Organization for Associate Degree Nursing, 177
National Paralegal Association, 129
National Rehabilitation Association, 82
National Rehabilitation Counseling Association, 82
National Renewable Energy Laboratory, 187, 191

National School Public Relations Association, 167
National Science Teachers Association, 40
National Society of Genetic Counselors, 82
National Society of Professional Engineers, 186, 187, 191
National Student Nurses' Association, 15, 177
neonatal nurses, 172
network architects, 42
network engineers, 42
network or integration specialists, 54
network systems analysts, 42
neurosurgeons, 155-156
Nontraditional Employment for Women, 21
North American Board of Certified Energy Practitioners, 186
North American Securities Administrator Association, 94
nuclear pharmacists, 134
nurse anesthetists, 10, 172
nurse educators, 173
nurse practitioners, 10, 172
Nurse.com, 13, 175
nurse-midwives, 10, 172
nurses, 10-17, 171-179
nursing informatics specialists, 173
nutrition support pharmacists, 134

O
obstetricians, 155
occupational health nurses, 173
ocean energy workers, 182-183
Ocean Renewable Energy Coalition, 191
Office of Special Education and Rehabilitative Services, 206
oncologists, 153
oncology nurses, 172
Oncology Nursing Certification Corporation, 12, 13
oncology pharmacists, 135
Ortegon, Nina, 16-17
Orthopaedic Nurses Certification Board, 12
orthopedic surgeons, 155
Osteopathic Medical College Information Book, 160
osteopaths, 153
otolaryngologists, 156

P
paralegals, 124-132
pediatric nurses, 172
Pediatric Nursing Certification Board, 13
personal financial advisors, 92
Phair, Judith, 169-170
Pharmaceutical Research and Manufacturers of America, 123
pharmacist informaticists, 135
pharmacists, 133-143
pharmacologists, 117
pharmacotherapists, 135
photovoltaic installers, 182
physical therapists, 144-152
physician specialists, 154
physicians, 118, 153-161

physiotherapists, 144
plastic surgeons, 156
Preparing Future Faculty, 38
press secretaries, 162
primary care doctors, 154
private accountants, 2
private bankers, 94
programmers, 54, 193
Project Connect, 204, 212
Project CRAFT, 22
project managers, 60
psychiatric pharmacists, 135
psychiatrists, 155
PT Centralized Application Service, 147
public accountants, 1
public affairs specialists, 162
Public Relations Professional Career Guide, 165, 167
Public Relations Society of America, 164, 165
public relations specialists, 162-170

Q
quality assurance testers, 54

R
radiologists, 155
radiology nurses, 171
Radman, Deborah, 167-168
real estate paralegals, 125
reconstructive surgeons, 156
Reed, Brent, 142-143
registered nurses, 171-179
rehabilitation counselors, 77
renewable energy and green industry workers, 180-191
Renewable Fuels Association, 191
RenewableEnergyWorld.com, 187
research epidemiologists, 117-118
respiratory nurses, 172
Robert Half International, 5, 45, 51, 57, 196
RX Career Center, 138

S
Schick, Kip, 151-52
Schmeling, Dotti Dixon, 82-83
school counselors, 75
Seider, Tara, 17
senior care pharmacists, 135
Sloan Career Cornerstone Center, 44, 50, 56, 194
Sniewski, Luke, 8-9
Social Security Administration, 127
Society of Cost Estimating and Analysis, 71, 73
Society of Hospital Medicine, 155, 160
Software and Information Industry Association, 197
software engineers, 192-200
software report writers, 54
Solar Electric Power Association, 191
Solar Energy Industries Association, 191
solar industry workers, 181
solar panel installers, 182
Solie, Caryn Loftis, 89, 91
special education teachers, 201-207
Start Here, Go Places, 4, 6

Structural Engineers Association-International, 31
structural engineers, 27
substance abuse counselors, 76
surgeons, 155
sustainable business consultants, 185
systems administrators, 41-46
systems software engineers, 193

T
tax consultants, 1
Taylor, Laurie, 105-108
Taylor, Marcene, 74
Teacher Education Accreditation Council, 210
teachers, kindergarten, elementary, and middle school, 208-214
technical support specialists, 47
Technology Services Industry Association, 52
TopSchoolJobs, 204, 212
Tradeswomen Now and Tomorrow, 21
Tradeswomen, Inc., 21
trail planners, 182
Training and Careers in Human Genetics and Solving the Puzzle: Careers in Genetics, 81
transportation engineers, 28

U
United Brotherhood of Carpenters and Joiners of America, 19, 20, 22
U.S. Department of Energy, 181, 183, 194, 189, 190
U.S. Green Building Council, 187, 189, 191
U.S. Department of Defense, 103, 137, 148
U.S. Department of Justice, 127
U.S. Department of the Interior, 127
U.S. Department of the Treasury, 127
U.S. Department of Veterans Affairs, 13, 137, 148
U.S. Food & Drug Administration, 137
U.S. Public Health Service, 13, 137
USteach, 204, 212

V
vocational counselors, 76

W
wealth managers, 94
West Point Bridge Design Contest, 33
Why Choose Computer Science & Engineering?, 44, 50, 56, 194
wind industry workers, 181
windsmiths, 181
Women Construction Owners and Executives, USA, 21
Women Contractors Association, 21
World of Opportunities: Career Paths in Infectious Diseases and HIV Medicine, A, 121

Y
Youthbuild, 22